'It is absolutely fundamental that journalists treat vulnerable contributors sensitively and with respect'

– Louis Theroux

'Dealing with personal tragedy is hard enough but dealing with the media often compounds the pain, trauma and powerlessness of uninvited experiences. It doesn't have to be like that. The insight and the guidance in this book reflect compassionate, ethical and professional practices that can only benefit journalists as well as those they work with and for.'

– Anne Eyre, Disaster Action

'Full of vital, sensible and practical advice. All journalists, especially those just starting out on their careers, would benefit from absorbing this clear, thoughtful and much-needed guide.'

– Adam Bullimore, Editor, BBC Breakfast News

'Families we have supported tell us the way they are treated by the media can have a massive impact on them. We welcome the level-headed and practical advice in this important book which will increase the confidence of reporters and reduce any unnecessary distress for families.'

– Child Bereavement UK

'The scoop-obsessed, noisy hack pack, forever ready to pounce mercilessly on unsuspecting people suddenly thrown into the media spotlight, is a stereotype beloved of Hollywood and television detective series. Countering that image, Jo Healey, drawing from wide-ranging interviews, academic studies and her own experience, shows that there is, indeed, a large, caring and reflective community of print and broadcast journos who strive hard to work sensitively when dealing with vulnerable children and adults – and with people suffering from all kinds of trauma. Healey also records moving testimonies from people who, following some tragedy, have had to face the hack pack at their door. Both students and practicing journalists will find this text – packed with sensible and always clearly presented advice – of enormous, lasting value.'

– Richard Lance Keeble, University of Lincoln
and Liverpool Hope University

Trauma Reporting

Trauma Reporting provides vital information on developing a healthy, professional and respectful relationship with those who choose to tell their stories during times of trauma, distress or grief.

Amid a growing demand and need for guidance, this fascinating book is refreshingly simple, engaging and readable, providing a wealth of original insight. As an aspiring or working journalist, how should you work with a grieving parent, a survivor of sexual violence, a witness at the scene of a traumatic event? How should you approach people, interview them and film with them sensitively? *Trauma Reporting* features guidance from some of the industry's most successful news correspondents and documentary makers, including Louis Theroux, Lucy Williamson, Tulip Mazumdar, Richard Bilton, Jina Moore and many more, all sharing their experience and expertise. It also features people who chose to tell their sensitive stories to journalists, giving readers invaluable insight into what helped and what harmed.

The book also includes:

- What your interviewees may be going through and how best to respond, by trauma expert Professor Stephen Regel.
- A discussion on ethics, rules and regulations by Dr Sallyanne Duncan of the University of Strathclyde.
- Making sure you look after yourself, by Dr Cait McMahon of the Dart Center for Journalism and Trauma.

Insightful and innovative, this book is essential for new and established journalists across all media, students of journalism and broadcasting, and anyone who wishes to share the stories of those affected by trauma.

Jo Healey is a senior broadcast news journalist for BBC TV, specialising in highly sensitive human-interest stories. She developed and delivers training for BBC staff in working with emotionally vulnerable interviewees. She began her career in weekly newspapers, moving as a chief reporter to daily papers. Her broadcast career began in radio where she worked as a reporter, producer and acting news editor before moving to TV as a reporter and presenter.

Trauma Reporting

A Journalist's Guide to Covering
Sensitive Stories

Jo Healey

Routledge
Taylor & Francis Group

LONDON AND NEW YORK

First published 2020
by Routledge
2 Park Square, Milton Park, Abingdon, Oxon OX14 4RN

and by Routledge
52 Vanderbilt Avenue, New York, NY 10017

Routledge is an imprint of the Taylor & Francis Group, an informa business

© 2020 Jo Healey

British Library Cataloguing-in-Publication Data
A catalogue record for this book is available from the British Library

Library of Congress Cataloging-in-Publication Data
Names: Healey, Jo, editor of compilation.
Title: Trauma reporting : a journalist's guide to covering sensitive stories / [selected by] Jo Healey.
Description: London ; New York : Routledge, 2019. | Includes bibliographical references and index.
Identifiers: LCCN 2019009485 (print) | LCCN 2019022271 (ebook) | ISBN 9781138482098 (hardback : alk. paper) | ISBN 9781138482104 (pbk. : alk. paper) | ISBN 9781351059114 (ebk.)
Subjects: LCSH: Disasters—Press coverage. | Violence—Press coverage. | Victims—Press coverage. | Journalistic ethics.
Classification: LCC PN4784.D57 T78 2019 (print) | LCC PN4784.D57 (ebook) | DDC 070.4/33—dc23
LC record available at https://lccn.loc.gov/2019009485
LC ebook record available at https://lccn.loc.gov/2019022271

ISBN: 978-1-138-48209-8 (hbk)
ISBN: 978-1-138-48210-4 (pbk)
ISBN: 978-1-351-05911-4 (ebk)

Typeset in Goudy
by codeMantra

For Andy, Frankie and Anna

And for the many families who have shared their experiences in this book

Contents

x   Contents

Acknowledgements

This book has been built on a bedrock of goodwill. Very many hugely talented journalists, documentary makers and camera operators from several news organisations, or working freelance, have generously taken the time out of hectic schedules to hand on their experience, expertise and invaluable insight. They've done so to offer support to aspiring and working journalists faced with the often daunting task of sensitive reporting. They are all named in the book, and I am truly grateful to each and every one of them.

Thank you to my inspirational friends and colleagues at BBC East Midlands, particularly Emma Agnew and Kevin Hill, a great management team, who have backed me all the way in this work. Thank you also for the much valued support of Sarah Ward-Lilley, Managing Editor of BBC News and Current Affairs, and Occupational Psychologist Susannah Robertson-Hart.

The book would not have been possible without the excellent Dart Center for Journalism and Trauma, an incredible global network of expertise, which has supplied much valued support and information. My thanks and appreciation, in particular, to Gavin Rees, Dart's Director Europe for his insightful help, patience and guidance with both the trauma training and the book.

Thank you to the specialist contributors, Gavin, Sam Dubberley, Suleman Nagdi, Caroline Brant and Neil Evans, for the *Extras* sections, giving added expertise to the chapters.

A huge thank you to those who not only combed through early chapters to give me an idea of how the book may be viewed in their worlds, but also offered time and support along the way: Cheslyn Baker (newspaper feature writer), Anne Eyre (Disaster Action), Dr Sallyanne Duncan (author and journalism senior lecturer), Professor Stephen Regel (trauma specialist), and Jane Keightley of Child Bereavement UK, who has embraced and backed this work from the start.

My added thanks to Sallyanne, for her support and for contributing the Ethics chapter, and to Stephen for writing the *Trauma Awareness* sections. I am very grateful too to Dr Cait McMahon, director Dart Asia Pacific, for contributing the Self-Care chapter. It is so important that we journalists look after ourselves and each other when covering these emotional assignments.

More than ten major UK and US charities have been involved. They are all named in the book and I am very grateful to them for allowing me to pass on some of their media guidance and research. In addition to those already mentioned, key players have been Rose Dixon of Support after Murder and Manslaughter, Lorna Fraser of Samaritans, Fay Maxted of The Survivors Trust, Minh Dang of Survivor Alliance, and Bernie Fennerty of Scope. Huge thanks to all of you.

Many thanks also to my research assistant Anna Matthews for painstakingly transcribing interviews, giving a student's perspective and suggesting we ask Louis Theroux to take part – thus proving the time-honoured journalistic principle, particularly relevant in this work: never assume they'll say no. Louis, thank you so much for saying yes.

For my family and friends and their unstinting willingness to listen, I am inordinately grateful. In the five years of research involved, my husband Andy has been a constant, towering and patient source of support. All massively appreciated.

My thanks to Margaret Farrelly at Routledge, for believing in this book, and to Jennifer Vennall for steering me through the publishing process.

Thank you for the grant aid from the National Union of Journalists and the Society of Authors, which enabled me to take some unpaid leave to complete the book well ahead of deadline – always a pleasing, if rare, position for a journalist to be in.

But most of all, my profound and heartfelt thanks to the families, victims, survivors, sources, contributors, interviewees who all said 'yes' to reporters at dreadful times in their lives. Their generosity in reliving those moments, to hand on constructive advice to journalists, to help us do our job better, bowls me over. They know words fail me in expressing my appreciation. They also know they have been my motivators to produce this book. The texts from bereaved mothers and survivors of abuse, telling me, 'Go girl, you can do this', have spurred me on. They are all truly an inspiration.

It has been written in a tremendous spirit of goodwill. I hope you will listen to them all, and I hope it helps.

1
The introduction

Do your job, do it well, do no harm.

'It is absolutely fundamental that journalists treat vulnerable contributors sensitively and with respect,' Louis Theroux tells me, and the aim of this book is to give you the confidence to do just that. Try to keep an open mind because the way sensitivity may *look* to your interviewees and how *they* say they wish to be treated may, at times, surprise you.

At the heart of the book are the many ordinary people to whom something extraordinarily bad or difficult happens and who choose to speak to journalists about it. Also, the many ordinary journalists who regularly approach them, build relationships with them, interview them, film with them, write about them and follow up their sensitive stories.

As a journalist, you may spend hours filming with vulnerable people at different locations for a documentary or news feature, talking to them at length on the phone or face to face for a print or online piece, recording with them for a radio package, doing live studio or location interviews, or approaching them at the scene of a traumatic event.

No matter what your beat – news, health, education, crime, social affairs, even politics or sport – the chances are you will spend time working closely with people who may be bereaved, shocked, injured, hurting, or trying to handle a tough time.

Sometimes it can be sudden and unexpected. Mark Shardlow, who is now a BBC sports editor covering events from the Olympics to the Commonwealth Games, was working as a young sports reporter when he was thrust into the scene of a disaster. It was the FA Cup semi-final between Brian Clough's Nottingham Forest and Liverpool and the date was 15 April 1989. 'We all know what happened at Hillsborough that day. Our sports coverage became a breaking tragedy in the days before rolling news,' he tells me. 'Unprepared, we had to deal with emotional and distraught interviewees and eye-witnesses.'

Ninety-six people died in the Hillsborough disaster and it became the worst stadium-related disaster in English sports history. Journalists would be covering the loss and outrage felt by their families for decades to come.

From disasters to disease, attacks to abuse, lost livelihoods to lost lives, the way you work with the people at the heart of your stories matters. It matters personally, as one human being responding to another, but it also matters professionally. By treating people decently, you are more likely to get a stronger story, better access and shots, more insightful interviews, and they are more likely to come back to you as their story unfolds. Tragic stories can run and run, sometimes for years, as we have seen with Hillsborough.

Dr Mary Self is a psychiatrist who had terminal cancer and her book *From Medicine to Miracle: How My Faith Overcame Cancer*[1] charts her recovery. Her story made international headlines in the late 1990s, and having given nearly forty media interviews, she is well placed to give her take on what was helpful and what was not. 'Approximately half of the journalists who conducted these interviews acted professionally and with incredible empathy and understanding. It worked both ways and I gave them a much better story,' she says, adding that she had a lot of bad interviews which in every case greatly distressed her through 'loss of trust and loss of control.'[2]

How it all started

As a journalist, I have covered hundreds of sensitive stories across three decades. It struck me that our traditional approach of practising on the hurting public and sending reporters routinely to knock on the doors of the newly and tragically bereaved, without any formal training in what that may mean to them or to us, is at best outdated and at worst risky and potentially harmful. Health professionals can undergo years of training before asking emotionally vulnerable people the probing questions reporters can be tempted to ask them in an interview.

Some practices are clearly bad: sticking cameras in the faces of people who are grieving, breaking the news of a death, or bullying and bribing people to talk. These levels of intrusion are becoming potentially more exposed, with journalists being held to account through such means as Leveson,[3] Kerslake[4] and through social media.

However, there are more subtle ways in which you can hurt your interviewees in the way you interact with them. Dr Self describes how a loss of *trust* and *control* harmed her, but what did she mean by *control*? What do we actually *do* to our contributors which can be harmful, and why? How may good and bad practice *look* to them?

In 2012, Faith's teenage son Joshua was knocked off his bike by a car as he cycled to school. He died eleven days later in intensive care. Faith was at his bedside. She chose to speak to several reporters about his death, to help raise thousands of pounds to build a skate park in Josh's memory. 'It's often the little things. They don't realise how hurtful it is, not knowing my son's age or name when they get here,' she explains. The effect was that she would clam up, so it was counterproductive on all levels.

Yet a reporter, arriving under-prepared, under pressure and dispatched at the last minute, may not grasp the importance of knowing these details or the impact of other harmful behaviour: Why do families react with such fury to seemingly small inaccuracies in their accounts? Why did one woman, who spoke to reporters about the deaths of her children, describe the experience as akin to being *raped* because they did not contact her after the interview? Why did a survivor at the scene of a terrorist attack struggle to answer technical questions and object to being called a hero? Why was a father incensed by the reporter who hurried him, a mother by the reporter whose phone kept beeping in her bag, and a survivor of sexual abuse whose interviewer appeared sceptical?

When covering sensitive stories, there are key things you need to be aware of. With this in mind, I banged the drum in the BBC and got backing to research, craft, develop and deliver training for reporters in working with people who are emotionally vulnerable or distressed. I linked up with Gavin Rees, director Europe of the Dart Center for Journalism and Trauma, who became a rich seam of information and support.

How sensitivity and respect may 'look' to our interviewees

I believe we tell our stories best through the people they affect, so I applied the same approach when crafting the training. Survivors of sexual abuse, parents whose children had been killed, and children whose parents had died, each of whom had chosen to be interviewed by journalists, went on film to spell out what they liked and disliked about the experience of working with them; what helped and what harmed. Their testimony is powerful for reporters to hear, offers constructive guidance and has quite an impact.

Hundreds of working reporters, correspondents, documentary makers, editors, producers, camera operators and researchers have chosen to attend the sessions and the appetite and the feedback have been overwhelming. This was the response from one senior editor who attended:

'While we still spend a lot of time teaching people how to write and use kit – how to deal with people and get the most out of them in difficult circumstances has been lost as a core skill. Without cracking interviews we've got nothing to work with – everyone in the newsroom who did the course was raving about it.'

The response from a senior lecturer, when I delivered the session to his investigative journalism students, was that it was *mind-blowing*. He told me they felt *empowered* by the training and there is a growing call for these skills to be embedded within student learning.

Reporters say they value *hearing back* from their interviewees, they appreciate clear dos and don'ts and guidance, they like that the course is delivered by someone who does the job so understands some of the pressures we can be up against. They also value being able to share their experiences and expertise with each other.

This book has evolved out of those responses. Many journalists from various news organisations have offered the benefit of their experience. Many survivors and families have also contributed in a spirit of generosity and a willingness to help us improve how we work with them.

During an early roll-out of my training, Faith contacted me with a strong follow-up to Josh's story. We sent a reporter, who had attended my course in the morning, to interview and film with Faith in the afternoon. Unsolicited, she sent me this email:

'Jo, I wanted to say thank you. It made me smile. He rang me and it was obvious to me he'd been in your training session. He made sure he had the information correct about my Josh and if he wasn't sure he said so and we clarified things. The simple "sorry" that makes it so much easier for me to move forward with the report you're doing. By the time we did the piece live, I felt he understood me, my story, my Josh.'

No one-size-fits-all

There cannot be a one-size-fits-all approach to how we work with people whose emotions are in turmoil. Each will have varied responses to what has happened to them and it is important to treat each person as an individual.

However, you can add to people's distress in the way you behave. It is, therefore, important to understand what they may be going through and glean good practice. This can be adapted to the different situations you find yourself in, so that you do your job, do it well and do no harm.

The charity Disaster Action has members who have been involved in, or bereaved through, nearly thirty disasters around the globe. Their book *Collective Conviction* explains how some people, in the wake of a tragedy, described feeling abused by reporters whereas others found the media useful. The authors, Anne Eyre, who is a survivor of Hillsborough, and Pam Dix, whose brother Peter died in 1988 when Pan Am Flight 103 was blown up over Lockerbie killing 270 people, say, 'the difference often comes down to the extent to which our engagement with journalists includes **acknowledgement, compassion, honesty, accuracy, consent and control**.'[5]

Covering sensitive stories is not about allowing your emotions to cloud your impartiality. As a journalist, it is your job to give all sides to the story, but treating your subjects respectfully does not compromise this.

In 2016 US journalist Ken Armstrong was the joint winner of the Pulitzer Prize in Explanatory Reporting for a long-form trauma journalism piece called *An Unbelievable Story of Rape*. In an article about the art of trauma reporting, he offers this advice to journalists:

'I don't think that there's anything about being respectful of people who have been hurt that in anyway undermines the journalistic mission. You want to know what happened, you want to be accurate, fair – none of those things is in tension with being open and transparent and respectful with people who have been hurt.'[6]

How to use this book

This book follows the process of what you may do when covering a sensitive story and applies good practice at each step of the way. The idea is not to teach the nuts and bolts of researching, interviewing, filming or writing but to explain why and how you may need to adapt your practice when the person you are working with is emotionally vulnerable. Sometimes this can involve turning traditional journalistic teaching on its head. Overly interrogative, challenging or incisive interview techniques, for instance, can be wholly inappropriate with people who are feeling disempowered by a traumatic experience.

Each chapter follows a format and each section will enhance your understanding. By the end of the chapter, you should have a clear idea of how to proceed when approaching, preparing, establishing relationships, working with children, interviewing, filming, writing about and following up people's sensitive stories.

The format for the chapters is as follows:

- *The guidance*: some clear dos and don'ts.
- *Extras*: added tips about areas such as cultural considerations, safeguarding children, approaching people through social media, and anonymous filming.
- *Focus*: how experienced journalists tackled assignments relevant to the theme of the chapter.
- *Insight*: constructive observations from our interviewees – what helped and what harmed them at each stage of the process.
- *Overview*: how a high profile journalist goes about covering sensitive stories.
- *Trauma Awareness*: what your interviewees may be going through.

Journalists involved in the book have covered stories such as mass killings, terrorist attacks, disasters, health epidemics, wars, refugees, riots, murders, human trafficking, fires, floods, drownings, kidnappings, radicalisation, trials, inquests, inquiries, suicide, rape, alcoholism, traffic collisions, drug abuse, mental health issues, serial killings, homelessness and many more.

Asking the experts

The book includes two contributed chapters. In doing this work you can regularly be facing raw, visceral emotion head on. A single story which resonates for you, or your relentless ongoing coverage, can hit you when you least expect it. Or it can be a slow burn. I often find interviewing children who are hurting can affect me. Look after yourself, it is essential. To handle tough emotional assignments and do them justice, you need to be in good mental shape yourself.

Dr Cait McMahon, a psychologist and the Asia Pacific director of the Dart Center for Journalism and Trauma, has written the Self-Care chapter. It gives you clear advice on what to look out for, what to do about it and why it matters. Cait received the OAM, one of Australia's highest civil accolades, for her work with journalists and trauma.

Our profession has editorial guidelines and codes of conduct around covering sensitive stories which can be honed further within news organisations. In the Ethics chapter, senior lecturer, researcher and author Dr Sallyanne Duncan spells out what ethics are, why we have them, and tackles some ethical grey areas. Sallyanne is the co-author of *Reporting Bad News: Negotiating the Boundaries between Intrusion and Fair Representation in Media Coverage of Death*.[7]

Professor Stephen Regel has written the *Trauma Awareness* sections in the book. Stephen is the Director/Clinical Lead of the Centre for Trauma,

Resilience and Growth at Nottingham University/NHS. He set up the UK's first academic Trauma Studies programmes and has been involved in Red Cross emergency response missions across the world, from tsunamis to terrorist attacks. In 2013, he started an ongoing project to raise awareness of the impact of traumatic experiences on the lives of survivors. He also co-wrote *Post Traumatic Stress (The Facts)*.[8]

... to reassure

We are journalists, not trained psychologists or therapists, and intense emotions can make some reporters feel insecure and out of their comfort zone. Here are some of the more common concerns which crop up and my responses to them:

- I don't really do touchy feely stuff or hug people, should I make myself? – No, this book does not advocate that. Be genuine, be professional and be kind.
- I'm worried I'll screw up, say something stupid and upset them even more – We all make mistakes, I have and you will, but the fact you are worried about it means you care, and your interviewees will appreciate that. Your attitude is what matters when this happens.
- I tend to try to fix people's problems and I may want to make things better for them – You are not there to sort out their lives or cheer them up, nor would you be able to. The best comfort you can give is to treat them well and do a decent job of telling their story.
- I'm terrified of intruding – This is not uncommon, see the Approach chapter.
- What if I cry when they cry? – This can and does happen occasionally and, though not ideal, is not necessarily unprofessional. It is a human response. Check out the Self-Care chapter if you are regularly over-empathising, as we do have to protect ourselves from being drained by these stories.
- People's strong emotions make me nervous and want to run away – It is important to deal with this. It can help if you think about it as a job which needs doing and needs doing well. Think about them and their responses rather than your own, and never let them feel embarrassed or uncomfortable if they become emotional. Use your nerves to inform your work rather than hinder it.
- I'm on a short-term contract or freelance and under pressure to deliver: am I a reporter first or a human being? – A human being first every time, the two need not be mutually exclusive. You will hear this echoed throughout the book by journalists who are at the top of their game and

are proof that if you treat people well, you are more likely to get better interviews and stories. Bad behaviour is not the way to get a story and, in the current climate, you may well be held accountable.

- Sometimes people think that by making their story public, I'll achieve great things for them or get involved in their campaign – This is an expectation which needs managing so they appreciate your role is to report their story. Remember that you are not their best friend nor their advocate.
- I just want to get in there, get the story, get out and keep my editor happy – As reporters, we are programmed to deliver. But think for a moment if you were the one who was suffering. Which reporter would get the better interview from you: the one who hurried you and treated you like a story, or the one who treated you like a human being and took time to listen? Which one would you return to with your strong follow-up stories? Which result would please the editor most?
- Sometimes, when I'm covering these sorts of stories, I feel protective towards my interviewees. Is this unprofessional? – No.

Depending on your level of experience, different elements of this book will resonate for you in different ways. It does not attempt to suggest strategies for news organisations, when big stories break and the media descends. Instead, it concerns itself with aspiring and working reporters out on the road, who can regularly find themselves face to face with the people affected.

It is not, of course, an exact science and it would be impossible to cover all eventualities. The idea is to increase your awareness of what you may be dealing with and to empower you with a sense of good practice. Adapt it and apply it to different situations and to your way of reporting. Some of it may validate how you are already working.

It may also help to remember that when reporting the stories this book is concerned with, and we cover many of them, you are rarely there to *hold* people to account, but to *hear* their account and to hear it in the best way you can, for them, for you and for your output.

Notes

1   Mary Self and Rod Chaytor, *From Medicine to Miracle: How My Faith Overcame Cancer*, HarperCollins, 2001.

2   Mary Self, 'Tomorrow's Fish-and-Chips Paper,' 1 June 2005, https://dartcenter.org (accessed 24 January 2019).

3   'Leveson Inquiry: Culture, Practice and Ethics of the Press', archived 22 January 2014, www.webarchive.nationalarchives.gov.uk.

4   The Kerslake Arena Review, www.kerslakearenareview.co.uk.

5   Anne Eyre and Pam Dix, *Collective Conviction: The Story of Disaster Action*, Liverpool University Press, 2014, Ch. 10.

6   Alex Hannaford, 'The Art of Trauma Reporting', 27 September 2016, https://dartcenter.org (last accessed 24 January 2019).

7   S. Duncan and J. Newton, *Reporting Bad News: Negotiating the Boundaries between Intrusion and Fair Representation in Media Coverage of Death*, Peter Lang, 2018.

8   Stephen Regel and Stephen Joseph, *Post-Traumatic Stress*, 2nd edn, Oxford University Press, 2017.

2
The approach

'It's someone approaching us in a compassionate way, not in a hurried way. Approaching us and saying I'm sorry for your loss, if it's not too painful would you mind talking to me about it and giving us time. You can immediately pick up from someone whether they're being respectful.'

Rose Dixon, a bereaved mother and CEO of
Support after Murder and Manslaughter

In this chapter

Why and how we make an approach.

What to do and what not to do.

Focus on reporters who secured sensitive interviews.

Insight from families who chose to speak to the media at difficult times.

Overview from Lucy Williamson on how she covers sensitive stories.

Trauma Awareness: traumatic events and common responses.

Ordinary people, extraordinary experiences

From stabbings to shootings, traffic accidents to terrorist attacks, muggings to murders, floods to fires, you tell your stories most effectively through the people they most affect. Louis Theroux describes them as the people who are 'grappling with it directly, whose lives have been upended by something deeply affecting, deeply traumatic.'

'It is a feeling of total shock, disbelief, numbness,' Rose Dixon tells me when describing the sudden death of her daughter Avril, who was 22. 'Whatever we do, there's always an empty chair there.' Rose heads up the charity SAMM and works with many families bereaved through murder and manslaughter.

She chose to speak to reporters about what happened to Avril. Others may choose not to speak to you but you will only find out by asking them.

When attempting to interview people whose lives have been shattered because they have experienced something traumatic, painful or shocking, you have to approach with care and avoid distressing them further. In the aftermath of the Black Saturday bushfires in Australia in 2009, researchers from the University of Melbourne looked at the impact of media exposure on survivors. Overall, they found the coverage had done more good than harm, prompting donations and putting pressure on the authorities to fix problems. But they concluded, 'There is a responsibility on the profession to minimise doing harm … there is certainly much to discuss.'[1]

Unlike politicians or celebrities, people at the centre of these events do not choose to be newsworthy and rarely have any experience of the media. In his book *Journalism, Ethics and Regulation*, Chris Frost explains, 'Their involvement in the story has been thrust upon them and they would prefer to be elsewhere.' He adds that doesn't mean journalists should not interview them, but they should treat them with particular sensitivity.[2]

For journalists, making an approach can feel daunting, as Quentin Rayner, a chief news reporter with more than thirty years' experience, tells me. 'The sense of dread never recedes. You always feel you are impinging. No one wants to do it. You have to hang onto your humanity. What you are most worried about is how they are going to respond. Will they see it as a massive intrusion or will they embrace the chance to share what has happened?'

It can be helpful to view it as part of your job. In an article for *The Independent* newspaper, the journalist David Barnett says it is an essential task for reporters when covering news. 'They have to. That's what they're paid for. It's just not a pretty part of the job and it's certainly not the whole of the job and it might surprise you that often it's actually welcomed by people on the receiving end.'[3]

Research by journalism academics Jackie Newton and Dr Sallyanne Duncan, who have worked extensively with journalists and the families they interview, bears this out. 'It is well known within the industry that most approaches are met with approval from the family, who are often glad of the opportunity to talk about their loved one and let the community know what has happened.'[4]

You make approaches to people in many different ways: by phone, through social media, through a third person, at the scene, by email, by letter, by knocking on their door or putting a note through it. Your interviews may be for print, online, radio or TV, or for all outlets, and they may be live or pre-recorded.

The trickiest approaches can be as the story is breaking or in the immediate aftermath, when you are under pressure to deliver, hordes of journalists have descended, and competition is fierce. But you may also try to make contact after time has elapsed, by approaching people at a court case, an inquest or an anniversary, or you may want to ask them to take part in a documentary, news feature or live phone-in, exploring a wider issue or investigation. You may be focusing solely on their story, or wish to reflect the impact of what has happened on a community or even a nation.

Be mindful that the sensitivity you show in the early days still applies when covering the story further down the line. Take care not to assume, as you make your approach weeks, months or even years later, that they will have got over it. 'As soon as a family starts talking about the murder of their loved one it's like the murder has just happened at that moment in time and they're really into the pain and trauma,' explains Rose Dixon.

Why do we approach?

- *It's about people:* Talking to those affected will transform your story from a sad litany of facts and statistics into an account of human experience. It will provide the emotional narrative and allow insight into the impact of what has happened. 'Journalists know that every story needs a "who," a person who will humanize the event, and stories about violence and victims of crime and disaster are no different,' say Roger Simpson and William Cote in their book *Covering Violence: A Guide to Ethical Reporting about Victims and Trauma.*[5]

- *Getting answers:* There may be a need to hold authorities to account, and the families or survivors will strengthen your mission. Politicians may put off a persistent journalist, but it is much harder for them to ignore families who are grieving and angry and demanding to be heard.

- *Verifying facts:* The information which has been made public about victims may not be correct. It is important to check with a reliable source so that your report is accurate. Getting even the smallest facts wrong, when reporting these stories, can cause immense distress.

- *Giving control:* Families have told me of their anguish when reporters lift material, such as party pictures or inaccurate comments, from social media, without asking or checking. Some can also find it distressing to be ignored and not consulted at a time when their story is being widely reported. 'My name was never mentioned and I was never once asked for an interview. I was just a sibling, I didn't count,' one person told researchers in Northern Ireland who were exploring how the media reports murder and manslaughter.[6]

- *Expectation:* When people hear of an accident, earthquake, bombing, shooting, flooding or any other major news story, they expect to read about, watch or listen to people caught up in it. 'Better reporting about trauma can help readers and viewers gain empathy for the suffering of victims,' say Simpson and Cote.[7]

Why do people choose to speak to reporters?

- *Tribute:* For some families, it can be a comfort to be involved in how the person they have lost is depicted and described publicly. As Richard Keeble points out in his book *Ethics for Journalists*, 'Sometimes people welcome the attention of the reporter and use the interview as an opportunity to celebrate the life of the deceased person.'[8] By being included in the report, they also have some control over the photographs and images that are used. The charity Disaster Action was created by the bereaved people and the survivors of nearly thirty disasters across the world. They asked their members to share with the media why they appreciated being interviewed. 'By listening to my story I felt someone was at least acknowledging the importance of my brother's life and death,' one person said.
- *Awareness:* Someone may have a rare illness, be the victim of medical negligence, be homeless or jobless at Christmas or a survivor of slavery or trafficking, and by bringing their experiences directly into people's homes, via news reports, they instantly draw attention to their plight or to a wider injustice. 'We really wanted the system changed so that others could benefit from our experience,' was another comment by a Disaster Action survivor.
- *Campaigning:* Some families want to spare others from a similar experience. They focus their energies on campaigning for change and can welcome the chance to get their message out. 'It was nice to feel I could make a difference by helping to learn lessons. I tell myself this is one way to try to reduce some of my guilt at surviving,' another survivor shared.
- *Holding to account:* In the same way as journalists want answers, so can people who feel strongly a tragedy should never have happened, and they too can welcome working with reporters. 'We wanted people to know the truth about what had happened,' another family told Disaster Action.[9]
- *Appeal:* There are times when people choose to give interviews because they want to appeal for information and keep an ongoing police investigation in the media spotlight. The rapist, attacker or hit and run driver may still be out there, and hearing from their victims can intensify the search. These interviews can often be managed by police press officers, sometimes through press conferences. Sometimes they are pooled,

where one media outlet will do the interview and the material is given to all news organisations, to avoid the victim having to speak to multiple journalists.

- *Fundraising:* Although it is not a reporter's job to campaign or fundraise, there can be stories in which a family chooses to speak publicly because they want to raise money for a charity, trust or memorial connected to what has happened to them. These efforts can become part of their on-going story.

Good practice

Applying good practice when approaching people who are hurting will not guarantee that you seamlessly secure an interview, but it will allow you to do a difficult job as well as you can. It also allows you to be able to do the job and still look yourself in the mirror afterwards.

If they do not feel able to talk to you immediately, treating people decently can mean that when they are ready to talk, it is you they may choose to come to with their story. As Washington journalist Scott North says, when a child is murdered, the parents are in a fog. 'They hurt so much they can hardly feel for a while. They're not always ready to talk to me.' He adds that survivors don't heal on newsroom deadlines. He also makes the point that murder cases run for a long time, so there is no pressure for them to talk immediately.[10]

These pointers for good practice when making your approach can be adapted to all the means by which you make contact, at all the various times.

- *Preparation:* Before approaching, check the facts that are available. People are unlikely to warm to you if you don't know the name of the person they have lost or the basic circumstances of what has happened. Being well prepared can also help to calm your nerves.
- *Appearance:* If you are approaching face to face, think about the impression you are giving if you are scruffy, as it may be considered disrespectful. You are a professional person doing a professional job. When covering an ongoing attack, make sure you are warm and can move fast.
- *Attitude:* Approach with humanity and compassion and be gentle. Do not rush or be dismissive even if you have a tight deadline. Think how you would feel being approached in similar circumstances.
- *Transparency:* Be clear and honest from the outset about who you are, who you work for, and why you are contacting them. They can be in turmoil and may have had several journalists approaching them, so clarity and honesty are important.

- *Open mind:* Make no assumptions or judgements because people respond differently to traumatic events. Treat them as individuals and respect their reactions. Christine Haughney was a young reporter on the *Washington Post* when she found herself covering the 9/11 attack on the World Trade Center. 'The biggest lesson I have learned from this experience is not to judge how people process tragedy,' she says.[11]
- *Acknowledge:* Some reporters consider it disingenuous to say they are sorry for a person's loss or situation, yet families tell me they value the acknowledgement. It can be a decent human connection to make but must be genuine. 'Do not feign compassion. It can't be faked. Offer sincere condolences early in considerate supporting terms,' is the advice given by the Dart Center for Journalism and Trauma.[12]
- *Apologise:* You are intruding during what is possibly the worst experience of their lives. It may be appropriate to say you are sorry for disturbing them at such a difficult time and you don't wish to intrude, but you have to do a report on what has happened and would like them to be involved.
- *Control:* Their lives have been upended, so families can value you offering them some involvement and control. After a death, this can mean choosing their favourite photographs, checking how they would like you to refer to the person they have lost, and taking the time to verify the all-important facts. 'After a murder the bereaved family are totally out of control. They have to do what the police tell them, they have to do what the coroner says, they have no control over the situation and anybody who comes in and actually gives them a little bit of control, they value that very highly,' Rose Dixon tells me.
- *Confidence:* You may be feeling nervous and anxious but try to manage it. Take a deep breath and approach with quiet confidence and courtesy. It is more likely to reassure people that you will tell their story well.
- *Pressure:* If they do not wish to speak to you, accept it and make it clear there is no pressure. Leave them your contact details and say you would very much like to speak to them should they feel ready. As Scott North explained when approaching the community affected by the Oso mudslide in Washington in March 2014, a major landslide in which forty-three people were killed, 'We accept their answer and we always tell them, "Maybe now isn't the time. Maybe someday it will be the time. And when you're ready to tell us about this person, we'll be ready to listen."'[13]

Bad practice

It may seem obvious, but any behaviour that causes further harm or distress to a potential interviewee would be bad practice. When approaching people to talk to you, this includes subtle or blatant bullying, threatening, intimidating, pressurising or persisting. It also includes coercing, bribing or paying.

Never deceive, manipulate or exploit people. This includes clear acts of deception such as impersonating an official. It also includes subtle manipulation such as suggesting your report will achieve the outcome they want, or being dishonest about how you intend to portray them.

Although you may have a deadline, be careful not to appear hurried, forceful or dismissive. Do not approach children or film them without permission (see the Ethics and Children chapters). Be careful not to reveal more than people may know, or pass on rumours or second-hand information.

In May 2017, a suicide bomber attacked the Manchester Arena injuring hundreds and killing twenty-two people. The youngest was 8. The attack followed a concert by the US singer Ariana Grande and prompted an international media frenzy.

The subsequent Kerslake Arena Review examined the role played by the media in the aftermath of the attack. Families spoke about being 'hounded' and 'bombarded' and put under pressure to appear in TV programmes. Staff at a hospital were given a tin of biscuits containing a note offering £2,000 for information about the injured.

One person was approached by someone claiming to be a bereavement nurse, another told how a reporter rammed a foot in their doorway trying to get access to their home. In two cases, children were given condolences on their doorsteps hours before their families had been officially notified of the deaths.[14]

The Kerslake Review[15] added a further layer of accountability to behaviour which would once have gone under the radar, as does social media where some families can and do express their anger if treated badly by reporters.

How we approach

There are different ways in which you may have to contact people. Alongside the good practice, these are some added points to consider when you are making specific approaches.

Face to face

This can be known as the *death knock* because reporters knock on the door of a bereaved family unannounced. If you are a TV reporter approaching the door with a camera operator by your side, ask them to hold the camera down, not on their shoulder, as this can be off-putting and intimidating. You are not there to ambush them for a statement, but to ask if they would like to talk to you about what has happened. Some reporters prefer the cameraman to hang back altogether and will knock on the door alone.

When people answer the door, don't crowd them, but step back a little and give them some space. Unless you are one of many reporters who have been knocking on their door, they won't be expecting you, so introduce yourself. Think beforehand about what you are going to say and be honest and straight with them. Treat them with dignity and do not record without permission.

'I'd knock on the door, it would open a crack and someone would answer,' the newspaper reporter Sue White says in Emma Lee Potter's book *Interviewing for Journalists*. Then she would say, 'Hello I'm Sue White from the *Birmingham Evening Mail*. We've heard from the police about the dreadful accident last night. Could I come in and have a word with you about it?' Almost everyone would invite her in, she says. 'I felt if I talked openly in as friendly and sympathetic a way as possible – one person to another, making clear I just wanted to confirm some facts – people would give me the information. I was usually right.'[16]

You are trying to make a human connection. One journalist, who had followed a stream of reporters up the garden path, tells me she made her approach and simply said, 'You must be so sick of people like me knocking at your door, I'm so sorry about all this,' and the woman invited her in.

The award-winning US journalist Chip Scanlan describes an assignment as a young reporter, when he was sent to the family home of a woman who had accidentally been killed in crossfire between a prison parolee and police. 'An idea came just before I knocked. When the woman's father opened the door I identified myself, apologized for bothering them at this terrible time and said I wanted them to know that the paper was going to write a story about what had happened to their daughter. Then I added, "I just didn't want you to pick up the paper and say, 'Couldn't they at least have asked us if we wanted to say anything?'"'[17] He adds that taking the 'tough guy' approach rarely works and 'a softer more human one is more effective.'

The editor of the *Press Gazette*, Dominic Ponsford, is unequivocal about reporters making these approaches. 'I would argue that when you are writing a story about someone's death or serious injury it would be disrespectful not to contact the family.' He adds, 'It is a task which no journalist enjoys but it has to be done. And as a mark of respect it should be done face to face.'[18]

It can be controversial but, although you have to expect rejection, don't assume they will say *no*. No matter what response you get, treat 'people in extremis with the utmost grace and respect', says Andrew Hogg, a former news editor of *The Sunday Times* newspaper, and he adds that sometimes interviewees can find it therapeutic to talk about what has happened. 'I am not suggesting that when you … are going to interview widows and widowers that you are going to be providing some kind of surrogate therapy for them. But … don't be frightened, don't go and hide in the loo when you are confronted with the request from your news editor.'[19]

Although they can readily dispatch you to these homes, editors and producers rarely advise you how best to go about it. The only 'helpful' tip one reporter tells me he was given by his editor when he started out on a local newspaper was, 'always shut the garden gate.'

Approaching 'at the scene'

When covering an unfolding disaster make sure you and your crew are safe and that the people you may want to interview are safe.

You may get any number of responses from people, but remain calm and respectful. 'A distracted fire fighter waves me away with a gruff, "Not now,"' recounts Heidi Singer from when she was reporting on 9/11. 'A familiar stress twists in my stomach: I need to do my job and I don't want to be a pest.'[20]

Journalists can be under intense pressure to gather eyewitness interviews, tweet updates and do live slots from the scene. Amidst all of this, the BBC's Paris correspondent Lucy Williamson, who has covered countless disasters, tells me it is important to trust your instincts as a human being. 'Firstly because you have to live with yourself after you've covered the story and secondly because I don't think putting the journalist first gets you the story anyway.' Richard Bilton who reports for the BBC's current affairs flagship programme *Panorama* has also been in these situations many times and adds, 'You're expected to deliver but that oughtn't to change the way you behave.'

The heightened sense of awareness can make people keen to talk about what has happened to them initially. 'In the hours after a violent event a victim, survivor or witness may want to apprehend a violent person, stop a pattern of violence in a community or give voice to the emotions aroused by the devastating fire, flood or earthquake,'[21] say Simpson and Cote, who also emphasise the responsibility journalists have in these circumstances. 'Reporters are not trained to assess the emotional state of a person, but they can take pains to assure that the people being interviewed know who is asking the questions and understand why the interview is taking place.'

Be mindful that people can have varied reactions to shock. Some can be calm and appear rational, others may be overcome, angry or frozen. People 'may not be in a fit state to be interviewed, filmed or photographed, to give anything like informed consent to an interview, so go easy on them,' advises the Dart Center for Journalism and Trauma.[22] Take a look at the *Trauma Awareness* section at the end of this chapter to get an indication of what your potential interviewees may be going through.

Equally, be aware that you may witness sights which are hard to forget, as the journalist Nick Spangler did when covering 9/11. He was 25 at the time and a student at the Columbia Graduate School of Journalism. 'I saw two bodies fall and I saw four that had already hit. I saw one fall on the opposite edge of the square, arms out and legs straight.'[23] Be mindful of the effect these experiences can have on you and have a read of the Self-Care chapter.

When asking an eyewitness, who seems calm enough, to speak to you for an interview, ask them first of all if they are all right. Apply the good practice of explaining who you are and, if you are filming, introduce the camera operator too. Ask simple open questions and do not ask them to speculate. See the *Focus* and *Insight* sections in this chapter, and Lucy Williamson's account of how she covers sensitive stories, for more on this.

Despite the pressure you may be under and the potential chaos around you, it is important to take a moment and recognise that your behaviour may impact on the people you approach. When a Swedish study examined survivors' experiences of being approached by journalists at two separate train crashes, it found their reactions were mixed. One group of passengers described feeling violated. 'This group of survivors felt dizzy, shocked and unable to judge the significance of being interviewed or photographed during a stressful event.' They found it offensive to have to keep turning interview requests down. Another group found the interaction helpful. 'The journalist became a listener in the midst of chaos and was perceived as caring.'[24]

Approaching by phone

Although establishing a rapport can be trickier by phone, you can make an empathetic connection without eye contact or body language to help you.

Newsrooms can be noisy places, so if you are about to ring a family, try to find a quiet spot. Bursts of laughter or live broadcasts happening around you will be distracting for you and for the person you are calling.

Be warm and maintain a softer tone of voice and have your facts to hand before making the call, to avoid trawling through them as you are speaking. As a planning journalist, Rosemary Harding can make several sensitive approaches by phone each week from her newsroom and gives good advice in the *Focus* section of this chapter.

Always be clear with people about what you are asking and don't assume they understand the process. If you are ringing to ask if they would mind doing a TV interview, take a little time to explain what that involves. It isn't unusual for people to think they'll be overrun by a team of lighting and sound guys, directors and producers, and will have to do a live outside broadcast, when the reality is much more discreet.

Explain that it would simply be you, or you and a camera operator. Tell them that it would be at their home or wherever they choose and it would be very low key. Your main consideration is that they are comfortable with everything and you will talk it all through with them. This way, you take away the fear of the unknown and they will be more likely to agree to the interview.

Written approaches

Be careful with your use of language and your tone in any written approach, whether through social media, by email, letter or a note through someone's door. Follow the good practice by being clear about who you are, where you are from and why you are making contact. Ask a colleague to cast an eye over what you have written. Re-read it yourself as if you were the person about to receive it and imagine how you would feel if you were emotionally vulnerable and read what you had written.

If you have called round at someone's home address and had no response you may wish to leave a note through the door. Again, think about how the look and tone of your note may appear to them. One reporter I spoke to will keep writing drafts in her notebook until she's happy with the finished note and will always make sure it is neat, tidy and grammatically correct. It is about being re-spectful. Dashing off a scrappy note because you are under pressure is unlikely to be well received or effective. Another reporter told me she keeps smart notepaper in her car for just this reason. It may seem like a small detail, but if the note is what secures you the interview, then it is worth writing it with care.

Families have told me they can find a business card put through their door too impersonal. One mother, whose 6-year-old son had died in hospital, told me three separate journalists sent her sympathy cards with business cards inside. Not surprisingly, she felt sickened.

Third person approach

This can be viewed as the most sensitive way for journalists to approach peo-ple. Making contact through the person's school, college, employer, the police, their lawyer, a family friend, a neighbour or vicar can give the person you wish to interview a little time and distance to consider your request.

There are situations when a direct approach would not be appropriate. You wouldn't normally 'door knock' a rape victim, but would be more likely to make contact through the police. In his book *Journalism: Principles and Practice*, Tony Harcup tells how the award-winning *Times* newspaper journalist Andrew Norfolk made sensitive approaches. He was carrying out his ground-breaking investigation into the grooming of girls for sexual exploitation in Rochdale, Rotherham and elsewhere. The newspaper's chief investigative reporter wanted to show how the girls and their families had been repeatedly failed by the authorities. 'Norfolk had to tread very carefully ... and did not approach victims directly because of their vulnerability and young ages. Instead he contacted family support groups and gradually built up sufficient trust to allow one-to-one meetings and interviews to take place.'[25]

There are tips on approaching at inquests and court cases in the Follow-ups chapter.

EXTRAS: Approaching through social media

Sam Dubberley co-founded First Draft News which gives practical and ethical guidance on how to find, verify and publish content sourced from the social web. He is the co-founder of Eyewitness Media Hub. He co-authored a global study exploring the use of user-generated content, or UGC, in TV and online news and is special advisor to the Crisis Response team and manager of the Digital Verification Corps at Amnesty International. Here he gives advice on approaching sensitively through social media.

- Have you read all the comments? Often someone sharing content online from a breaking news event will reply to requests from media to use their content – and give widespread permissions. Don't contribute needlessly to the flood of messages they will be receiving – most importantly from their friends and family asking if they are safe.
- Is the contact safe? If you are the first to find someone sharing content online, understand that, just because someone involved in a breaking news situation is communicating on social media, this does not mean they are safe. Always consider this before attempting to contact them and in the questions you ask.
- What language do they speak? If you're trying to contact someone on social media, remember that your native language may not be theirs. Try and communicate in their language if at all possible – online translation platforms can be a real help here.

- Can we communicate offline? If someone is sharing content publicly from a breaking news event, they are likely being inundated with messages – try and communicate with them directly and privately if at all possible.
- Did you capture the content? Remember also that the person sharing content might not be the person who captured it. You need informed consent to use it from the person who captured it, not the person who uploaded it.
- Do you understand where I will be publishing your content? Make sure that you explain where else your contact's content could appear if you use it. People don't understand what affiliates in other countries are, or what providing content to a news agency really means – so make sure you explain in clear language, so they are not surprised (or placed in danger) if they see their content online or broadcast in other countries.
- To credit or not to credit? Ask if a person wants to be credited if you use their content – they may want to be or may not want to be – don't assume either way, as this can have different repercussions to different people.
- Have you verified the content? Ensure that the content is really from the event in question before publishing anything. Failure to do so can really hurt if you're wrong.
- Can't I just 'fair deal' it? Fair dealing or fair usage laws vary from jurisdiction to jurisdiction – so don't assume you can rely on those if you can't get informed consent to use the content – especially if you're using the content after the event is no longer headline news.
- Make sure you're okay afterwards! Covering breaking news events can take its toll on all of us even if we're not there. Be aware of what vicarious trauma is, how it builds gradually, and make sure to look after yourself.

FOCUS on journalists

Caroline Lowbridge is a former newspaper reporter who works for the BBC's news online service. In 2017 and again in 2018 she won Digital/Online Journalist of the Year at the Midland Media Awards.

When a sensitive story breaks, Caroline's first step will be to put the name of the person involved into social media. Facebook would be her first port of call though she says Instagram is becoming more popular with younger people.

She can often see who their friends and relatives are and can make contact. Her approach will vary depending on the circumstances but she will often start with an apology. 'I'll write something like "I'm sorry to contact you via

Facebook when something like this has happened, however we're reporting on the story about X and we wanted to give you the opportunity to say something." I explain who I am and sometimes acknowledge the fact they're probably being bombarded by lots of media,' she tells me.

Caroline will always message people privately. 'I've seen reporters commenting underneath people's posts or underneath people's pictures and I think they do that because people are more likely to spot the message, but I feel that's a bit too insensitive. It's a balance, but I think I'd rather wait longer for a response than send something insensitive which they might not reply to anyway.'

Caroline was due to cover an inquest into the death of a woman who had killed herself after being abused by her ex-boyfriend. Concerned about approaching the woman's family at the inquest itself, she decided to make contact beforehand via Facebook. 'I thought if I approached the family at the inquest they're going to be really upset and they probably won't want to talk to me because inquests can be very emotional,' she explains.

She sent the woman's mother a private Facebook message to introduce herself and let her know she would be at the inquest. They exchanged a few messages but Caroline could sense the mother was hesitant. She has since learnt the mother was wary initially because she thought the ex-boyfriend may have set up a fake account and be using it to message and taunt her, pretending to be a journalist.

At the inquest, Caroline introduced herself. 'I told her I was really sorry for what had happened to her daughter and I was here if she wanted to talk to me afterwards but if not, I understood as it can be really upsetting. I could tell she was glad I had gone over and spoken to her.'

The mother did do an interview with Caroline for online news, and several follow-up stories which were covered by national newspapers. 'She was really glad that the story was out there because she felt like someone was listening to her.'

> Helena Lee started out doing work experience at national newspapers and local radio stations during her holidays. Her first full-time job was at IRN (Independent Radio Network) before moving to LBC independent radio, then into the BBC as a news correspondent. Here she explains how she approached people after the Grenfell Tower fire in London in June 2017, in which seventy-two people died.

Helena says the Grenfell Tower fire is a story no reporter can forget covering. The day after it started she was sent to one of the hospitals where some of the injured had been taken. She was reporting live updates for the BBC News Channel.

When she spotted a couple leaving the hospital, she asked the cameraman to hold back, as she thought it would be off-putting, and made her approach. The man and his pregnant wife had been in the tower block and had managed to escape.

'I was trying to judge if they would be happy if we asked them for an interview and whether they would be all right to speak about it because clearly this had just happened some hours earlier,' she tells me.

'I simply told him where we were from and asked what his story was. He and his pregnant wife were happy to talk but it was about being very sensitive, asking if they were okay and I often do this. It might sound simple but asking how are you? how are you coping? often starts the conversation and they can be willing to talk about it.'

Helena was sent to cover a march in the wake of the Grenfell fire where the crowd was tense and emotions were running high. 'There were hundreds of people who had been affected, who had perhaps lost somebody in the fire and they wanted answers.'

In that situation, Helena advises playing down your presence. 'When I wanted to approach somebody, I didn't show them the microphone, I simply asked them if they would like to have a chat without sticking a camera in their face. It was a volatile situation so keeping a low profile was important. You come across all sorts of people and some are more vulnerable than others.'

She spoke to an Australian man who had gone into the tower to rescue people. He was confident and was prepared to be interviewed for TV. 'I explained it would be live and they would want him to describe what had happened and what he had seen. He was happy to talk about what he had been through, but I was also very aware that he had experienced something horrific so I don't think you can be naive in that sense. You have to be mindful that somebody has been through a traumatic event even though they appear confident.'

If you have approached people to talk to you, take the time to say thank you, says Helena. 'Often with stories in those kinds of situations, you have to get back to the truck to feed the interviews but I still like to take the time to have a conversation off air with them. They've taken time to speak to you about something that's been very difficult.'

Kathleen Mullin studied journalism in Belfast before working for the local independent radio station 6FM and as a parliamentary reporter for Hansard. As a researcher and assistant producer for BBC TV's current affairs department in Belfast, she has worked on documentaries for BBC Three, BBC Two and Panorama, the BBC's investigative documentary programme.

The *Panorama* team was on the ground early after the Grenfell Tower fire, as were many reporters. Kathleen's task was to get a sense of who they needed to interview and whether those people would want to talk, while also being aware that nearly everyone she spoke to was traumatised.

She describes two approaches she made, one where they chose to speak to her and another where they didn't.

'I was taken by a member of the community to the mother of a child who had not made it down from one of the top floors of the building. In that particular instance, I was aware I was in an incredibly privileged position to have been asked there to experience their grief with them. Because I was dealing with people from an African country, their expression of grief was different culturally to what I am used to, much more open,' Kathleen tells me.

The family chose not to be interviewed. 'I left my details and all professional bases were covered. But the fact I didn't put any pressure on them, and I was involved with them on a more human level, meant parts of the community became aware of that attitude. We were conscious of the sensitivity of our role and the fact we were human beings first was appreciated. So even though I didn't get the interview, the communication was important.'

Another approach she made was to a man who felt able to be interviewed about rescuing a neighbour on his way down the tower. 'In the midst of this incredible trauma you have someone who wants to talk about it, because it's a natural human need to talk about something extraordinary that's happened to you, even if it's extraordinarily bad.'

In her years of experience, Kathleen has found that motivation is the key to people choosing to speak to reporters and, if they feel their story will be useful to others, they will generally be cooperative. This was the case with her interviewee at Grenfell. 'He wanted to make sure that telling his story was going to be beneficial to the community as well. That was very important to him.'

> *Rosemary Harding is a senior journalist who has worked in newspapers, radio and TV. She is a planning producer heading up a regional news-gathering team so is constantly setting up stories and approaching potential interviewees.*

When setting up a sensitive story, prepare as much as you can beforehand. 'Step back for a moment. Read any documents that you've got, do a bit of research. It's really important that you don't go into making that phone call on the back foot. You've got to feel confident that you're not going to make things worse by not knowing the story fully,' Rosie tells me.

There is a balance to strike between gaining their confidence and maintaining your objectivity. 'You want to approach it professionally. You're dealing with it in an impartial way but you also want to make sure you can make a connection with the person so they feel confident in your ability to be professional.'

Knowing the background will help to establish a connection and build trust. 'You're going to be talking to them about something very personal and very important to them. I always remember from my journalism training days many years ago that, as a journalist you are talking to people every day about stories. But for them that could be the only time in their life that they ever speak to a reporter and potentially are on television or on radio or on a story online. For them it's a really big occasion and incredibly important and we should never forget that.'

Consider your environment when making a sensitive approach by phone. 'If you're in a busy newsroom where people are laughing or joking it can be embarrassing or off-putting if you're ringing somebody about a tragic or sensitive story and they can hear the background noise. It can throw you and it doesn't sound professional,' explains Rosie. She also advises having the relevant paperwork or information ready on screen. 'Think about that so you're not furtling around while you make that call and you can give them one hundred per cent of your concentration.'

Check if they are all right to talk to you, because if you are ringing their mobile they could be anywhere. 'Asking if it is convenient is a good way to make contact without barging in. It shows you are being considerate and not assuming they've got to tell you anything. Then I would explain who I am and why I'm phoning and the programme I work for and what I would like to discuss with them. You learn over time and there's a degree of instinct. Some people want to be quite factual and matter of fact and others need to talk round it a lot more before you get to the main point.'

A good way to connect with your potential interviewee can be to refer to an aspect of what they are going through. 'If it's about a child and they're in hospital you can say something that shows you appreciate and understand where they are, perhaps talking about their journey to and from hospital every day to visit and the traffic. It can be something, not central to the actual story, but central to their life. You're not saying you know what it's like to go through the trauma, but on a practical level you can identify with some of the day-to-day things they might have to deal with.'

Use a gentler tone and be compassionate. 'You don't have to be hard. It's about making a connection and being genuine. You can show kindness and still get the story.'

Nerves can be a good thing because they heighten your awareness. 'If you're not nervous then you're probably not appreciating how important the story really is. See it as being your natural reaction to something that's slightly out of your comfort zone. It does become easier.'

Tony Roe is a veteran news reporter who started out in local radio before moving to TV as a reporter and documentary maker. He has covered stories nationally and internationally and is currently a regional BBC Political Editor.

Tony describes a story during the first Gulf War when he was a young TV reporter. He went against the news pack when making an approach and it served him well.

Tony had filmed Flight Lieutenant Robbie Stewart telling primary school children, at a morning assembly, about his job. A month later, Robbie Stewart was the navigator in an RAF Tornado bomber shot down over Iraq and Tony was dispatched to his home to get a reaction from his family.

'Part of me thought yes, go and camp outside Robbie Stewart's home in a small village along with the rest of the media pack which gathers at times like this. A bigger part of me thought it's not the right thing to do. One organisation had put lights up outside. The family were in there, Robbie's wife and two young children,' Tony tells me.

Instead, he interviewed the vicar who knew the family and could talk about the shock felt by them and the community. 'I wrote an old-fashioned letter to Robbie's wife explaining how we'd been filming with him and expressing our regret at what had happened. I said if they ever wanted to talk in the future I would be happy to but I wasn't going to pester them and left it at that.'

Shortly afterwards, the war ended and some allied prisoners were freed – Robbie Stewart was one of them. He had ejected and landed in the desert, shattered his leg and been held prisoner at the notorious Abu Ghraib prison in Baghdad.

Reluctant to talk to the media on his return home, he did agree to an interview with Tony who then went on to follow his road to recovery and to flying again. When Robbie retired, after more than forty years' service, Tony was there to cover the story. Robbie was flying with his daughter Kirsty who was now also in the RAF and became the first female pilot in the world-famous Red Arrows.

Another story Tony followed over many years was the case of the serial child killer Beverley Allitt. In May 1993, Allitt, a hospital nurse, was convicted of murdering four children in her care and attacking nine others. Tony's job was to approach and work with the children's families. 'There were a lot of people and I had to approach them all over time. It was a process helped by the fact that the families had formed a group together to push for a speedy conclusion to the police investigation. It meant a couple of leaders emerged who would tell their story but also help liaise with others who were perhaps more reluctant. Going through a third party often helps,' he advises.

Tony also attempted to approach Allitt's family for a comment. 'It's clearly not the easiest task to track down and then try to secure an interview with an alleged killer or their family. Her father later gave me short shrift when I tried to persuade him to talk.'

> *Nick Southall is an investigative radio reporter. He won the BBC Frank Gillard Journalist of the Year award in 2015. Here he talks about approaching people during the search for April Jones in Wales. In October 2012, the 5-year-old was abducted and murdered.*

The huge search for April made national and international news and her home town was awash with reporters. 'I hate media scrums, they are so intrusive for the community,' Nick tells me. 'A couple of times I decided to let the scrum happen and I waited on the sidelines. When it had died down, I went up to the person afterwards. I made a more personal kind of approach and found I got exactly what I needed to get out of it. That was very effective.'

Nick joined in with the search and was profoundly affected when the missing person story became a murder hunt. 'People were in tears and it was finding the right way to approach. What are you looking to get from interviewing them? I guess it was trying to portray that sense of shock from the community and give the listener or viewer a real feel for what it's like there. Then the story would change a bit, because people would raise money for the family, so you can start focusing on some of the more positive angles of the story.'

INSIGHT from interviewees

> *Holly found herself caught up in a terrorist attack and shares her insight to help journalists who may interview eyewitnesses at the scene.*

In June 2017, eight people were murdered when three attackers drove a van into pedestrians on London Bridge, then attacked people with knives. The killers were shot dead. Holly was on the bridge that night and the van drove straight at her.

'I can't describe fear like it. I remember just freezing to the spot thinking I'm potentially going to die and it was almost as if the whole world zooms down on you and it's so very overwhelming,' she told me. Holly leapt out of the way just in time. 'I looked down the bridge and I could just see it hitting all these people, bodies going in the air. It was insane, like dominoes. It's just something your mind can't contemplate.'

Her first tip for reporters is to avoid putting ideas into the minds of witnesses. 'At that point you are so confused that if a reporter tells you something, you can think it's the truth when it's not. Be careful not to speculate. You want my opinion and you want to know what I saw and you don't want to jeopardise that.'

Think about the questions you are going to ask and keep them simple. For Holly questions such as what did you see? are you okay? what happened? all worked well, but what didn't work well were technical questions such as how fast the van was going.

'I said it was going about fifty to sixty miles an hour. Now that wasn't the case, it wasn't going that fast but when you have a van hurtling towards you, the speed and time don't make sense because you're so frightened. So be careful with questions about facts and figures,' she advises.

Her quote about the speed the van was doing was on the front page of newspapers the next day. 'To be honest I felt quite guilty because that information was wrong. Asking me what speed it was going was a technical question and those are hard to contemplate. I didn't even have a clue what time it was, so avoid the finer details so close after it's happened. Treat your victims with the respect they deserve. They aren't going to know the finer facts if it's a breaking story. Be quite broad with your questions,' she advises.

Holly agreed to be interviewed at the scene and, although profoundly shocked, was relatively calm, but she advises reporters against talking to people who are clearly in a state of heightened distress. 'A man got out of his car and started screaming, people were in tears or being sick or lying on the floor shivering whereas I was okay to talk. Everybody reacts differently.'

Not surprisingly, the national and international media pounced and Holly was in great demand as an interviewee for weeks after the attack. When making an approach she advises journalists to be honest and clear from the start about who they are and what they want. 'If you have a bad experience with one of them that's it, you don't want to speak to anyone.'

Most hurtful and infuriating were her experiences with journalists who were deceitful when making their approach. They rang pretending to be from a different news organisation or were not straight about what they wanted from her. One international news organisation she had agreed to talk to said they would send a car for her but refused to say why. 'About an hour beforehand, they finally told me the interview would be on London Bridge. I was so mad, just so angry and I felt betrayed because you feel like you are doing the media a favour by doing these interviews. The main reason I did them was to let people know I was safe and to let the victims' families know what had happened,' says Holly.

Being honest and open at the scene is equally important, says Holly. 'Keep it all very clear. When you go up to the victim, introduce yourself. If you've got a cameraman, introduce them as well. It's very intimidating at the best of times to have a camera in your face and being asked to be interviewed, never mind when you've just experienced this.'

The final piece of advice Holly gives to reporters is to check your eyewitness is safe, particularly in an ongoing attack, and be very careful not to put them in danger.

> Rose works with hundreds of families internationally who are suddenly and brutally bereaved, through her charity Support after Murder and Manslaughter. Here she shares her experiences to help reporters who approach families after a violent loss of life.

'It's someone approaching us in a compassionate way, not in a hurried way. Be human rather than "I'm a busy reporter and I've got to get this story out,"' says Rose.

She adds that humanity and compassion will make a big difference. 'It's not so much what you say to a family, it's the way you say it. Approach us and say I'm so sorry for your loss, if it's not too painful would you mind talking to me about it. Give us time. You can immediately pick up from someone whether they're being respectful. It is asking them all the time, what is comfortable for you?'

Rose adds that little things in your approach will make a big difference and your attitude is key. 'After a murder, the bereaved family are totally out of control. They have to do what the police tell them, they have to do what the coroner says, they have no control over the situation. Anybody who comes in and actually gives them a little bit of control, they value that very highly. So asking me how would you like me to refer to your daughter, that gives me a little bit of control.'

Often it is when reporters take control away that they can cause distress, such as lifting material from social media sites without asking the family's permission. 'That makes most people feel very angry,' says Rose.

'Don't treat me like someone who's got a story to tell, treat me as a bereaved mother, or a bereaved father or wife. Show me that little bit of respect and compassion. Don't tell me you know how I feel. You may have lost your granny but that bears no comparison to losing somebody through murder. When you are in that quagmire of pain and grief and trauma, things like that come over as being very painful and insensitive.'

'I had someone say to me once, I know exactly how you feel, I lost my dog recently. I just looked at him and thought my goodness, is this man for real.'

The following experiences are shared by families whose children were murdered and who wished to pass on their insight to reporters, while remaining anonymous.

'I would prefer to be approached by email or via the police press office as this gives me the chance to think it over and decide whether to respond. My motivation was to represent my daughter, pay tribute to her, give the human story, the impact on families, insight into our experience and to ensure all facts relating to my daughter and my experience were portrayed correctly. Once I had established contact with any filming companies they would explain format, timings, location for the interview, expenses and sent links or CDs of previous programmes. This was very helpful in making a decision as to whether to be involved.'

'We felt invaded by the press when pictures of our daughter had been taken from her social media sites without our approval. We would have liked the opportunity to choose. Many were out of date and we found it very upsetting to see pictures of our daughter together with her murderer.'

'We had many offers to tell our story in magazines, tabloid papers, TV programmes and documentary programmes. The murder programme production teams' written correspondence was either through Facebook or postal letters. They were the most insensitive and intrusive because they were written in a threatening tone and manner. These would start with their "sincere" condolences and sadness for the loss of our daughter but would then lead into threats if we didn't appear in their TV programmes, saying they would still continue to film without us anyway … we found all this very upsetting, causing us deep distress at a time when we didn't need it.'

HOW I COVER SENSITIVE STORIES: LUCY WILLIAMSON

'Put people before stories every time.'

Lucy is the BBC's Paris correspondent. She has covered stories of violence and human suffering across the globe. Her career began at the BBC's World Service in London where her first foreign reporting role was as a Middle East reporter, working for much of the year in Gaza and the West Bank but also covering stories in Iraq, Iran, Lebanon, Jordan, Egypt and the Gulf.

She was then the Jakarta correspondent for three years, followed by a further three and a half years in Seoul, covering the North and South Korea story.

Just before she left South Korea, she covered the Sewol ferry disaster in 2014: 304 people died when the ferry carrying schoolchildren sank.

'Their parents would gather on the quayside and wait for these boats to come in, ferrying the dead bodies back to shore, to find out if it was one of their kids,' Lucy told me. 'There were thousands of parents and grandparents and family members. I don't think I've ever seen so much shock and desolation. It was partly the limbo that made it so painful for them – not knowing yet if your child had died, not having a body to hold and grieve. It was very, very difficult to approach them for an interview. My cameraman and others got attacked and chased and kicked by some people. It felt incredibly intrusive.'

Making an approach

Trust your instincts as a human being is Lucy's advice. 'When you find yourself reporting on situations like that where the human emotion of it is overwhelming and you recognise that, the journalist in you has to come second. Firstly, because you have to live with yourself after you've covered the story but secondly because I don't think putting the journalist first gets you the story anyway.'

Following the ferry disaster, Lucy kept the cameraman back, and if parents were open to being approached, she went to sit with them on their ground-sheets. 'You almost have to wait for them to invite you in to that situation because they are so raw. Parents who don't know if their child is alive or dead and whether they'll get their body back.'

The invitation may be as simple as a moment of eye contact which acknowledges you are there. 'You have permission then to say "I'm very sorry. Do you mind if I talk to you?" It's about going very slowly, feeling very softly where they are and what their response is to talking about it. That repays you. If they do want to talk, you can establish that respectful relationship and that trust, and then they are likely to trust you with their feelings and their story.'

Covering terror

When Lucy moved on to Paris her work was dominated by covering terrorist attacks, around a dozen so far. Among them were the Charlie Hebdo and Hypercacher attacks, the November Paris attacks including the Bataclan, plus attacks in Brussels, Nice and Copenhagen. 'You have to keep safe,' cautions Lucy. 'Not all attacks are over when you are covering them.'

Unlike the Sewol ferry disaster, people in these situations may be hyperaroused. 'There are very strong opinions about what's happened, who's to blame and the information isn't always accurate. So be careful of that. Be careful of jeopardising ongoing police operations with what you're reporting. It's always a bit chaotic after a sudden news event and getting accurate information can take time. If you're doing "live" news, on a breaking story, there's a strong pressure to piece together a narrative very quickly, but the story can change once information starts coming out.'

Approaching at the scene

Approaching people is always a judgement call but Lucy advises sometimes making the approach alone, without the cameraman or producer. 'Treat them with gentleness, you can do a lot of harm in that situation if you're not careful. If you find that someone isn't ready to talk at that time, try and keep in contact with them if they're willing to do that because you can often build a relationship afterwards. Suggest that you text or call later on, or the next day, and stick to what you've agreed.'

People sometimes want to bear witness to help them make sense of particularly traumatic events. 'Telling their story to a public audience is sometimes healing for people,' she says. 'Remember you're pressing on a wound when you approach those close to a traumatic event, they haven't chosen to be in the public eye. You're looking for their consent and to win their trust, so don't bully or blackmail them.'

Even if you have just minutes to do the interview, Lucy says it is important to take a moment at the start to connect with them on a personal level and acknowledge what they have been through. 'Give them a safe space in which to speak. If you don't have long to do the interview, cut your cloth accordingly, don't try to rush them through a whistle-stop tour of the whole event. Be gentle in focusing them in on the core points.'

Another key point Lucy makes is to avoid over-promising in terms of your impact on or involvement in their lives, and to be careful when asking eyewitnesses to describe traumatic incidents. 'Dial it back a step if they seem overwhelmed or upset. Keep your focus on them and watch your own reactions, even if what they're telling you is very disturbing.'

Sensitive interviewing

Consider the location in which you may be talking to your interviewee. 'Be careful taking them back to the scene, especially if it is the first time they've returned there. Don't ask them to re-live something or pressure them to get the perfect quote, or push them to get something more graphic.'

Equally, be mindful of your response if your interviewee does share something which is difficult to hear. 'Just be careful of how you are reacting to that because, if they're telling you for the first time what's happened to them, you don't want to be a robot but neither do you want to react so strongly that you make them feel more isolated, more marginalised, as if they'll never get back from where they are. They're the focus, you're not the focus.'

Always get permission for an interview and do it somewhere your interviewee feels comfortable. 'When you sit down next to them, it's about that human to human contact and going in softly and almost letting them lead the conversation. Doing interviews is like doing a three-dimensional jigsaw; you've got the issues in your head, you've got the questions and how best to frame them, and you've got what the person in front of you actually says and how you respond to that. With someone who may be traumatised, it can work better to let them lead you through the forest and not push them through in a particular way, because you'll get to whatever the heart of it is, our brains work like that. You'll get to the most important things because that's how it works, you don't have to push them there.' You just need to be alert and listen out for what those important things are.

Sensitive interviews are very different from interviewing politicians where you may have to push for answers, explains Lucy. 'With this conversation, the thing that has affected that person most will rise to the surface if you give it space to do so. It will make the interviewee feel better than if you are channelling them down a particular path. So how many limbs were hanging off? How bad was it? How much blood was there? That sort of stuff can make a lot of interviewees shut down. And you have to live with yourself afterwards.'

If you have time, her advice is to start at the beginning and let them tell you their story, take you through what happened. 'If they get stuck at a particularly horrific point you make a judgement call as to whether to try and keep them there or whether now is not the time and you let it go. It's the old thing we come back to all the time as journalists which is the conflict that sometimes arises between being a decent human being and being a decent journalist.'

People before stories

If it comes down to a direct choice, it is the person before the story for Lucy, but she adds, 'I don't think it's a zero sum game. Often you can get some of your best insights into what someone's been through by giving them the space to be human first. The same is true when you are reporting something. Why does any story matter? It's because we relate to the individual experiences that the person has gone through.'

'So even with something huge and overwhelming that hits a whole country or city, it's the individuals that people will connect with. Make it about the people; that person, that individual, that story because it's too big otherwise.'

The Bataclan experience

In 2015 in Paris, gunmen and suicide bombers hit a concert hall, a major stadium, restaurants and bars almost simultaneously, killing 130 people and wounding hundreds more.

The story was overwhelming and had a particular impact on the Paris team. Lucy was no stranger to violent breaking stories, from Gaza and Iraq to coups and civil unrest in Asia. Her cameraman had covered Bosnia, yet the Bataclan attack felt unique. 'One was the scale of the attack in Europe. It was multiple locations, there was a very high number of deaths and the style of violence was highly sadistic and personal. That made it very difficult. And the threat was ongoing that night, so when we were outside the Bataclan, reporting the siege, some of the attackers were still at large in Paris and it was very chaotic.' For both Lucy and her cameraman, that attack – more than any other in France – brought back difficult experiences from earlier in their professional lives.

Her advice to young reporters, who may find themselves covering such stories, is to protect the things that enable you to do justice to the story. 'Top of that list is empathy. Without empathy for the people you're reporting on, you won't get the full story. It's easy to deal with the horror of what's happening by pretending it doesn't affect you, or locking it away, but unless you can allow yourself to feel some of it and be open to the people you're interviewing and the stories they're telling you, there's a good chance you'll miss something.'

Understandably, this work takes its toll on reporters, and Lucy relied on the strong bonds with her team at the bureau who supported each other through attack after attack. 'It's often the case that those who experience the events with you are well-placed to understand how you're feeling, so don't be afraid to acknowledge it,' she says. 'I think we found it very difficult and doing some of those graphic interviews in the days and weeks afterwards, often quite relentlessly, compounded how difficult it was. We'd felt horror and fear in our home city that night and then we interviewed people about their experiences over and over again.'

The fear factor

In these situations it is absolutely normal to be scared. 'The trick is to try and harness that fear and all the emotions that you're feeling and channel it into telling the story. You're trying to communicate that horror to an audience back home. You need to be comfortable feeling it in order to communicate it. You can let it filter into the writing or into the "two-way" without losing the journalistic analysis of it, the perspective. These things are horrific. I don't think you should try and not feel them or try and expunge it from your reporting of the event either.' But try to find a detail or a story that illustrates it, rather than just stating how awful it is.

Making contact

After the terrorist attacks in Paris, many people had been affected and Lucy worked to get introductions to those people through both personal and professional contacts. 'Also, very quickly, groups spring up, victims come together and I think that can be a good way in. It gives people a measure of control and safety.'

Don't forget to keep in touch once you have made contact. Lucy would text, email, maintain the connection via Facebook, phone or meet for coffee. 'There may be further developments later on, but it's also so people don't feel dropped after they've served their purpose and sometimes you are a link with that event that they might value.'

Key advice

Put the person first. If you're going to harm the person mentally or emotionally by doing something that's good for the story but bad for them, don't do it. That would be my take on it. No story is worth a person's mental health or a person's life, not yours and not theirs either.

Lucy offers further advice on writing and framing stories in the Writing chapter.

Trauma Awareness

A traumatic event can be defined as when an individual, family or community is exposed to actual or threatened death, serious injury or sexual violation. It can be sudden, such as an accident, assault or robbery. It can be a mass traumatic event such as a terrorist attack, earthquake or war. Or it can be ongoing, such as child sexual abuse, domestic violence or torture.

It includes witnessing something terrible or hearing about it happening to close family or friends. It can make one feel fear, horror and helplessness as well as creating shock, confusion and disorientation.

At the scene of an event, there are often three survival reactions: fight, flight or freeze. It can also be common not to feel any of the responses described below. They are often determined by a variety of factors such as the degree of involvement, proximity to the event or the experience of loss.

Here are some common responses your interviewee may be feeling in the hours, days and weeks after a traumatic or extremely stressful event.

Psychological reactions

- Anxiety: fear and restlessness, feeling anxious and panicked when faced with reminders. Concern about losing control or not coping. Worry it may happen again.
- Hyper-vigilance: scanning around for danger cues, being overly protective of loved ones.
- Sleep disturbances: vivid dreams or nightmares.
- Intrusive memories: images of the incident which can come with or without apparent triggers.
- Guilt: regret about how they acted or coped. Guilt because they survived and their friend or loved one didn't, known as 'survivor guilt.'
- Shame or embarrassment: a sense they weren't good enough in some way and a wish to go into hiding.
- Sadness: low mood and tearfulness.
- Irritability and anger: a sense of injustice, wanting someone to accept responsibility or blame. It can be directed at friends and family.
- Emotional numbness or blunting: feeling detached from others.
- Withdrawal: retreating and avoiding social contact.
- Disappointment: feeling people don't really understand how you are feeling.
- Mental avoidance: avoiding thoughts associated with the trauma by trying to push them away.
- Behavioural avoidance: avoiding all physical reminders of the event, e.g. places or people.
- Increased startle response: becoming jumpy or easily startled by sudden noises or movements.

Physical reactions

- Shakiness and trembling.
- Tension and muscle aches.

- Insomnia, tiredness and fatigue.
- Palpitation, shallow rapid breathing and dizziness.
- Nausea, vomiting, diarrhoea.

Points to discuss

Read through these common responses to trauma and consider the allowances you may need to make when working with people who have had a traumatic experience:

If they are exhausted, finding it hard to concentrate or feeling a sense of shame or guilt, how may you need to adapt your working practice and the questions you ask?

How important is it that you remain calm and reassuring and why?

Which signs or reactions would indicate that you should not approach somebody at the scene?

Notes

1 Executive Summary, 'In the Media Spotlight: The Survivor Stories,' University of Melbourne, August 2011.

2 Chris Frost, *Journalism, Ethics and Regulation*, 4th edn, Routledge, 2016, p. 177.

3 David Barnett, 'Inside the World of the "Death Knock",' 4 June 2017, www.independent.co.uk (accessed 4 November 2018).

4 Sallyanne Duncan and Jackie Newton, 'How Do You Feel? Preparing Novice Reporters for the Death Knock,' *Journalism Practice*, 4 (4), 2010, 439–453.

5 Roger Simpson and William Cote, *Covering Violence: A Guide to Ethical Reporting about Victims and Trauma*, 2nd edn, Columbia University Press, 2006, p. 99.

6 University of Ulster, 'An Exploration of Media Reporting of Victims of Murder and Manslaughter in Northern Ireland', for Support after Murder and Manslaughter Northern Ireland, www.webarchive.nationalarchives.gov.uk (accessed 4 November 2018).

7 Simpson and Cote, *Covering Violence*, p. 8.

8 Richard Keeble, *Ethics for Journalists*, 2nd edn, Routledge, 2009.

9 Disaster Action, 'Personal Reflections and Guidelines for Interviewers', www.disasteraction.org.uk.

10 Simpson and Cote, *Covering Violence*, p. 245.

11 Christine Haughney, *At Ground Zero: 25 Stories from Young Reporters Who Were There Tell Their Stories*, edited by Sam Erman and Chris Bull, Thunder's Mouth Press, 2002.

12 Dart Center for Journalism and Trauma, 'Working with Victims and Survivors', 22 February 2011, https://dartcenter.org (last accessed 24 January 2019).

13 Scott North, 'Oso's Mudslide: Five Journalists Speak', 14 April 2014, https://dartcenter.org (last accessed 25 January 2019).

14 Manchester Arena Bombing: key points from the official report, BBC News, 27 March 2018, www.bbc.co.uk.

15 The Kerslake Arena Review, www.kerslakearenareview.co.uk (last accessed 7 February 2019).

16 Emma Lee Potter, *Interviewing for Journalists*, 3rd edn, Routledge, 2017, p. 27.

17 Chip Scanlan, 'First Rule of Interviewing: Be Human', 1 September 2002, www.poynter.org, category:archive (last accessed 25 January 2019).

18 Dominic Ponsford, 'Why "Death Knocks" Are a difficult but Essential Part of the Job for Journalists,' 24 May 2017, www.pressgazette.co.uk.

19 Andrew Hogg, 'The Power of Listening', 13 November 2012, Dart Center for Journalism and Trauma, https://dartcenter.org (last accessed 25 January 2019).

20 Heidi Singer, *At Ground Zero*, edited by Erman and Bull.

21 Simpson and Cote, *Covering Violence*, p. 100.

22 Dart Center for Journalism and Trauma, 'Working with Victims and Survivors', 22 February 2011, https://dartcenter.org (last accessed 25 January 2019).

23 Nick Spangler, *At Ground Zero*, edited by Erman and Bull, p. 41.

24 Liselotte Englund, Rebecca Forsberg and Britt-Inger Saveman, 'Survivors' Experiences of Media Coverage after Traumatic Injury Events', *International Emergency Nursing*, 22, 2014, 25–30.

25 Tony Harcup, *Journalism: Principles and Practice*, 3rd edn, Sage, 2015, p. 212.

3
The preparation

'Do some background so you know my son … The reporters who came in and didn't really know what had happened … I used to think, why am I doing this?'
Faith, whose teenage son died after being hit by
a car as he cycled to school

In this chapter

Preparing to meet your interviewee.

Extras on cultural considerations.

Focus on how news reporters prepare to cover emotional interviews.

Insight into what families need from journalists.

Overview from Jina Moore on how she covers sensitive stories.

Be briefed

If you have approached the family yourself, you should be across the story. Yet it isn't unusual, in a multimedia newsroom, for the approach to have been made by a researcher or producer, and you can be dispatched, sometimes at short notice, to interview the family, survivor or victim.

Take a moment to do as much research as you can muster and check the details carefully. If the story is about a death, it will not be acceptable to turn up at a family's home without knowing the name of the person they have lost and having some idea of what has happened to them. 'Things like that make such a difference when you are in this state of mind,' explains Faith, who spoke to numerous reporters after her 14-year-old son Joshua died.

Details can be sketchy in the early hours and any information you can glean, often via social media or police reports, will need verifying. Names, nicknames, ages, spellings, chronology, inter-family relationships are all of immense importance to people. They are entrusting their story to you, they can be feeling powerless and vulnerable and, as psychologist and director of the Dart Center Asia Pacific, Cait McMahon, tells me, 'Inaccuracies or misspelled names and incorrect ages are just one more hurt or insult.'

When you talk to your interviewee, you will need to run through the details you've gathered and double-check them. An apparently simple name can have numerous spellings or alternatives. Is it Katherine, Katharine, Catherine, Catharine, Cathryn, Kathryn, Kate, Katey, Katy, Katie, Cate, Cat, Kathy or Cathy? If you guess, it is highly likely to be wrong and this will cause offence.

In 1993, just short of his third birthday, James Bulger was abducted and murdered by two 10-year-olds. It was a shocking crime at the time and continues to shock to this day. In an article for the *Guardian* newspaper, Simon Hattenstone wrote that James's mother Denise Fergus had reason to be angry at many things surrounding her son's murder. But one of them was 'the way newspapers insisted on referring to her son as Jamie, when he had always been James.'[1]

It can be worth adding a note to your copy, to emphasise a particular name spelling. Sometimes sub-editors and social media editors can make changes which the reporter can't always control. A strong working relationship with your news team will help avoid distressing mistakes.

Be clear what your news editor or producer is expecting from your interview. As Emma Lee Potter points out in *Interviewing for Journalists*, 'The last thing you want is to interview someone about one thing and discover at a later date that the editor was expecting something completely different.'[2] Conversely, the story you are expecting to find may well change when you meet and begin listening to your interviewee, so avoid having a strict agenda.

If you are doing a TV interview, will it also be used by radio and will news online be expecting a piece? These each require a slightly different approach. In general, TV reports use short clips of audio, often, but not always, without the questions, whereas radio may require a longer interview to include questions. Online or print tend to use short quotes but can require more detailed facts and information.

Map out the sorts of questions you may like to ask, but keep an open mind. Think about possible shots too, as pictures can be challenging when covering these stories. Are they likely to have photos, film footage, letters, documents or campaign leaflets you can use to help illustrate their story? They may need advance warning of this so they can seek out the material before you meet them.

If you are a video journalist, check and double-check the kit, as this is not a job to arrive at with a flat battery or a missing microphone. If you are working with a camera operator, brief them and arrange to meet them outside the house before going in. Crews can often be dispatched from a different story and different location and have scant idea of the task ahead. Take a moment to explain the sensitivities of the piece you are about to film.

Be focused

A few years ago, I interviewed George who was dying and wanted to do an interview in favour of euthanasia. Months earlier, I had been with my own Dad on his deathbed. George was the same age, 83, and when I arrived he was wearing a similar dressing gown. I share this because some sensitive stories will be tougher for you to cover than others. Many of us have experienced grief and some stories may resonate for you, as George's situation did for me, or you may have a relentless run of covering emotional stories.

Take a look at the Self-Care chapter and make sure you prepare yourself mentally and emotionally, but in the context of covering the story, it has to be about them and not you. Temper the urge to share your own experiences of grief. If you are speaking with a parent whose child has died, don't share that you've lost a mother, father or spouse. It is not the same and parents have told me they struggle with this. Even worse, Rose Dixon tells me how one man, on discovering she was a bereaved mother, told her he knew exactly how she felt because his dog had died.

You may, however, work with an interviewee over a longer period of time on a story featuring, for example, their road to recovery from illness. In those instances, it may be appropriate to share if you too have had a similar journey. It may seem odd *not* to have mentioned it.

Square it

Be clear in your own mind *why* you are covering the story (see the Approach chapter). If the reason for doing it is not clear, some reporters tell me they feel they are intruding, even though the family has agreed to the interview. Yet taking a sense of guilt or shame across their threshold is counterproductive. This work needs to be done with a sense of quiet confidence.

If you are feeling nervous or shy, take a leaf out of the US journalist Beth Winegarner's book. Painfully shy herself as a child, she suggests letting your curiosity override your anxiety, preparing well to give yourself confidence and using your job as armour. 'As a journalist it's your professional responsibility to talk to people,' she says.[3]

Your task will be to put the people you are about to interview at ease, treat them carefully and allow them to feel safe with you so they can share their story.

Be ready

People react in many different ways to a traumatic experience. They may be feeling an exhausting raft of emotions such as fear, guilt, helplessness, agitation, anger, sadness, numbness. This may or may not be evident when you meet them. (See *Trauma Awareness* in the Approach, Relationship, Children and Follow-ups chapters.)

In teaching people to become trauma literate, Cait McMahon cautions them not to expect any specific response. 'Different people react to traumatic experiences in different and often unexpected ways, from hysterics to stoicism, from silence to talkativeness. Some will appear in control and even to be unaffected but may fall apart when the journalist is gone and reality sinks in.' She adds it is important not to make judgements.

Prepare yourself for people's reactions and, whatever emotion they show, treat them with respect and do not let them feel awkward or embarrassed.

EXTRAS

Suleman Nagdi MBE DL is an international figure on human rights and community relations and serves on inter-faith forums contributing to a number of UK government consultations. His book *Discovering through Death: Beliefs and Practices*[4] details how a large number of faiths and religions view death, mourning, grief and loss. While acknowledging there cannot be a one-size-fits-all approach here, he shares some important considerations for journalists when preparing to work with the black, Asian and minority ethnic (BAME) communities.

- *Removing shoes:* As you enter the house, take notice if people are wearing shoes. If they are not, it may be polite to remove your footwear simply because they may pray on the carpet by putting their forehead on it. It is for hygienic reasons.
- *Shaking hands:* Before shaking hands, particularly with someone of the opposite gender, wait first to see if they offer their hand to shake. If not, then refrain because the idea of invading personal space can be important in minority communities. Some from a conservative background rarely

shake hands with people of the opposite gender, simply out of respect. Some may not make eye contact for the same respectful reason.

- *Being accepted:* If you are working with a conservative family ask beforehand how you can best be accepted. Ask if there is a more modest dress code or if you should cover your hair. These simple things go a long way to showing the family you have done your homework and you are there as a human being, not there to treat them as a commodity or story.

- *Hierarchy:* In some families you will find a hierarchy of authority; by this I mean certain family members who speak for the family as a whole. This person may well be the eldest brother or senior member of the family.

- *Being non-judgemental:* Be accommodating and accepting of other cultures even if it may feel different or alien.

- *Suicide:* This is often a taboo subject. Families may not feel comfortable speaking in front of other people because of the whole idea of guilt and blame. In such tragic situations, try to speak to them privately and give them space to talk.

- *Photographs:* To ask within the Muslim community for anything that has any imagery in it, such as photographs, may be insensitive. It will depend on the family. That's not to say they won't provide a photograph but it isn't the same as asking people of other or no faiths.

- *Physical contact:* It can feel the most natural thing in the world when someone is hurting to reach out to comfort them, such as putting a hand on their arm. But if it is someone from the opposite gender I wouldn't do it as the risk factors are far greater than any possible benefit.

- *Funerals:* Funerals within BAME communities can be quick and in Jewish and Muslim communities the funeral is within twenty-four hours so this can be a time when people are making preparations. If you don't get an answer to your request immediately it is because they have more pressing things on their minds and they may have hundreds of people coming from all over the country. Allow them time and ask when would be more convenient to contact them.

- *Dress:* Don't expect people to wear black. Some may wear colourful clothes and it is not unusual for the Hindu community to wear white as a sign of loss. What is important is that they've lost a loved one and it may be how they connect spiritually with that individual.

- *Labelling:* Avoid referring to an individual's religion unless it is important to the story. Rather than saying 'a young Muslim boy passed away', simply say 'a young boy passed away' and avoid attaching labels.

- *Cards:* If you wish to write to say thank you, giving cards is quite a Western concept. A handwritten letter or a small note or email would be preferable.

- *Be human:* Above all when covering these stories, I think the more human side of the journalist should be uppermost.

FOCUS on journalists

Daniela Relph worked as a reporter for local radio before moving to regional TV then on to network, first as a news correspondent for the BBC, then as a sports news correspondent. She was Washington correspondent for three years before moving back to London where she combines general news reporting with being a royal correspondent.

Be prepared to expect the unexpected when reporting. In March 2017, six people died in a terrorist attack. They included a policeman and the attacker, who had driven a car into pedestrians on Westminster Bridge in London.

A few days later, Daniela was sent to interview the family of a man who had been killed. He and his wife had been visiting from the US, as part of a tour of Europe. The interview was to be at the Metropolitan Police headquarters at New Scotland Yard. 'I always think before going into something like that: What's it going to be like? How should I behave? What do I want to ask them? I probably felt a bit like I was bracing myself for it because it had been such a terrible event,' Daniela tells me.

She arrived having prepared herself to interview a couple of the man's relatives who would be shocked and grieving. Instead, she was met by thirteen people including siblings, nephews, cousins and nieces who had flown in and who all wanted to speak to her. The dynamic in the room was not what Daniela was expecting. 'They smiled and shook my hand. They weren't tearful or obviously sad. They were all Mormons and talked about their faith and felt that, in this moment of grief, the best way to deal with it and overcome it was to work together as a family.'

Rather than being evidently grief-stricken, Daniela found they wanted only to speak in positive terms about the life of the person they had lost and how amazing he was. 'When I asked them how did they feel about the incident and the person that did it, they said they felt only forgiveness, their faith was so deep.'

A week after the attack, they allowed Daniela to film them on the bridge holding hands in a circle and praying. 'They were incredibly strong and united and very clear about how they were dealing with it. I felt I really had to reflect that in the way I reported it.'

Be prepared to be flexible in these situations. 'Use your common sense and react to what you are seeing in front of you. Take your lead from them and accurately reflect how they are feeling. I did ask them to explain why they feel like this because, as an outsider looking in, it's not what I expected.'

Conversely, when covering Hurricane Katrina in New Orleans, in August 2005, Daniela had to be prepared to deal with people's anger. Admittedly, she felt conflicted when having to deliver an even-handed report while reflecting the fury and frustration felt by families who felt abandoned by the US government in the wake of the disaster.

'In a post traumatic event, there's the level of anger people feel and they want to blame everybody. You just had to let them work their way through the anger and understand why they were so absolutely furious and upset with what was happening. You didn't want to dilute the anger in any way, but you wanted to find out what had happened to them.'

She says, where possible, she would take time away from the camera to sit with people and ask them what was going on, what particularly was upsetting them, why they were so angry. 'You have to work out what is the best thing to do with people who are in front of you and want to talk to you. Do you take some time out with them and sit down and explain or do you just go with that raw anger and let them explain it to you in that way? You can only judge that through experience or time or trusting your instinct.'

Navtej Johal is a video journalist working in BBC TV. He covers many sensitive stories and here he explains how he prepares to work with bereaved families.

When preparing to interview the family of someone who has died, Navtej will try to find out all he can about the person they have lost, often through their Facebook page or Twitter account. 'There was one story I did where a young woman was murdered while she was backpacking across Australia. She was a very keen social media poster and had an active Instagram page. Checking that and getting an idea of who she was before going in to talk to the family was really important, because it shows you have done your research,' Navtej tells me.

Equally important was checking the facts such as her age, knowing how to spell her name and how to pronounce it. For months, the media had reported the young backpacker as being 21 years old but, when Navtej finally interviewed her mother, he double-checked what had been reported, and she was 20 when she died.

'All of that enables the interviewee to trust you more. They feel like you have taken the time, it's not just another job for you,' he explains.

Preparation begins the moment you hear about the story. 'If someone has died, it's a case of finding the address or location of where that person may have lived and then building the story and contacting the parents or family.'

When making contact via email or Facebook or speaking to families, Navtej's first advice is to acknowledge the loss. 'Often it can be difficult to know what to say but it can be as simple as saying: I'm really sorry to hear about your loss, if you would like to talk, if you would like to pay tribute, if there's something you feel you'd like to say, here is my number.'

He will also try to prepare his producer for the fact that the interview may take time. 'I'll say that, if they want a really good story they have to take the pressure off, because it might be that you spend the first half-hour or hour just talking to your interviewee and getting them to feel comfortable around you.'

Kathryn Stanczyszyn is a political and news reporter covering breaking stories for BBC network news: radio, TV and online. She worked closely with mothers whose sons had been stabbed to death for an in-depth series on knife crime. Here she explains how she prepared to cover the story.

When covering a story in greater depth, Kathryn says it is important to take time to build the relationship. She went to meet the mothers first without recording anything. 'We're human beings based on human relationships and body language. If you can sit there and openly have an informal chat first, so that people know who you are and where you're coming from, it just takes a lot of tension out of the actual interview process.'

She adds that part of the preparation is working out what you are trying to achieve through doing the interviews.

'We're all guilty of running around and having a million things to do. But you're doing yourself a disservice if you're going into what could be an extremely powerful interview, without having a clue about what you're trying to get out of it. You're doing them a disservice because the whole point is, you're trying to get their story out there and you're going to be rewarded with some amazing content. You need to have thought about that beforehand,' Kathryn tells me.

She says research is particularly important when covering a story in depth, such as knife crime. 'It's certainly about knowing about the crimes relating to the people you are going to interview. If there's been a court case, know your stuff. It shows a lack of respect for what's happened to the victim if you know nothing about them.'

INSIGHT from interviewees

Rachel's teenage daughter suffers with severe anorexia. When she needed a bed in a specialist eating disorder hospital, the only place available was 300 miles from home. In her frustration, Rachel decided to go public and she shares her observations about how preparation was key to her working successfully with the media.

'It was probably one of the worst scenarios you could imagine being in,' Rachel tells me. 'Having a very ill daughter, then being told the bed was three hundred miles away. I felt anger, disbelief and helplessness. I was very vulnerable.'

The first thing she advises any journalist to do is to read the media guidelines for reporting on mental health and specifically eating disorders, in her case.

If you turn up unprepared, be honest and take guidance from your interviewee. 'A national newspaper photographer came. He didn't know we were only allowing anonymous pictures of my daughter, but instead of panicking and getting on his phone and checking, he just took me at my word and did them as we wanted them to be done. That was excellent because he listened and he trusted me.'

Rachel also valued being shown articles and a documentary she took part in, before they were printed or broadcast. 'It's not always possible with a news item but it's really important if it is a possibility. When they've been going through stuff like this, nobody wants to sit down and be watching it for the first time with everybody else in the country.'

When preparing for an interview, Rachel found it less helpful to have a list of what she would be asked. 'That would make me over-think and feel anxious so I think in some ways "live" radio interviews have been easier for me.'

Rachel struggled when her expectations were not managed. She was not prepared for the fact that only a small portion of what was filmed would actually be used in the broadcast. 'They must have been here for half a day,' she explains. 'So you prepare yourself, you do your best and you literally see a flash and you think well that just doesn't seem like it was worth it to me.' This made her less inclined to do further pre-recorded interviews.

Communication is key, says Rachel, who wanted to be kept informed and contacted after being interviewed. 'What I find really hard, whether it's radio, TV or papers, is the silence. They've got what they want and then there's just silence. Particularly when you're vulnerable and it was difficult for you to talk and painful. Then to have this wall of silence is probably one of the worst things I think. You've just poured your soul out to somebody and then you almost feel like you've been dropped.'

It worked best for her to have a way of contacting the reporter or producer, so she could check what was happening to the piece and when it would be printed or aired.

Spelling out exactly what you are asking of your interviewee could make the difference between them agreeing to the interview or declining. They can easily make assumptions about what you are asking of them, so you need to be clear. Initially, when Rachel was asked to do network radio interviews for 5 *Live*, *The*

World at One and the *Today* programme, she was asked, 'Can you go into the studio?' or 'Can you do a down the line interview from your local radio studio?'

'My idea of being in a studio, is being with lots of people with microphones and headphones all looking at you and firing questions at you. I thought there's no way I've got the confidence to do that.'

When she finally discovered the reality, that it simply meant going into a small sound-proofed room, popping on some headphones and talking into a single microphone, she became an instant fan. 'Nobody explained or prepared me for what it meant to be in the studio. I came out thinking I would do this every week if that's all I've got to do.'

> *Faith's 14-year-old son Joshua was knocked off his bike as he cycled to school. He died in intensive care when Faith had to agree to his life support being withdrawn. She gave many interviews to reporters to help raise funds to build a skate park in Joshua's memory.*

'Complete, utter, devastation,' is Faith's description of her grief at losing Joshua. To steel herself to do media interviews and to be able to talk about her son, she had to be consulted and prepared.

'You had that initial conversation over the phone and I then needed time to get my head sorted out. If they gave me an idea of what the questions were going to be, I felt that I could prepare myself without getting too emotional or upset about it,' Faith tells me.

She says that allowing her time to tell her story was an important part of the preparation. 'I wanted to know how long they expected to be there for, an outline of what they were trying to achieve. The more preparation the better for me, so I could be more relaxed. It was lovely to do the interview at my home. I didn't find it easy going out and I didn't like giving information over the phone, I felt caught on the hop. I used to say give me half an hour and ring me back just so I could collect myself and my thoughts.'

Faith says reporters who wanted to get the best from her needed to do some homework. 'For them to have done a bit of research so they know your son's name when they get here and they've got his correct age. Things like that make such a difference when you are in that state of mind. Do some background so you know my son. It was the reporters who came in and didn't really know what had happened. I used to think, why am I doing this?'

She also felt reporters should be prepared to make allowances for her emotional turmoil. 'Speak slowly because it's just processing information when you're like you are and maybe repeat what you're saying and use a softer tone of voice and just sound like you care.'

As part of their research, Faith says reporters need to check dates. 'Be aware of anniversaries of particularly difficult times like when it happened because then it is very difficult to even talk about it. So don't come and interview me when it's Joshua's birthday or if it's approaching Christmas.'

> Rose, who shared her insight in the previous chapter, also advises reporters to be prepared when working with families whose loved one has been killed.

Rose stresses the damage which can be done if reporters fail to focus on getting the facts right. 'Spelling the name incorrectly, getting the wrong age, getting the school incorrect are all very hurtful.' She also points out how off-putting it can be for families if reporters are continually checking their phones or leaving them 'pinging away' in their bag.

She says it feels as if the reporter is telling her, 'I'm a very busy important person, I can't afford to turn my phone off, I might miss an important call.' Her response to them is this. 'Well hello, my daughter's death is very important to me. If you want to talk to me about it, you give me your full attention and you deal with your phone when you leave this house. It is very disrespectful to do that.'

> The following insight is from parents whose daughter was murdered and who wish to remain anonymous. They describe how they felt hounded and invaded by reporters before finally agreeing to be interviewed for a background piece to run after the murder trial.

Initial reports about their daughter's death were inaccurate. 'That was very damaging for us and the memory of our beloved daughter. It caused more upset and worry, when we were trying to cope with our unbearable grief. We could not have the right of reply as it could damage the evidence used in the court process.'

They agreed to an interview to run at the end of the murder trial.

'We were treated with respect by our local ITV news reporter. She had already asked our police press officer how we would like to be addressed, "formally" or "informally". We preferred the latter, using our first names throughout the interview. We were told if we didn't want to answer one of the questions, we could move on to the next question, and if we were unhappy with one of our replies, then we had the opportunity to record that answer again. It was done slowly and not rushed. We were given some of the questions prior to the interview which helped us prepare in advance.'

HOW I COVER SENSITIVE STORIES: JINA MOORE

'Never let them feel powerless.'

After studying at Boston then Columbia University, Jina Moore began her journalistic career as a freelancer in Rwanda. She worked her way up to become the Global Women's Rights Reporter and Africa Bureau Chief for BuzzFeed News, then the East Africa Bureau Chief for *The New York Times*.

As well as being a multi-award-winning journalist, Jina also lectures at universities and presents at conferences internationally on reporting trauma, mental health and human rights. She is leading the East African Initiative for Trauma Journalism, focused on peer support for African journalists covering violence and tragedy in their hometowns and countries.

Jina says her mission is to hold the powerful to account by telling stories about the people around her. She explains that, to do this often challenging work, she has had generous collaboration from her sources, fixers and fellow journalists in the field, from Cambodia to Liberia to eastern Congo.

'I do a lot of interviews with people who've been through trauma and tragedy,' she tells me. 'Quite a lot of my work in conflict settings and post-conflict settings has been around sexual and gender-based violence ... rape as a weapon of war, rape in the refugee crisis – alas, a lot of different rape.'

Making a connection

When Jina was working for BuzzFeed, she wanted to make contact with women refugees who would talk to her about being vulnerable to sexual violence while fleeing from Syria and crossing Europe. She knew they would be suffering but was struggling to stand up her story.

Eventually, she found a female refugee who had worked in Syria as an English translator. She was living inside one of the refugee centres in Germany and she became Jina's fixer. Jina could not get into the camp, so each morning she would meet her fixer and a woman the fixer had found who was willing to be interviewed. Jina would then drive her interviewee downtown for a coffee and they would sit and talk.

'It turned out to be very important culturally. I didn't think about this at all, but Syrian women like their coffee. It's a morning ritual, a friendship ritual and they hadn't had a proper cup of coffee in months. So that opened things up in a way I didn't anticipate but worked really well. We would sit and talk until they didn't want to talk anymore.'

When working generally with women who are vulnerable, Jina tries to take an all-female approach. 'I'm a female reporter, I work with a female translator to talk to women in a place with no men and, if possible, no children because they're not going to want their children to overhear these stories.'

Meaningful consent

Jina believes consent is essential in trauma interviews. By this she means the person you are interviewing must understand why you are interested in their story; what you, as the journalist, believe their story will say about the broader situation and why it is important that a wide audience of strangers understands that situation.

Most of the time, introductions are made to sources by interlocutors – fixers, or charity workers, or others. 'That means that by the time I'm sitting down with a woman who survived the Rwandan genocide, she'll probably already know who I am and why I'm there.' But Jina goes through it again. She says it is important for them to hear it directly from the journalist, who should explain how and where the material will be used. 'If I'm talking about *The New York Times*, I would tell them it's a newspaper that has two million readers, or when I worked for BuzzFeed that it's an online website that's full of news. And I would always have a screenshot of the site so that, even if I don't have the internet, I could show them what it looked like.'

It can be harder as a freelancer to know where the article may end up, but as a staff reporter Jina would explain to her interviewee, 'It's going in this publication, it will appear on the internet, we have this many readers, it will be in English. If I'm recording someone, I will explain it is just for print and I'm not going to put their voice on the internet or radio. There are some cultures where that is really important. To say "I will talk to you" and "I will let you put my voice on the radio" are not the same consent process.'

She also tells them she will do her best to follow up with them and make sure they get a copy of the article or a link to it.

Jina's next step is to be clear on confidentiality. She asks her interviewee if she can quote her by name but will then check again at the end of the interview. 'I'll say, you were very open and honest with me and I appreciate it. Are there maybe things you ended up telling me that you didn't expect when you said I could use your name. Is it still okay that we put your name to everything you said?'

Preparing for the interview

The more preparation you do before the interview, the more your anxiety about doing it will be reduced, Jina explains. You can acknowledge when you are there that these interviews are difficult.

She will explain to her interviewee, 'Some of this will be uncomfortable and I'm sorry, I don't want to have to put you through this but for the story it's important that we're clear about X,Y or Z.' Jina says it is important to be assured when doing the interview. If you are unsure it will make them uncomfortable. 'You can be polite and compassionate but still confident about the information that you need to get.'

Significantly, Jina takes time to explain that they are in control. 'I tell them I'll be asking questions and I know there are certain pieces of information that I'm going to need. Some of the questions may be uncomfortable. It's okay to say "can we stop?" It's okay to say "I don't want to answer that question" and it's okay to change your mind.'

It is important to make no assumptions, and to adapt your practice as you go. Jina had been taught to avoid euphemisms as they can be viewed as disrespectful. 'If you're talking about rape, you call it rape, you don't call it something else,' she explains, but she then discovered this is not always the case. One interviewee found the use of the word extremely upsetting and asked her instead to refer to what happened as 'the incident.'

Working with vulnerable sources

If she is going to interview someone who is a survivor of rape, Jina will try to clear her diary for the rest of the day so she can give the encounter enough time. 'I don't want to be rushing them or cut them off, or in any way make them feel like their story wasn't important or I got what I needed and now I'm leaving. I want them, as much as possible, to run themselves out and we close the interview when they've said what they have to say and I've got what I know I need.'

She gives a lot of thought to where she sits in the room and makes sure she is not blocking the exit. 'It creates more psychological safety for someone if you are able to give them that direct line and you aren't a physical obstacle to getting out.'

She makes sure she is always at eye level or lower than the person she is speaking to, never standing above them, which creates a power imbalance. She will also sit next to them rather than directly in front of them, as she says sitting alongside signifies congeniality and equality.

A different kind of interview

If her vulnerable interviewee asks Jina not to use something she inadvertently told her, she will honour that request. She explains that these situations are not like interviewing a politician. 'The rules are completely different. In fact they are completely backwards, a total inversion. We have "on the record" rules with politicians or powerful figures because it makes the playing field a little bit more even between the men (usually) who control the world, and the humble journalist trying to ask tough questions or get accountability.' With trauma survivors, the journalist is the one with control, she explains.

'So I will take things off the table if they ask me to because ultimately the story, and agency over that story, belongs to them. The important thing is that what appears in print is something they're comfortable with. Because if they are not comfortable with it, then the fact that it is public, is very likely going to be re-traumatising and that is not what we are trying to do, even if it's the most amazing quote or detail.'

Jina's guides and articles

Jina has also written widely giving advice for reporters. In her training guide 'Covering Trauma,'[5] she writes that because of the psychological impact, reporters have to make allowances when interviewing survivors of violent attacks.

They may not follow the chronological order of events, or they may omit things or change details. 'These are not necessarily signs of an untrustworthy source. They could be symptoms of trauma,' she explains. It is also important to manage their expectations and not pretend that your story provides your interviewee with a solution.

Other key guidance she gives when interviewing sensitively is to avoid implying blame. 'If a woman says she was raped on the road late at night, don't ask her, "Why were you out late at night, anyway?" If a child was abducted when getting water alone, don't ask him, "Why did you get water alone?"' Researchers have found that these questions can cause psychological damage to survivors because the questions imply that the trauma is the survivor's fault, she explains. 'No matter what piece of information you need, word your questions carefully to avoid the language of blame,' she advises.

She describes the responsibility which falls on journalists when reporting on a society which is recovering from violence. 'Communities depend on us for reliable information and stories that rebuild trust in the country and each other. They do not need us to be cheerleaders for a specific politician or a specific programme; neither do they need us to retell, day in and day out, stories of destruction from which everyone is trying to recover.'

Key advice

Contact your interviewee the day after you have interviewed them. Jina will always do this with a phone call or a text and say,' I just wanted to check in and see how you're feeling. Thanks again for your time yesterday, I hope everything is going well.' This shows that you didn't just leave them and forget about it, she explains.

She also says trauma is about power and powerlessness. 'Journalists should never, ever, make their subjects or sources feel powerless.'

Notes

1 Simon Hattenstone, 'My Son, James Bulger,' *The Guardian*, 20 January 2018, www.theguardian.com (last accessed 25 January 2019).

2 Emma Lee Potter, *Interviewing for Journalists*, 3rd edn, Routledge, 2017, p. 53.

3 Beth Winegarner, '5 Ways Journalists Can Overcome Shyness during Interviews,' 23 April 2012, www.poynter.org (last accessed 26 January 2019).

4 Suleman Nagdi, *Discovering through Death: Beliefs and Practices*, MBCOL, 2011.

5 Jina Moore, 'Covering Trauma – A Training Guide', 2011, www.sfcg.org.

4
The relationship

'I fervently believe it's the acknowledgement that something horrific has happened but not dwelling on that and talking about the person who is lost, that's key.'

John, whose teenage daughter Jess died from a brain tumour

In this chapter

Connecting with your interviewee.

Focus on reporters who have built successful professional relationships.

Insight from families on what helps when we meet them.

Overview from Louis Theroux on how he covers sensitive stories.

Trauma Awareness: responses to traumatic bereavement.

Thank and acknowledge

Journalism is a competitive industry, so it is important to get the relationship with your interviewee right first time. Tragic stories can run and run and, if you lose a family's confidence at the start, it will be hard to regain it further down the line. Equally, many journalists maintain strong and rewarding professional relationships across years and even generations as stories unfold. As the American journalism professor Julia Lieblich says, 'If I can give advice to journalists, I suggest it's all about relationships.'[1]

When you have made your approach and done your preparation, you will go to meet your interviewee. Be punctual and if you have arranged to meet the camera operator outside their home to brief them, be sensitive to how it may seem if you are joking together. As the award-winning documentary and filmmaker Sacha Mirzoeff tells me, 'We always say we're on duty the moment we step out and we're in their road. They might be looking out of the window, so we conduct ourselves the way we conduct ourselves when we're talking to them.'

Introduce yourself and the camera operator and, if you have a technical team of people, introduce each person individually and explain, in simple terms, why they are here and what they do.

In doing this work, you will meet people from all walks of life. Some, such as people who may be homeless, recovering from addiction, former prisoners, or living in a refuge or hostel, may have issues with their own sense of self-respect. Do not judge or make assumptions. Be respectful, polite and considerate as you introduce yourself and explain what you would like to do. Sit with them and listen closely to their needs and opinions.

Thank your interviewee for agreeing to talk to you, shake their hand and make eye contact. If your story is about a bereavement, acknowledge the death with sincerity. Reporters are not always inclined to say, 'I am sorry for what you are going through,' but families tell me that acknowledging what has happened to them is really important. 'The simple "sorry" that makes it so much easier for me to move forward with the report you're doing,' explains Faith, whose son Joshua died 11 days after being knocked off his bike as he cycled to school.

Navtej Johal is a TV news reporter who has covered many sensitive stories. He believes acknowledging that something terrible has happened is the first step in building the relationship. 'I spoke to a couple who had lost their daughter in a horrific incident a decade earlier. She had been murdered by someone with mental health problems,' he tells me. 'Judging by their mood, I felt it was appropriate even at that point, ten years on, to tell them I'm sorry for your loss and I think immediately they did appreciate that. The fact that I'd acknowledged it just made our conversation from that point on a lot more comfortable.'

Accept their hospitality

This can be another good starting point in establishing your relationship. If they offer you a cup of tea, accept it because this deceptively simple interaction can achieve many things. Making tea or coffee is a ritual people tend to be familiar with. It allows them a valuable sense of control while they get used to having a reporter and camera operator in their home. It also allows you to sit with them in the kitchen and clarify the all-important facts. If you have limited details, be honest about this and ask them to help you fill in the gaps.

Be careful not to pre-interview. In an article for Nieman Reports, the US radio and print journalist Karen Brown cautions against it, saying, 'I always want them to be telling me their story for the first time when I have my tape recorder out and it's on the record.'[2] An account is unlikely to be so powerful second time round. It can also be hard for an interviewee to have to keep repeating what they are going through. At this stage, simply run through the facts and details with them and explain what you would like to do.

Sharing hospitality also helps to make a human connection. Melody is a survivor of childhood rape and spoke to several reporters after the trial in which her stepfather was jailed for eighteen years. She shares her experience of the media in the *Insight* section of this chapter. She points out how important it is to build a human connection and suggests doing so by discussing things over a cup of tea.

The discussion will also give you space to gauge how to proceed. If you are covering a death, some people will appear relatively calm when telling you about the person who has died. For others the grief is so raw, they can barely articulate the person's name. Listen to them and use your judgement carefully. If you are filming with them, this conversation can also help with ideas for shots which will illustrate their story. They may tell you for instance that each day, they light a candle in front of a photograph or tend a memorial in their garden.

In my experience, families who have agreed to share their stories want to support you in doing the best job you can. They can be astonishingly tolerant of TV crews traipsing through their homes, of rooting out photographs and documents for you, but you have a responsibility not to take advantage of their good will. Make allowances for the emotions they may be grappling with beneath the surface. Take a look at the *Trauma Awareness* section at the end of this chapter.

Control

'Journalists should never, ever, make their subjects or sources feel powerless,' says US journalist Jina Moore in her guide to covering violence.[3] Because of the disempowering nature of traumatic events, allowing people some control over how you are working with them is fundamental.

This can include asking them where they would prefer to be interviewed, asking them to choose their favourite photographs or video, asking how they would like you to refer to them and to the person they have lost. It can also include allowing them to guide you round their home before the cameraman sets up his equipment and explaining what you would like to do and why.

Giving them an idea of the questions you would like to ask them before the interview, and taking the time to listen to their opinions, is another way to give them a sense of control. If you are filming with them, it is even more important to involve people in the process. Take care not to overwhelm them with technical detail, because the effects of grief and trauma can also be exhausting. (See the Interview and Filming chapters for more on this, and the *Trauma Awareness* sections.)

In their submission to the Leveson Inquiry in 2012, the team from Dart Center Europe explained how people can lose their sense of control. 'Traumatic incidents typically disempower people. Bereavement, violent assault, sexual abuse or other forms of personal tragedy, can affect people's sense of security and of self in disquieting and subtle ways.'[4]

Check with your interviewee that they are comfortable with what you are asking them to do at each step of the way. Giving control can be particularly important when working with people who have been raped or sexually abused. Melody offers insight on this in the Filming chapter.

Remember that, although filming and interviewing people is routine for you, it is likely to be alien to them, so *explain* and *involve* but don't *overwhelm*.

Empathy not sympathy

When building a rapport, be empathetic. Empathy is non-judgemental and is the ability to understand another's emotional position, to put yourself in their shoes and to show them you hear what they are saying and feeling. It is not the same as sympathy which can imply you feel sorry for them or pity them or even that you are siding with them.

'Empathy is a quality all interviewers need,' says journalist and author Emma Lee Potter. 'It is imperative to try and understand what they have experienced and how they feel.'[5]

Empathy is not about *knowing* how they feel. Never be tempted to say you know what they are going through, you don't. It is about trying to understand, and to do that, you have to listen without making assumptions. Active listening skills will be explored in the Interview chapter.

Show empathy rather than detachment, but be careful not to over-empathise and do try to control your own emotions. If you have had a similar experience, there can be a temptation to identify too closely with your interviewee. 'The danger is that this leads the journalist to cross professional boundaries and become a confidante or advocate,' explains Cait McMahon who says their prime responsibility is to focus on understanding and reporting events accurately.

In Mark Masse's book *Trauma Journalism: On Deadline in Harm's Way*, the photojournalist and documentary filmmaker Molly Bingham, who has covered global conflict, violence and tragedy, tells him a successful trauma journalist has to understand and to feel the emotional impact of what they are seeing but also do the job. 'You have to be there. You have to witness it and you have to feel it. But you cannot let those feelings overwhelm you.'[6]

You are not there to comfort, diagnose, rescue or cheer them up and this approach can prompt inappropriate and insensitive comments. Pam Dix's brother Peter died in the Lockerbie disaster. In an interview with Gavin Rees, director of the Dart Center, Europe, she recalls how someone said to her mother, '"Well at least you have three other children." The suggestion was that she should get over the loss and focus on us remaining three instead. And she replied, "Which one of your children could you afford to lose?"'[7]

Be careful not to over-connect by 'siding' with people and fuelling their sense of injustice. It is not your job and they may well quote you. A correspondent who specialises in health stories recalls how a woman he interviewed was claiming to be the victim of medical negligence. He spent a couple of hours filming with her and, as he was leaving, she told him she had recorded the whole interaction, including their conversations, on her phone. Had he over-sympathised and joined her, off camera, in decrying the management at the local hospital, she could have tweeted or used his comments, particularly given his speciality. Thankfully, he maintained his professional boundaries.

Managing expectations

When people have agreed to be interviewed for a news report, feature or documentary, they need to be clear about consent. Some news organisations have consent forms but in day-to-day news it can be up to you, as the reporter, to manage expectations. Remember how important it is for people to feel a sense of security and control.

Avoid running through a checklist at the start, as this would be off-putting and you don't want them to pull out of doing the interview. However, during the course of your interaction, there are things you need to make them aware of. Remember they are rarely media savvy and can be in turmoil, so you may need to repeat yourself or remind them. Be truthful, transparent and tactful. They need to know:

- Who else you are planning to include in the report. It is important to reflect all sides, but you need to make them aware of this.
- Where else the interview is likely to appear. If it is a TV interview, will it also be on radio news bulletins or programmes and are there plans for a phone-in about the subject? Will it appear online, in which case it may be permanent and people may post comments.

- If they are talking to a local or regional reporter, is the material likely to be used on network TV and radio or in national newspapers or on national news websites?
- When the piece is likely to be published or aired. If they are being interviewed about a death, they need to know if a photograph of their loved one is likely to appear suddenly on their TV screen or in a national paper or magazine, for instance.
- If the interview is live or recorded. Always be clear when you have started and stopped recording.
- That you can only use short clips of the interview in a TV piece, so they don't expect you to use all that they have said or, worse, assume when they see it, that they didn't do a good enough interview.
- That the care you are taking with the filming is necessary, if time-consuming. It can be hard for people to equate the time it takes to film, with the duration of the piece which finally airs, so reassure them. I would caution against giving them the actual duration. People outside broadcasting rarely understand that a two-minute news piece is a substantial and effective chunk of airtime. You can, however, explain that when they see the report, they will understand why you needed to film certain sequences (but do avoid over-filming).
- That there are no guarantees and no promises should they believe your report will achieve a specific outcome for them such as raising funds, prompting an inquiry, changing a policy or making their attacker see the error of his ways.
- If there is a chance the report may not be published or broadcast. Sometimes a piece may be commissioned but not used – sometimes news features can be overtaken by a breaking story. If there is a chance of this happening, it is really important to make people aware early on.
- If other people in the newsroom will be involved in how the story is told and you are unlikely to have control over the finished article or report, its context or headlines.
- If you have agreed to send them a copy or a link to the piece, that you will do so.

Prepare them too for any images you may be using in your report, particularly if they are of a child or adult who has died. Talk it through with them, ask their opinions and explain how they may be used and why. As the charity Child Bereavement UK, whose staff work with hundreds of families, tell me, 'It can be very upsetting to see a picture of the person who has died, for example, lifted from social media without prior knowledge that it is going to be used. This is especially important if the picture is of the child with the person who has died.'

The Children chapter has more on informed consent when working with young people. The Follow-ups chapter has more on managing expectations when working with survivors of rape and sexual abuse.

Language and body language

Communication is key when establishing your relationship. Nerves can make you speak faster but this can be confusing for someone who is struggling to concentrate. 'Speak slowly,' says Faith. 'It's just processing information when you're like you are and maybe repeat what you're saying.' She also suggests using a softer tone of voice and sounding like you care.

They may also be nervous, so focus on putting them at ease. Make allowances if they react in unusual ways, such as laughing at an odd moment – their emotional expressions may be awry. If they don't meet your eye or they take time to answer you, it is unlikely they are being shifty or evasive. They may be trying to grasp what you have asked them and struggling to remember the sequence of events.

Avoid at all costs saying, 'I know how you feel, I understand what it's like, I know what you are going through.' Even if you have been through something similar, you cannot know how they feel and families say they find these platitudes offensive. In the Poynter article, 'From the ER to the Newsroom,' the US journalist and former nurse Mary Pitman says she prefers to say the more appropriate, 'I can't imagine what you are going through.'[8]

Working with tragically bereaved families was part of Detective Sergeant James Greely's role in 25 years of police service. During that time, he investigated murders and serious road traffic fatalities. As a family liaison co-ordinator, he also managed the victims' families throughout criminal investigations and the court process. 'It's about setting the right environment for speaking to people. I always sit at their level, so I'm not standing looking down at them. It's about using open language with people. So we will freely use the word *died*, we refer to victims by their names, we don't refer to them as victims,' he tells me. 'We always refer to collisions as collisions, we don't refer to them as accidents.'

As a rule, avoid euphemisms. As one grieving father explained to me, 'I haven't lost her, she died.' But, as ever in this work, you have to adapt. Some people will prefer phrases such as 'passed away.' As former *New York Times* journalist Jina Moore discovered, when interviewing a survivor of rape, sometimes the word itself can feel too harsh. Her interviewee flinched at the word *rape* and asked for it to be referred to as *the incident*. If you have established a collaborative relationship, and need to use specific terminology to tell their story, it should be possible to ask them gently which words or phrases they would prefer.

When talking with your interviewee, use appropriate eye contact to show interest, engagement and encouragement. Sitting alongside them can feel less threatening when chatting to them, though when recording a TV interview you would generally have to sit opposite them. Be mindful of encroaching on their personal space, particularly if your interviewee has been attacked or abused.

Keep your body language open, receptive and unthreatening. Crossing your arms or legs can act as a barrier and appear defensive. Mirroring the way your interviewee is sitting can be empathetic and you may find you do this naturally during the interview.

Remain warm, kind and considerate throughout the process, both in what you say and how you behave. Tune in to their needs, stay calm and unflustered and take care not to over-react to what people are telling you. There will be more about this in the Interview and Filming chapters.

Take Your Time

John, whose teenage daughter Jess died of a brain tumour, found it insulting and insensitive when a reporter hurried him. He says that, even if you are in a rush because of your deadline, 'you can't let the person be aware of that in any way, shape or form.'

Put your phone on silent and out of sight and focus on the people who have been good enough to share with you what is probably the worst experience of their life. 'However urgent your deadline, however impatient your editors, allow the people you are interviewing to set the pace, to take breaks, to end the interview,' says Mark Brayne, in his guide to trauma journalism.[9]

There are occasions, however, when the deadline is tight and looming and the time pressures are intense. In those cases, it may be appropriate to share this tactfully with your interviewee and ask them to work with you. It is a fine balance and still important not to let them feel rushed. In my experience, people who have chosen to share their stories will make allowances, but it is then essential to contact them after the piece has aired and give them time and space to talk to you, and to apologise if they felt at all hurried.

Leaving and after-care

How you *leave* someone who has entrusted their story to you, the impression you give as you head off, really matters. Much of the good work you have done to build the relationship, in the preceding hours or minutes, can be broken if you then leave in a hurried or dismissive way.

You may be distracted and worrying about delivering the report on time, having the shots you will need, technical issues, the details of a graphics sequence, having time to edit it, write it and select your interview clips, but it is important not to let this show. It can be damaging for people to be left with the feeling that you got what you came for, your concern was short-lived and, to you, they were little more than a story for the day.

In the *Insight* section of the Follow-ups chapter, Jeff describes the impact of being interviewed for the many anniversaries since the Aberfan tragedy of 1966. Coal slurry engulfed buildings including the junior school in the Welsh village, killing 144 people. Most of them were children and Jeff was the last child to be dug out alive. Global media interest has been intense since it happened, with many journalists returning to mark anniversaries of the disaster. Jeff explains how violated some villagers feel when reporters encourage them to spill their emotions only to disappear with their stories. He talks of how one bereaved mother equated the experience to being *raped*. So be attentive as you are leaving, thank them for their time and tell them they can contact you with any questions or concerns.

An important tip is this: take a moment, after the piece has aired or been published, to get in touch with them, say thank you and check they are all right. Few journalists do this because, in our fast-paced world, we move quickly on to the next story. However, if you do take the time to text, call, message, or email them, you will be the reporter the family return to with important follow-up stories.

Rachel spoke to many journalists because her teenage daughter, who had anorexia, needed a hospital bed and the nearest unit was 300 miles away. After giving an interview, she tells me she found the 'wall of silence' from reporters distressing. 'You've just poured your soul out to somebody and then you almost feel like you've been dropped.'

To contact them matters professionally, but crucially it matters at a human level because families can often feel vulnerable once their story is public, so they value being thanked and given a chance to talk about it. It also reassures them you were not simply viewing them as a story, to be forgotten as soon as it had been broadcast or published. It only takes a moment, but it really does make a difference.

FOCUS on journalists

Sacha Mirzoeff is an award-winning filmmaker who specialises in social issue documentaries that are shot over long periods of time. He is the Creative Director of Marble Films and was a former documentary Executive Producer at the BBC.

On occasion his work focuses on challenging or traumatic situations such as child abuse, exorcism, drug use, racism, war, conflict and religious extremism. Here he explains how he and his team build relationships with the vulnerable people they are working alongside to film.

A vast amount of legwork goes into planning one of Sacha's documentaries. Securing responsible access is a time-consuming process. He will often begin with any professional agencies involved and pan out from there into working with the frontline staff and then finally the vulnerable people they help support. 'There are several stages of separate engagement to do this in a protective way. What's at the heart of that, is giving everyone really clear and informed information about what's involved so they can make an informed choice. We never, ever put any pressure on anyone to take part. That's really important to us,' Sacha tells me.

Motivation is one aspect to consider in the people who might want to take part. Why do they want to? What might seem appropriate for them may not necessarily be right for the filmmaker/broadcaster – and vice versa. Sacha feels it is crucial they are treated with dignity and respect during the entire process whatever their circumstances, but will not shy away from difficult areas relevant to the narrative. 'We're very clear that we want to engage with them but we don't sugar-coat it. We'll say we'll be there at the good times but we'll also want to be with them at the bad times and, at that point, they may feel that it's particularly challenging. But the reason we want to be there at those times, is to document the relevant ups and downs of life. Of course there may well be many other difficult parts of their life, that don't feel central to an overarching narrative, that can be safely ignored.'

Sacha believes his films are only as strong as the strength of the relationships they build. 'It's a really interesting paradox because you want it to be a meaningful strong and real relationship, and yet you need some clear boundaries.'

An example would be when they were working with drug users. 'It's inevitable a hard drug user is going to ask you for money at some stage, which wouldn't be morally acceptable for us and we don't pay our contributors anyway. But in this case, it would be particularly worrying. We have to lay it out at the beginning and the clearer our parameters and understanding, the better the long-term relationship is. Those early conversations will play out in very real ways later on when challenging situations present themselves,' explains Sacha.

His team will have ongoing conversations about consent and what it means throughout the filming process, which can stretch out for months or even years. What is relevant at the beginning of a filming relationship will be different from what would be talked about when approaching broadcast. 'The handshake where we're saying you know what we're about, we know what you're about is more important than any form that anyone signs. Honesty and clarity is absolutely key.'

They have filmed at times when tempers have flared in highly tense situations, such as some contributors being arrested and the crew turning up with the police. 'We did turn off the camera when asked to by the contributors but five minutes later, while the arrests were still going on, we were able to continue filming with them because they remembered those conversations that we had had months before at the front of the project. We didn't want to film them to be gratuitous. We wanted to demonstrate how tough their lives were.'

Staying calm in the face of high-octane emotion is really important. 'If a situation becomes fraught and tense and somebody starts shouting or kicking off in front of you, you might naturally start getting jumpy. But the argument is rarely with you, so most of the time you can with confidence remain relaxed and remain focused on what you are doing.'

Listening and communicating with appropriate language is essential. 'It's a way of being human, understandable and respectful, using language that's meaningful for the people you're talking to. So the way we might approach someone who is living in a car park and our approach to a Chief Constable would share some elements, but also have some differences. I want both people to feel at ease. So I meet them on their terms, in a way which is most comfortable and understandable for them.'

When following a story for months and months, the team is waiting for an extraordinary narrative to unfold in front of them. If the relationship is strong, tough emotional situations can take place and the crew can blend into the background. 'We've been there at the point where a mother finds out that she'll lose custody of her child forever, or situations where people are dying in front of us. It simply wouldn't be appropriate to be there unless we felt that everyone felt fully comfortable with us and fully understood what we are doing and why. Relationships, relationships, relationships … it's why all of our work is long-form.'

Putting a documentary together on this scale is like building a picture with jigsaw pieces of people's lives. It involves anticipating different twists and turns and preparing people at each step of the way. Often contributors become comfortable with the whole process, even getting involved with technicalities: fixing on a radio microphone becomes as normal as making a cup of tea.

With the vast majority of the films he makes, Sacha will show them to his contributors before they are broadcast. 'We are not in the business of surprising people or playing games or twisting reality – quite the opposite. We want them to be proud of the work as much as we're proud of it. Fortunately, with the safeguarding process in place, that always seems to be the case.'

Jeremy Ball is a regional BBC Social Affairs correspondent specialising in crime, immigration and homelessness. He won a Royal Television Society TV Journalist of the Year award in 2014. Here he explains how he secured an exclusive interview with a woman who had been trafficked as a child.

Modern slavery is a growing subject but finding people who have survived it and are prepared to talk to reporters about their experiences is rare, explains Jeremy.

Many journalists were keen to interview a university academic who had been trafficked for sex as a child by her parents. She was setting up a global network for fellow survivors. They wanted to hear her story of abuse but she refused to be portrayed as a victim, so she turned down flat any requests which focused on her past trauma. She did not want to keep telling her story repeatedly because she had come out of slavery some years ago.

The dilemma for Jeremy was how to tell her story fully, while honouring her request and securing the interview. 'I got into negotiation with intermediaries saying we can't ignore the elephant in the room and can't do the story without touching on what happened but wouldn't go into sordid details,' he tells me.

Experts he had worked with on similar stories were able to vouch for him and he also involved a university press officer. An informal phone conversation followed. 'We had a chat about what she might be happy with, what was newsworthy for us and how we might square that circle. When we met, I told her the subject areas I would like to ask about but explained I would clearly need to ask what had happened to her.'

Jeremy built up trust and secured the interview. He began by encouraging her to tell him about her current work before broaching her experience of slavery. After an initial brief answer, he prompted her and she gave a strong account of what had happened to her.

The challenge for Jeremy would be for him to maintain control of his material. It would now go to different news outlets, such as radio and online, and it was essential that they adhered to the agreement Jeremy had made when securing the interview. She did not wish to be seen as a victim.

He managed it by using the BBC's fairness guidelines. 'Under the rules, we had agreed the context of the story was that she was an academic using her experience to set up a survivors' network to tackle the problem, so anything she said about what happened to her had to be used in context.'

He took responsibility for checking all the output. 'I put out a note to all the editors who may try to use the material, explaining why it was so sensitive and saying anything they were running had to be run by me first. I was particularly worried about short headlines, short radio clips. So it was about maintaining control to honour the agreement.'

Jenny Johnson is an investigative journalist working on a team in BBC Wales which produces news stories across TV, radio and online. She began her career working for a local newspaper, then an evening paper, before becoming the crime correspondent for the national newspaper of Wales. Many of her stories involve people who have been through traumatic times.

Often the people Jenny is interviewing have been bereaved in terrible circumstances. 'These are the situations requiring the utmost sensitivity and care at each stage of the process, from finding the right form of words for that first phone call or email, right through to thanking them and checking they're happy once a story has finally aired,' Jenny tells me.

Jenny has learnt that the after-care, and how you treat people once the cameras stop rolling, is as important as how you treat them before securing the interview. She describes a story she covered in which a father's young son and stepson were killed by his estranged partner, who then took her own life.

The father was unhappy with the subsequent official review but was powerless to challenge it so he agreed to an interview. Jenny and her team spent several hours with him, allowing him time to tell his story in as compelling a way as possible. 'He was a very private man who hadn't spoken publicly about the tragedy before. He became tearful at points and I was aware that we had put him through the mill to get all that we needed.'

Concerned for his welfare, Jenny rang him that night to thank him for his time and his openness but largely to check in with him. 'We only had a brief conversation but he confirmed that while it had been upsetting for him, he was glad that he'd given us the interview and felt that it might even have helped him a little.'

She contacted him again after the piece had aired and sent him the copy he requested. 'This extra duty of care, checking on their welfare and perhaps keeping in touch intermittently in the months that follow, costs nothing but might make a difference in terms of how the interviewee remembers their experience of engaging with the media. And whether they are willing to engage again in the future.'

INSIGHT from interviewees

John's daughter Jess was 15 when she was diagnosed with a brain tumour. She died ten months later. John spoke to journalists because he wanted to raise awareness of brain tumours in children and raise funds for research as well as campaigning for improved hospital services for teenagers on cancer wards. Here John offers his insight into what he valued from the professional relationship with reporters.

John says that watching Jess die was something no parent should have to go through. 'The loss of a child is the worst thing, period. There is nothing worse,' he tells me. As a reporter, you have to be aware of the enormity of the feelings you may be walking into. 'It's not just someone's home, but you're coming into this huge emotion, this raw emotion, this bereavement. The house is empty.'

He advises always accepting hospitality, if it is offered. 'The whole act of making a cup of coffee or tea, whether or not you drink it, for me breaks the ice. It's what we would normally do when someone comes in.'

Everyone reacts differently, but for John, giving an interview was a chance to talk about Jess and release some of the emotion. He gives this advice to journalists who come to homes such as his. 'I fervently believe it's the acknowledgement that something horrific has happened but not dwelling on that and talking about the person who is lost, that's key. You could come in and perhaps spot a picture and ask is that Jess? Oh she's beautiful, tell me about her, what did she study at school? What did she like doing? Then that leads someone like me onto a positive. Oh she loved music, you ought to hear the songs she sang.'

Being empathetic and sharing this conversation with John beforehand allowed him to give a better interview. 'By the time you've had your cup of tea and sat down with me, I will be more at ease with the questions you are about to ask me because I now feel that you understand a little about Jess.'

Do not overlook siblings. Jess has two brothers and John says it's important to involve them if they want to have their say.

Taking time to listen is fundamental and John describes an experience with a bustling reporter who hurried through the questions at speed before disappearing. 'They want their piece, they want their copy, they want their photo. That is just insensitivity at the height of insensitivity.'

He adds, 'A reporter, for what I can understand you are always busy trying to go from one story to another. But in this instance there has to be a massive degree of sensitivity and time must be allowed. This is not a five-minute job and that is really important. So even though you might feel you're in a hurry, you can't let the person be aware of that in any way, shape or form.'

Melody is a survivor of childhood rape. In her later forties, she plucked up the courage to walk into a police station and tell an officer what had happened to her as a child. In the investigation and court case that followed, eleven other victims came forward and Melody's stepfather was jailed for eighteen years. After the trial, Melody waived her right to anonymity and gave several interviews to journalists. Here she explains how she wished to be treated.

One of Melody's most momentous days was when twelve strangers, the jury, said guilty. They *believed* her and it is essential to recognise how important this is when working with survivors of abuse. As a child, Melody was told by her abuser that no one would believe her.

When the verdict came through, it prompted a whole gamut of emotions. 'I've exposed myself in court of the most delicate and scary things that have happened in my life. There's a lot of shock, a little bit of horror that I'm sending someone to prison and, at the same time, this whole thing of being believed. So there's a lot going on emotionally and psychologically,' she tells me.

Melody decided to waive her right to remain anonymous so she could speak openly to other victims of abuse. She wanted to show them they too can bring their cases to court and be believed. This involved sharing her story with journalists.

The reporter she was never going to talk to was the one who confronted her in court after sentencing. 'I have no idea who he is or where he's from and there's nothing to identify him as a reporter and he's literally right in front, within inches of my face, pushed through everyone else and calling me by name,' she recalls.

The professional relationships she valued began with openness; reporters who introduced themselves, clearly identified themselves, gave her their contact numbers and showed her some manners. 'Please tell me who you are and what you're about, where you're from and what you are actually wanting from me. Be direct, be honest because then I can inform you whether I can give you what you want or not.'

Once she had agreed to be interviewed, Melody explains how she wished to be treated. 'The first thing I needed them to do was accept that: okay I'm a victim, I *was* a victim. However, I still needed to be treated like a normal human being who you would care to or dare to sit and have coffee and cake with. So it was about building rapport, building a connection and about those sensations you get when you do sit with somebody and say: okay, let's have a cup of tea and discuss how we're going to do this the best and to be handled in this way.'

Melody also advises reporters to be mindful of how they listen to her and others who have been sexually abused. 'Be prepared that you're going to be shocked and, while the victim appreciates that, if you physically recoil, that is going to be awkward. Your listening skills and empathy are important because, if anything, the victim needs to feel that they've been heard and understood in a positive way.'

She adds it is vital you don't simply see her as a story. 'You treat that victim as a sound and solid person in their own right that still has value in this world, rather than seeing them as "the incident."'

> *In the previous chapter, Faith explained why it is important that reporters do basic background research. Her teenage son Joshua died after being knocked off his bike as he cycled to school. Here she gives advice to journalists coming to her home to interview her.*

In common with a number of the parents I have interviewed, Faith asks that reporters make a point of acknowledging what has happened right at the start. 'The most important thing, the first thing you say is "sorry." I know it's a very difficult thing to talk about, we've all been there and felt awkward in a situation like that but just a simple "sorry" says a lot,' Faith tells me.

The reporters she didn't speak to were the ones who rang the hospital while Joshua was in intensive care, trying to obtain information about him by pretending to be a member of the family.

She also advises reporters against saying they understand what she is going through or know how she feels because they have lost a parent. 'I've lost those but this is my child and you can't compare. You just shut up, you clam up and you think they haven't got a clue so you stop talking,' explains Faith.

What she did appreciate were people who told her they couldn't begin to imagine what she must be going through.

When establishing the relationship, sincerity is key. 'When it's fake I can't stand it and I can spot it a mile off, the ones that are overly effusive. It's getting that balance between acknowledging the grief and being professional in what you do, but still having that empathy with what's happened.'

HOW I COVER SENSITIVE STORIES: LOUIS THEROUX

'Sensitivity and respect are fundamental.'

As a celebrated documentary writer and presenter, Louis Theroux bears little introduction yet his career began as a journalist working for a free newspaper in California.

He studied History at Magdalen College, Oxford and after his stint at the paper in San Jose, he was hired as a writer for *Spy* magazine and became a correspondent on Michael Moore's *TV Nation* series in 1994.

When that ended, he began working for the BBC where he went on to become an award-winning documentary filmmaker with a huge international following and fan base. His series *Louis Theroux's Weird Weekends* and *When Louis Met …* were followed by a series of special documentaries for BBC Two and in 2016 he premiered a feature-length documentary, *My Scientology Movie*.

Through his work, Louis has tackled profoundly sensitive subjects, approaching them in his distinctive style of guileless curiosity: autism, dementia, alcoholism, heroin addiction, sex trafficking, anorexia, imprisonment, adoption and end of life care, to name but a few. His work on these subjects forms the basis of his advice to working and aspiring reporters.

Putting people first

At the core of his films are the people most profoundly affected and this is central to Louis's work. 'I've always attempted to tell stories through actuality and through direct experience. I sometimes call myself an immersive journalist or a participatory journalist and there are different ways of understanding that but one part of it is experiencing a problem or a situation or a psychological issue at first hand, through the people who embody it directly,' he tells me.

To achieve this, he resists drafting experts or pundits into his documentaries. 'We really try and organically engage with a story by following contributors who are grappling with it directly, whose lives have been upended by something deeply affecting, deeply traumatic.'

He will film with them over weeks or months, to see how their situation affects them and the people around them. 'I don't mean to say we never have doctors or psychiatrists but we always have people dealing with the person who is at the centre of the story, so they kind of branch off our main contributor,' he explains.

Handle with care

Louis is unequivocal about the need to deal with people carefully. 'It's absolutely fundamental that journalists treat vulnerable contributors sensitively and with respect.'

He says it can be difficult for people who are going through awful times to dredge up and express their emotions, yet sometimes doing so can be therapeutic and valuable. 'Very often people have agreed to be in programmes because they wish to share their story or because they want to get something off their chest but that still doesn't always make it easy. There's a tendency to pussyfoot in an interview with someone who's been through something awful, or is going through something terrible, which is understandable but you do also have to do your best to get the story. So there is a need to sensitively push and you can't just cower and shrink.'

For him, it is about remembering that the person is taking part in the programme for a reason. 'Trust your instincts about how you are managing to build a rapport, how you are getting along with the person. Try and go for what you find most interesting about the subject, while being aware that you may see a red flag at which point you may think twice.'

Edge of Life

Edge of Life was the second film in Louis's documentary series *LA Stories*, in which he visited Hollywood's Cedars-Sinai Medical Center to get a clearer understanding of how Americans deal with terminal illness and death. Several patients and their families agreed to take part.

Among them was Javier Galvan, a young man who would die from leukaemia shortly after being filmed. 'It was clear from speaking to him that because of the sensitivities around what he was going through and understandable reticence on the part of the doctors and family, he hadn't really been able to talk about what he was going through in a deep way with anyone he was close to. So he just relished the opportunity to really talk about what he was feeling and it was kind of an amazing and, for me, very fulfilling documentary relationship.'

Conversely, on the same shoot, the team were invited to film relatives being told there was a good chance their loved one was not going to wake up, and the family felt blindsided by the unexpected news. 'There was a feeling of, did we handle that right? Should we have been more careful? Clearly you want to see high impact moments but there's a balance between that and infringing on people's private grief.'

Managing expectations

Although Louis is the presenter, he describes himself as the lead singer of a band, giving full credit to his team, his associate producer and his director. They will form the initial relationship and proceed when they have the people whose stories they are happy to follow. 'I have always been briefed on roughly what the story is with the contributor I'm about to meet and from there it's up to me to be a sympathetic and attentive listener while also being an engaging presence for the audience at home and attempting to explore the story that I'm interested in.'

The bedrock is making sure the contributor is fully aware of the sort of programme they are taking part in and that they are okay with it, he explains. If they have not seen his documentaries they are sent programmes to have a look at to clarify what they are signing up for. 'From there, I often think it's just as basic as trying to be polite and a nice person and a little bit humorous. It's not witchcraft, it really is just about attempting to be respectful while also getting your questions answered in the kind of organic, free-wheeling way,' Louis tells me.

First meetings

When engaging one on one, Louis says there is no rulebook and sometimes it is simply about giving people a chance to relax and for him to find his feet. 'I'll say, as you know we're doing this documentary about people who are struggling with anorexia and I'm just curious to hear a little bit about what your journey has been like with this.'

He adds, 'There's a little bit of throat clearing on my part that allows them a moment to sort of settle in the idea of the conversation that's going to take place. I think that's maybe a more natural way of interacting. It can be a little brutal to go, so what's it like to have anorexia? But that's sort of what you want to ask. You're basically asking the same question but you're just trying to do it in a way that doesn't sound harsh.'

Asking and listening

Louis is unequivocal about the importance of taking time to listen to what people are telling you. Listening is so foundational, he says, that if you're not going to listen, don't show up. He also cautions against writing questions down, preferring instead to trust his instincts.

'Sometimes for people, questions are a bit of a safety blanket and certainly when I started I would write questions and I still might occasionally scribble some things and have them in my back pocket just so I don't at the end of it think, have I covered everything? But increasingly I don't even do that. I do think the key to the whole thing is listening because you just don't know what's going to come up.'

By listening you are able to follow up on any interesting points. 'You're a bit like someone picking a lock. You have to have your ear against the lock to hear the clicks and whirs so that you know what's happening out of sight. That's how you decide how to focus your energy on what's coming back from the contributor.'

Louis adds that it is only by listening, that you will notice whether or not you run the risk of annoying someone in an unhelpful way. 'If you're losing them in some sense or if they are becoming more distant, then the questions you're asking are wrong-headed or offensive or not doing what they're supposed to do. It would be like playing tennis with a blindfold if you didn't listen.'

Breaking down

Inevitably, when covering stories where people are hurting, there may be tears. 'You have scenes in which the contributors are affected and break down, start crying or become visibly upset. There's a sense in which that's effective story-telling because it creates in the audience an appreciation of what the emotional stakes are. At the same time, you've got a vulnerable person who is experiencing something profound and may need looking after.'

Louis admits he isn't a fan of TV in which presenters over-emote, and prefers not to see them hugging and comforting. 'I tend to err on the side of allowing the person their moment but not rushing to comfort. I think for the most part it's actually a solid way of doing things. Just because someone is crying and upset, it doesn't mean it requires anything active from you other than a respectful silence and maybe ask, do you need a moment?'

He recalls two situations when people got up and left during the interview and there was little he could do or offer to do. He simply accepted that they were adults and they were upset. One was in 'Heroin Town' when a father was talking about his daughter and the moments they were lost to each other because of her addiction, the other was in his documentary about autism when he was asking a father about his relationship with his children.

Louis is aware of the need to keep a bit of distance. 'Maybe this is more of a human question than a journalistic question, that someone who you don't know terribly well is crying and it is odd and it's a little bit awkward but in a way, it may not demand very much from you.'

Louis says he tends to tune into the most vulnerable person in a room, particularly when interviewing. 'I sometimes find that children are within earshot and that there's a risk to them being exposed to things they shouldn't be hearing. So I tend to be aware of whether the child is okay and if the parent is crying, whether the child is okay with the parent's tears.'

Experts on hand

Many of Louis's sensitive documentaries are placed in a clinical setting. 'You have a hub for what your story is and you have an almost soap opera of people coming and going which creates stories and allows you to build a long-form narrative. I'm not generally weaving stories together from popping up in people's homes.'

They may be set in hospitals, prisons, rehab centres, secure units and educational facilities which allow him to have clinical expertise close at hand. 'I did one about a maximum security mental hospital in Ohio with people who, in psychotic episodes, had killed their loved ones and done awful things. Some of the interviews I did one on one, but often I found it helpful to have a three-way conversation, a chance to bounce off a third party who's got expertise.'

Mind your language

He advises being aware of the terms you use when covering these stories. 'You're often going into subjects where you can say the wrong thing quite easily, just because the language that's considered sensitive has changed, in the way that language does change. Terms that were previously considered acceptable, sometimes go out of date and people will usually correct you. Where possible, try and observe and don't annoy people unnecessarily.'

Lessons learnt

Louis described a long interview when he was filming a documentary about alcoholism in which a patient took offence and spun out of control. 'It does feel awful when you lose a contributor in that way and he was upset. Afterwards I thought oh wow, I've really let the side down, to be this deep into my story and into my career and to lose a contributor. I thought I might have damaged the access we had at the hospital because he was so upset. It turns out this was just one of his characteristics. I think they'd all been through the same thing with him.'

Another time he was doing a documentary on women who had been trafficked. He was interviewing a young woman in her hotel room but admits they made a fundamental error by having him, a cameraman and a male sound recordist in the room with her, and should have had a female producer. 'It didn't contribute to her feeling safe or relaxed,' he acknowledges.

Equally, there have been times when he has offered to turn the camera off because he felt intrusive, only to be asked to keep filming. It happened when a woman was dealing with an uncontrollable physical episode with her 15-year-old son who had autism and she was lying on top of him. 'I said would you like us to leave, thinking that she felt we were intruding on something that she hadn't signed up for us seeing. She said no, it's important that you see this, this is what true autism is, and we kept that scene in the film,' he explains.

Key advice

'In these kinds of stories, you are talking to decent people who are trying their best to recover from something or deal with something, and I think there's nothing to be gained from upsetting them unnecessarily,' says Louis. 'I do try where possible to extract some positives.'

Louis writes his own documentary scripts and offers further advice in the Writing chapter.

Trauma Awareness

Any loss of a loved one or close friend is traumatic, but a *traumatic bereavement* is often defined as that which occurs after a sudden, violent and unexpected death such as homicide, suicide, or accidental death. Often people affected experience a loss of control over events. It may cause longer-term psychological problems.

People's profound loss and grief can be compounded by factors which seem beyond their control. This can make the experience terrifying and shocking, particularly because they cannot prepare or protect themselves.

Many of us have experienced grief; we each express it in different ways and it is a natural reaction to a significant loss. It can be viewed in stages: numbness, shock, disbelief and feeling overwhelmed, followed by disorganisation, yearning, despair and hopelessness and then, in time, straightening up the mess and ultimately re-engaging with life. But everyone is different and their timelines will vary.

There are often gender differences in the way that individuals and families react. This will often depend upon a variety of factors which can be cultural, societal or environmental.

Although we are not really aware of it, we tend to have three basic assumptions about the world, others and ourselves:

- A belief we are invulnerable.
- A sense that the world is meaningful and comprehensible.
- A positive sense of ourselves and of others.

A traumatic death can shake or shatter these basic assumptions, which is why individuals, families or communities can feel violated or confused and a loss of identity and meaning. It is as if their world has been turned upside down.

Some reactions to traumatic bereavement:

- Profound feelings of sadness, helplessness, anger, rage, shock and numbing.
- Feelings of guilt or shame which is sometimes described as survivor guilt.
- Fear and dread of further violence and a strong sense of vulnerability.
- Hyper-vigilance and a compulsive need for reassurance that they and their family are safe.
- Difficulty sleeping and impaired concentration.
- Irritability and avoidance.

Bear in mind that reactions will vary, even within families, and there can be added stressors. Families can be trying to deal with the police, confusing legal systems at home or abroad, reading graphic and traumatic information, financial complications, as well as coping with their grief and the impact that can have on their lives, their livelihoods and their health.

Points to discuss

After a traumatic bereavement, how emotionally vulnerable may your interviewees be and why?

Why is it important to offer them control in the way you work with them, and how can you involve them?

What sorts of interview questions may provoke their potential sense of guilt or shame?

What is the difference between sympathy and empathy? In pairs, have a go at using active listening skills (described in the Interview chapter).

What allowances may you need to make, in terms of their responses, when you are working with people who have suffered a traumatic bereavement?

Notes

1 Julia Lieblich, 'A Journalist and a Survivor,' Nieman Reports, 15 December 2009, https://niemanreports.org (last accessed 25 January 2019).

2 Karen Brown, 'How to Do an Interview – When Trauma Is the Topic,' 2009, https://niemanreports.org (last accessed 24 January 2019).

3 Jina Moore, 'Covering Trauma – A Training Guide,' 2011, p. 4, www.sfcg.org (last accessed 25 January 2019).

4 Gavin Rees, Stephen Jukes and Bruce Shapiro, Dart Center Europe submission to the Leveson Inquiry, p. 4, June 2012.

5 Emma Lee Potter, *Interviewing for Journalists*, 3rd edn, Routledge, 2017, p. 79.

6 Mark H. Masse, *Trauma Journalism: On Deadline in Harm's Way*, Continuum International, 2011, p. 62.

7 Pamela Dix, Anne Eyre and Gavin Rees, 'Looking Back on Disaster,' Dart Center for Journalism and Trauma, 2 October 2016, https://dartcenter.org (last accessed 25 January 2019).

8 Chip Scanlan, 'Handling Emotional Interviews, Part 2: From the ER to the Newsroom: The Importance of Understanding Grief,' 28 February 2005, www.poynter.org (last accessed 26 January 2019).

9 Mark Brayne, 'Trauma and Journalism: A Practical Guide,' 24 March 2009, https://dartcenter.org.

5
The children

'Make sure to ask gently and not be too full on with the questions, ask them in an easy way to answer. You can feel under pressure if they are long confusing questions.'

Finlay, aged 12, whose Dad died by suicide

In this chapter

How to prepare, interview and film with children.

Extras on safeguarding children.

Focus on how a reporter told the story of a teenager who transitioned.

Insight from children about what helps them when being interviewed.

Overview from Tulip Mazumdar on how she covers sensitive stories.

Trauma Awareness: how children of different ages may be affected by traumatic events.

Giving them a voice

There are strict rules when interviewing children and it is essential they and their parents or guardians fully understand what they may be agreeing to. Having said that, children have every right to give their opinions and have their voices heard through your reports. Their testimony is often powerful, watchable and enlightening. They may want to speak, if you take the time to ask them, and some serious issues affect them more than adults. Some of the most affecting quotes in my reports into the death of a child or teenager have come from their young siblings or classmates.

Having said that, interviewing children about sensitive experiences has to be handled with great care. Avoid approaching young children at the scene of a disaster where they may need comfort rather than questions. 'Cameras and microphones can be intimidating. Even a journalist's scowl may communicate fear to a watching child,'[1] say Simpson and Cote. Do not assume children are well emotionally after a traumatic event, they add. A child may be more shocked and affected than they appear, so tread carefully.

When covering stories about children, always seek appropriate permission. Take a look at the Ethics chapter on this and on the ages at which someone is viewed as a child. Don't approach children directly, but do try to give them a say even if officials stand in your way. 'Their classic excuse for trying to stop children being interviewed is that the children are vulnerable and need to be protected. That's rather patronising. The same thing used to be said about women,' say Sarah McCrum and Lotte Hughes.

McCrum and Hughes produced a booklet called 'Interviewing Children' for the international charity Save the Children.[2] Young people in Barbados, Canada, England, Israel, Namibia, Northern Ireland, Palestine and Romania gave their views on the media, how they would like to be interviewed and what would make it easier for them. The booklet includes basic dos and don'ts when working with children and young people:

Do

- Listen.
- Treat children as equals.
- Take children seriously.
- Ask open questions.
- Ask if it's okay to use their real names.
- Take time.
- Explain what you'll do with the information.

Don't

- Patronise.
- Sit or stand at a higher level than the children.
- Put words in their mouths or let other adults do so.
- Interrupt.
- Talk too much about yourself, unless asked.
- Continue with the interview if a child gets upset.

The preparation

Find out as much as you can before you meet them. 'Children, like adults, are not impressed by ignorant visitors who waste time asking obvious questions,' say McCrum and Hughes.

The charity Child Bereavement UK explains that, when talking to children after a death, it is important to check how much the child knows, so you do not inadvertently reveal more. 'They may not have been told everything about, for example, the circumstances or cause of death,' they tell me. Find out if there are any areas they may struggle to talk about, plus details such as their term for the person who has died. Did they know them as Dad, Gran, Nan, Mummy, Mom? Clarify whether the child will be identified or not and if you will be using their full name. They and their parents need to be aware of the full implications if they are not speaking anonymously.

Allow plenty of time and if possible meet them prior to the interview, as children can be cautious with strangers. Sit with them or, if they're playing, get down and join in and have a chat about what you would like to do. Talk to them at their eye-level. There are key things to make them aware of:

- Who you are, where you are from, what you are doing, why you are doing it and how the interview will be used. Explain what your job is in words they can understand. It may help to bring a copy of the magazine or newspaper you work for or a screen shot or film clip to show them on your phone.
- You are there to listen to them, you are interested in what they have to say and they are in charge. This means they don't have to answer certain questions if they don't want to and they get to choose where they would like to talk to you and who they would like to be there. 'Children are very similar: if you treat them with respect they will give you something back,' explain McCrum and Hughes.
- If you are filming or recording, they can take a look at the equipment and have a go with it if they would like to. I have found this effective when using a large TV camera which can seem both fascinating and scary. It also shows them that you are there working and not as their friend.
- If the plan is for them to be identified, they need to be fully aware of possible consequences, such as reactions from friends or any likely repercussions. See the *Extras* section on safeguarding children.

Good advice is to relax and be open and honest. 'Children are quick to sense insincerity and won't open up to you if they don't trust you. If you feel unsure what to do or say, try asking them. They may be very willing to help you. Show your vulnerability,' say McCrum and Hughes.

If a child pulls out of doing the interview, do not let them feel bad about it.

The interview

Children can clam up when asked direct questions or say what they think the interviewer wants to hear rather than what they really think. You may sense they are searching for the 'right' answer to your question. It may take a while to get going, but it is important not to push them to speak if they don't want to and not to rush them. 'You can usually get the best from children when they feel they are in control. It helps to think of an interview with children as a conversation in which you are the least important person and they, naturally, are the most important person,' explain McCrum and Hughes.

Simple, unambiguous language works best. From its many years of supporting bereaved families, Child Bereavement UK offers advice on what to avoid saying:

- Whilst it is useful to reflect their language and terminology, it is generally unhelpful to use euphemisms with children such as: lost, gone to sleep, gone to the stars, passed away.
- Never ask questions which use expressions such as 'getting over it' or 'moving on.' It is better to talk about 'rebuilding your life after the bereavement.'
- Never try to empathise by saying 'I know what you're going through.'
- Don't assume that the person who died is a 'loved one' because people's relationships can be complex.

If a child becomes upset in the interview, they offer this advice: 'Give them time to allow a break and come back to the interview. Allow the adult who is with them to comfort them. Remember there is no time limit on grief so an interviewee may still be upset, even if the bereavement took place a long time ago.' Be prepared for them to show a range of emotions during the course of an interview. Children can move rapidly between being upset one minute and seeming all right soon afterwards.

Reassuringly for reporters, the charity tells me: 'Don't feel nervous that you will be upsetting the interviewee by asking them to talk about what has happened. When someone is bereaved, they are already carrying those emotions and as long as you are handling the interview sensitively, remember you are not creating those emotions, they are already there.'

Great sensitivity is needed when asking a child to talk about personal subjects, such as their experience of violence, sexual abuse, bullying, racism, family problems or living on the street, explain McCrum and Hughes. 'If they don't bring it up themselves, approach the difficult subject in an indirect way, don't ever say something as direct as: "Tell me about the time you were abused." Instead you could say something like: "I get the feeling you've had a pretty tough time and you've done really well to pull through. Can you tell me about that?"'

'Ask open-ended questions, such as "What was the hardest part?" rather than questions that deliver their own answers, like "Were you scared?"' advises US journalist Ruth Teichroeb in her guide on covering children and trauma.[3]

'Don't ask questions that imply blame, such as "Weren't you wearing your seatbelt?" or "Do you always walk alone at night?" That can make a child feel guilty or expose him to public humiliation,' she adds.

Plan how to finish the interview and ask if there is any more they would like to say. 'Let the children know when you're about to finish, so that they can get their thoughts together and say what they want to say. Don't leave bad feeling and disappointment behind you when you've gone,' say McCrum and Hughes.

Check if they have said anything they do not want you to use in your report and 'don't use information that would embarrass or hurt a child, even with her permission. Kids will tell you just about anything but that doesn't mean you have to print it, bedwetting for example,' explains Ruth Teichroeb.

This is also a good moment to tell them you can only use small bits of their interview. Assure them this is no reflection on how well they have done or what they have said, it is simply the way TV timings work. Always thank them and tell them their contribution was important.

Vox pops

Vox pops with children can be rewarding. In order to edit a coherent vox pop together, you will need to ask each child the same question. Let them know what you would like to ask, to give them a chance to think about their answer. I once asked a group of primary school children, who had taken part in an Armistice Day parade, what they thought about during the minute's silence. Their answers were moving and poignant, with several speaking in awed tones about the sacrifices soldiers had made for them.

Avoid 'voxing' too many children. You will not be able to use them all, and they may feel hurt if they are not included in your piece. Again, explain to them that you cannot use everything they have said and reassure them with positive feedback. Always try to make your vox pops inclusive and diverse reflecting a mix of ethnicity, disability and opinion.

Filming

When filming with children, think about moving into their space rather than expecting them to conform to yours. I filmed with a class of children with disabilities rehearsing a dance show. We had arranged to interview them in their break, at which point they had settled themselves comfortably sitting and lying on the floor. So I got down on my front alongside them, the cameraman squatted down too and the young dancers chatted away happily.

Unusually, when filming the dance rehearsal, it made sense to interview the children *after* getting the shots. Ordinarily, I would suggest doing the interview *first*, so they have told you what they want to tell you and the pressure is off. After the interview, filming shots and sequences should be enjoyable for children, so involve them. Let them have a go with the camera, let them have a look at the shots you have taken, and explain why you may be asking them to repeat actions. This has the added advantage of subtly bringing them back into the present moment, after revisiting their distress in the interview.

Sometimes the sequences, whether they are playing football in the garden, baking a cake or walking the puppy, can send a positive message about their resilience too.

If you are filming them anonymously, always show them and the supervising adult the shots and take care not to show any distinctive hairstyles, clothing, jewellery or tattoos. Take a look at the *Extras* section on anonymous shoots in the Filming chapter.

Writing

When writing or framing your piece, avoid cliché. 'Children tend to get put in a narrow set of boxes ranging from angels, innocents and brave little martyrs at one extreme, through to little terrors, tykes, tearaways, troublemakers, rowdy teenagers and downright delinquents at the other,' say McCrum and Hughes. They add that using the cliché repeatedly will lead to inaccurate stereotypes of children.

Children also told the researchers they don't like their serious comments used as light relief or for the amusement of adults and they don't like being lumped together as a problem group called 'youths.'

If at all possible, send them a copy of your piece or a link, but only make promises that you can keep, as one child told the Save the Children researchers, 'Journalists mess you around, they say things and never follow them through.'

As Ruth Teichroeb says, 'Violence shatters children's view of the world as a safe place and their beliefs that adults will protect them. Journalists can help adults recognise and respond to kids' emotional pain by providing information about post-traumatic stress, sharing their stories and providing a voice for our littlest citizens.' She adds, 'The bottom line: Treat kids like you'd want a reporter to treat your own children.'

Working with children who are hurting can take its toll, so look after yourself and read the Self-Care chapter. There is advice on writing about teenagers with mental health issues and eating disorders in the Writing chapter.

EXTRAS

Caroline Brant developed her expertise in child protection while working in the National Health Service. She has authored a number of Serious Case Reviews. She joined the BBC in 2013 in the wake of the Jimmy Savile scandal and led the whole-scale development and implementation of child protection and safeguarding practice across the BBC for over five years. Here she offers practical tips for journalists when working with children.

1. Don't think of how you can safeguard the child and yourself as an afterthought. Actively think through and risk-assess the environment, situation and context of what you are planning to do, the level of vulnerability of the child, what safeguards need to be put in place, and whether you should seek advice from someone with more experience or specialist knowledge. Make sure that you know what the child protection policy of the organisation you are working with is and that you have accessed relevant training on child protection and safeguarding so that you are equipped to know what to do. Working with children is a skill.

2. Establish professional boundaries. This will include not sharing your personal contact details with a child or young person or friending them on social media. Don't forget that to some children you'll be seen as a celebrity and they'll want to have you as their friend. But would you usually choose to hang out with a child under 18? Always remember this is a working relationship where the balance between you and the child is unequal. They may not be as confident or resilient as they appear to be.

3. Children and young people are all individuals and you will therefore need to adapt your approach dependent upon their needs. It is so important that you do not discriminate against a child. Every child should be treated equally regardless of age, disability, gender, racial heritage, religious belief, sexual orientation or identity.

4. Limit the physical touching with a child to the level that is needed to do the job. If the child is old enough to do things themselves, or there is a parent or chaperone present, ask them to help you. Always ask for the child's consent before you touch them and let them know what you are going to do.

5. Avoid being alone with a child whenever possible. Work alongside a colleague or ensure that the child is always accompanied by another adult such as a parent, teacher or licensed chaperone. If for any reason you find yourself unaccompanied, try and move to an open space or go and find someone to help you. Take the child with you!

6. Informed consent from the child is as important as consent from a parent or legal guardian. Use language that is appropriate to the child's age and

development to explain what is happening, and check with them that they understand what they are being asked to do. In sensitive situations, consent should not be assumed throughout, so it is a good idea to check with the child throughout your interaction, and post-production if necessary. Do make sure that when gaining consent you get it from the right people, i.e. the adults that have a legal responsibility for the child. If you think the person giving consent, whether it is the young person or parent/guardian, is not considering or understanding the child's best interests, you may sometimes, though rarely, have to stop filming or recording. Be sensitive to the fact that whatever you produce could be accessible for many years to come.

7.   Be prepared to think the unthinkable. If a child discloses information to you, try not to show shock, don't ask leading questions but do listen. It isn't easy for a child to disclose so this will be as hard for them as it may be for you. You will need to explain to the child that you can't keep this to yourself and will have to tell someone who will be able to help you both. Regardless of how you have become aware of a risk to a child, you will need to follow the child protection policy, which is usually to tell the child protection lead for the organisation. They will listen to you and decide what, if any, action will be taken. Have faith in the child protection policy and remember that whatever you have seen, heard or been told may just be part of the whole story. By sharing information you are helping to protect a child.

FOCUS

Marie Ashby began her journalistic career in local radio. She became a news reporter for ITV where she worked on national programmes and fronted the regional news half-hour programme. She moved to the BBC to front the current affairs programme Inside Out *and the regional* Politics Show. *She reports and produces documentaries often involving vulnerable contributors.*

Marie filmed a documentary with a 15-year-old who was transitioning from a boy into a girl. Although the teenager wanted to make the film, her parents were worried about the bigger picture and felt protective.

'She was very vulnerable, in her teens and just starting this process and it was highly charged emotionally because the family were just getting their own heads around what was happening,' Marie tells me.

'They were still very raw when I was talking to them and when we did the interviews with them they broke down. The dad was in tears, the mum was in tears, it was the first time they'd actually spoken to anybody outside their family to say what it was like to lose a son and gain a daughter.'

Marie empathised, imagining how she would feel if it had been one of her sons. 'It helped me to put myself in their shoes. I thought this is real and this could happen to any of us,' she explains.

Before any of the filming took place, there was a good deal of planning. She briefed the cameraman carefully and took him to meet the family. She also attended a session at their transgender centre. 'They were all weighing me up because there's been a lot of crappy reporting, sensational headlines and sleazy stories which haven't helped young people at all. I needed to show them I would treat the subject sensitively and that I wasn't in pursuit of headlines.'

Marie explains that trust between her and each of the people taking part was paramount. Honesty and transparency were the key as well as listening to them. 'There were editorial policy concerns because she was under-age and vulnerable. There were concerns about social media taunts and bullying and if there would be a backlash. So I had to prepare the family for that and my editor had a conversation with them as well.'

'We created an environment where they felt safe and protected because we did help them all the way through,' Marie explains. 'I find that I do get close to these people because it's inbuilt in me to have this duty of care. I would look after people as I would want to be looked after. I've got to be able to go home at the end of the day and feel I've done everything I can for those contributors. We can't do our jobs without them.'

They gave the teenager control in choosing where she would like to be filmed. They showed her shopping for clothes with her sister and sitting at her bedroom mirror putting on her makeup. Over the filmed mirror sequence, she explained what she saw reflected. 'She said she saw this boy who really struggled as a teenager and wasn't sure how he fitted into this world and now sees somebody who's finally happy with themselves,' explains Marie.

She was also filmed at school for an LGBT awareness session, and Marie spoke with students afterwards. 'That took a lot of setting up, with all the permissions for all the pupils in the school. They had to send letters home to all the pupils' parents. It took a bit of time but it was well worth the effort.'

Because of the sensitivity involved, in this individual case, they gave the parents the opportunity to view the film before it was broadcast. Marie felt this was kinder, given how heavily they had invested in it. It meant they didn't have to wait anxiously for the transmission date. 'The dad, at the end, was quiet then he just burst into tears and really sobbed in the edit suite and said, it's just so lovely and it just makes me realise how amazing my daughter is and how much she's had to cope with and how proud I am.'

INSIGHT from interviewees

> *Finlay was 12 years old at the time of doing this interview. His father had died by suicide five years earlier. Finlay gave interviews to radio and TV and offers his insight to help journalists when working with children who may be grieving.*

The death of his father was completely unexpected. 'I was very shocked because you don't think something like that would happen to you. I was incredibly sad,' Finlay tells me. 'I didn't say anything for ages, I just sat there. You realise you're not going to see that person again.'

He preferred being interviewed for radio rather than TV. 'With TV, I felt like I had to act which made me feel uncomfortable. When it's a camera, they see everything and it made me feel a bit nervous in case something went wrong. With radio, I could just sit and talk.'

His advice for reporters filming children is to have a reassuring chat beforehand, otherwise it feels like you're being asked to open up to a complete stranger. Tell them they can stop at any point and explain why you are filming particular sequences, talk them through it. 'I had to hang a decoration on a Christmas tree and it felt a bit weird having to act like we were doing it, a bit awkward.'

A great piece of advice is to involve children in the shoot. Show them the pictures you are taking, let them have a go with the camera so it becomes a little less scary.

In an interview, Finlay says simple straightforward questions are easier to deal with. 'I'm happy to talk about it but some people might be a bit worried about opening up. Make sure to ask gently and not be too full on with the questions, ask them in an easy way to answer. You can feel under pressure if they are long confusing questions.'

He says it's important to give children some control, explain they can stop at any point and they don't have to answer a question if they don't want to. 'If I'm struggling for an answer, it's nice to ask the questions again in case I've got a bit confused. I don't want to leave a silence so that helps quite a lot.'

'I feel when I cry about it I need to be left alone. Give them their own space because they might feel embarrassed crying in front of people. I would just ask to stop actually, just give me a minute. If I cry I do need to get myself together a bit before we carry on, have a minute to relax and gather my emotions,' explains Finlay.

He also liked having his mum in the room. 'It's a bit like if you walk into a room of strangers, it's quite nice having someone you know by your side in case it feels a bit awkward or uncomfortable.'

He also advises against being overly attentive and constantly checking, as some children don't like being treated too differently when they have lost a parent. 'Be a normal person,' he advises.

Managing expectations is crucial when working with children. Finlay hadn't been told that because of the way TV works, only little bits of his interview would be used. 'I was surprised because so much footage was gone. So much of what I said wasn't in it.'

He was happy with the piece but disappointed at what was left out. A simple explanation from the reporter could have avoided this.

> When Rebecca was 5, her mum died of breast cancer. She has given TV interviews including taking part in a network documentary about coping with grief.

'For a long time, I repressed everything and it made me very depressed,' Rebecca tells me. 'I learnt to accept those feelings of guilt, anger, extreme sadness and pain. I faced all my fears of being fragile and vulnerable and I overcame them.'

She says that, initially, it is really important for a reporter to have a chat. 'It is always good to get some rapport and make sure I feel comfortable. To have a friendly conversation settles any nerves and, to have a bond with your interviewer, allows you to answer their questions more honestly.'

Offering control is the key for Rebecca, who says she needed to be reassured she only had to answer the questions she felt happy with. 'Having that ability to say only as much as I want to is fundamental.'

Rebecca prefers direct questions but says she may not be typical in this. 'I don't like when people use euphemisms and edge round the subject without actually going into it. It makes it feel a bit trivial. What's happened has been serious and I deserve to be asked honest open questions so I can give very open and honest and direct answers.'

Equally, Rebecca prefers reporters to use terms such as death, died or killed. 'The problem shouldn't be lessened. It diminishes the death of my mother because she didn't pass away, she died. That's the reality of it.'

Rebecca values having someone she knows with her when being interviewed. She says that if she began to cry in an interview, she would want the cameras to keep rolling. 'To shy away from the rawness of the emotion is a disservice. It's important everything is included.'

To deal with their grief, both Finlay and Rebecca received support from Child Bereavement UK. They are young ambassadors for the charity.

HOW I COVER SENSITIVE STORIES: TULIP MAZUMDAR

'Reflect the positive too.'

After studying Sociology at the University of Liverpool, Tulip began her career as a BBC news trainee. She worked for local and national radio stations and was embedded with British troops in Afghanistan, travelling to Helmand for BBC TV in 2007 and 2008.

From there, she worked in South Asia out of the Kabul bureau, the Dakar bureau in Bangladesh and the Colombo bureau in Sri Lanka, as a producer. She went on to work in Islamabad before returning to London as the BBC's Global Health correspondent in 2013.

The many highly sensitive stories she has covered in this role include a documentary on the Islamic State branch in West Africa, Boko Haram, and the impact violence in northern Nigeria has had, particularly on women. She has covered stories on FGM (female genital mutilation) and acid attacks as well as outbreaks of disease including Ebola, Zika and ongoing diseases such as TB, malaria, and AIDS.

Approaching people sensitively

'You have to be very genuine with how you approach them. It sounds obvious, but remember that you are a human being as well as a journalist,' she tells me. 'Somebody who's been through some of the things people I've spoken to have been through, may not have actually spoken to anybody before about their experience, or have been asked in the way that we are asking.'

She says giving them time is important but can be tricky with a breaking news story and a tight deadline. However, 'when you are in the room with that person, be in the room with that person and listen to what they're saying and respond in a human way,' she says.

Contact and connection

Normally, when meeting her interviewee Tulip would shake their hand and introduce herself, but in the Ebola outbreak this wasn't possible. 'There was an additional barrier because there was a "no touch" policy in place in Sierra Leone during the outbreak. I was often speaking to people suspected of having the disease, or recovering from it. So the new greeting in that situation was to pat your chest and bow a little bit and that's how we could approach people. It was called the Ebola handshake.'

In some cases, her interviewees were behind a fence and there could be three metres between them. She would make sure that if they were sitting down, she would be too so they would be at the same level. If they were standing, she would also stand, 'Make sure you're not towering above them or hovering below them,' she says.

'A lot of survivors will have lost a number of people in their family so you acknowledge that and say, "I am so sorry to hear what's happened to you and your family."' But she would also add she was pleased that they were looking well, because they were recovering.

Tulip would then explain what she wanted to do and why she wanted to talk to them, telling them, 'I just want to ask a bit about your experience. I'd love to hear about your loved ones so we can help inform the world about what's happening here because I think it's very difficult for people from my country, the UK for example, to understand what it's like to go through this.' Once you have explained and they understand, you can start the interview, she says.

Sensitive interviewing

When interviewing, Tulip will always try to start on a positive and a time prior to the experience. She interviewed one girl who was in her late teens and her parents wanted her to undergo female genital mutilation or FGM. The girl had run away and was now in a school being educated and wanted to do the interview to encourage other girls not to feel forced into undergoing FGM.

Before the interview, Tulip made sure she prepared well with as much background information as possible. 'I didn't just go in on a fact-finding mission. I knew the key parts of her story, having spoken to her teacher first, and it was a case of facilitating her, to give her a global platform with the BBC because her message was very powerful and very important.'

Tulip began by asking her what her life had been like at home, before FGM had become an issue. 'She talked about it and she was smiling and reflecting on her parents that she clearly had a lot of love for. I smiled with her. You're not coming in and going, "I can't believe your parents did this to you."'

Tulip broached the more sensitive aspect of the interview with a 'when' question, by asking, 'At what point did you realise that this was something they wanted to do to you?' Tulip made it clear her interviewee should only tell her what she felt comfortable sharing, but wanted to ask her what had happened.

'I think you just put it in a very straightforward way and you give her the choice.' She told her interviewee, 'I'd like to talk a little bit about what actually happened that day to you, I know that it was obviously very traumatic and difficult. So please tell me what you feel comfortable with and if you want to stop at any point, then we'll stop and have a break, or move onto something else.'

It is important not to be judgemental or make assumptions. The girl understood the pressure her parents were under from their community for her to undergo FGM. She explained to Tulip it was from a place of ignorance but also love and she forgives them. 'That was also a crucial part of the story to get across.'

Be mindful of where you are doing the interview and make sure that you are both in a comfortable space, she advises. In the case of the teenage girl, 'I made sure that there weren't other students around, that we had privacy. It was really hot outside so we went somewhere that was cool and calm and there wasn't any commotion. You need to think about that.'

Follow-up contact

A key part of this work, says Tulip, is following up with the people and their stories. Ebola was an enormous story which had the world's attention for a number of months and then it fell away, she explains. 'I just felt it was so important to go back and talk to the people we spoke to at the height of it. It's not good journalism to just show the shock and horror and the biohazard suits and thousands of people dying and then not show what happens next. I think you need to go back and maintain these relationships and revisit people so that you can show how they move on.'

She would often maintain contact with people she had interviewed via WhatsApp which became a common way to keep in touch in the part of West Africa she was covering.

When revisiting their stories it is important to remember they are trying to move on and forget a difficult time, she says. 'Again it's that preparation, it's the fact that you've been speaking to them throughout. I think they appreciated that we'd followed them over a number of months and they trusted us and felt comfortable. It's also just genuinely caring about what they have to say. I wanted to know how they were getting on which, I think, came across. You are aware that you're raking all of this up again for them,' Tulip tells me. 'It's down to you to take your time and give them the space they need to tell their story.'

Filming with sensitive sources

Give them power, give them choice, talk it through first. Tulip will ask, 'Where would you like to do the interview? Is there anywhere in particular? Would you like to do it in your house, a café? Where would you feel most comfortable?'

She also says it is important to brief your crew, who may not have been as involved in the story, so they are aware of how sensitive it is.

If her interviewee is talking about a particularly difficult subject such as FGM, Tulip will explain to her beforehand if the camera operator is going to be male. 'You need to let them know who's coming, "the camera operator is a guy, we've worked with him lots, he's really lovely, he'll take his time with you but if there's anything you want me to do rather than him just let me know."'

Tulip gives important advice about fixing personal microphones onto vulnerable female interviewees and says she will always do it, rather than the cameraman.

Acid attacks

Sensitive stories can be a mix of suffering but also courage and resilience as with Tulip's story about a group of women from Bangladesh who suffered horrific facial disfigurements after being splashed with acid. 'Everybody had a slightly different story but the common theme was they were attacked by a male member of the family or a male love interest or somebody who had been rejected by the woman and had splashed their face for dishonouring them in some way,' Tulip tells me, yet she described the story as inspiring.

The women had come over to London to do a fashion show. 'They were supposed to run away and hide from the world and yet here they were on an international stage, strutting their stuff down a catwalk. Of course it's tragic but there was another side which was about taking control of their lives and not being defined purely as a victim of a horrific attack.'

Again, prior to interviewing the women, Tulip did her research so she knew what had happened to each of them and had photographs showing severe disfigurement from the acid attacks.

Initially, the women were reluctant to do interviews, so Tulip sat with them to talk it through. 'I speak a bit of Bengali, so I was able to communicate badly, which they found hilarious. I think that broke down some barriers.'

When the interview began, they were giving monosyllabic replies. 'You keep going and you start with easier questions, "Why are you here today? What are you trying to achieve?" So you start on a real "up." And then you go onto the more difficult parts of the interview and say, "I know this must be very difficult for you to reflect on, but could you tell us a bit about what happened to you that night?"'

By the time they reach that stage, Tulip explains, they have warmed up by making their point: '"I'm here, I'm not hiding, I want the world to know those going through this don't need to go and hide. I want to show the men that did this to us that we won't just shy away, that we will face it and campaign against it." By the time it comes to talking about the terrible thing that happened to them they feel more empowered.'

More than a victim

When writing or framing your sensitive story, Tulip guards against portraying people simply as victims. 'Unfortunately, horrible things happen to people all the time, but the resilience that people have is incredible. These aren't vulnerable Bangladeshi poor women who have been brutalised by men. These are strong women who have come out fighting.'

She adds, 'In every really dark situation there's always some light that can be found, acts of great bravery, love and resilience, and that needs to be reflected as well as the difficult experience they've had.'

Key advice

It sounds obvious but approach people like they're people, like it's somebody you know. Put yourself in their shoes, how would you like to be approached in a situation like that? And remember that some people won't want to speak to you and that's completely fair enough, but lots of people do. Don't be afraid to ask the difficult questions but ask them genuinely and sensitively.

Trauma Awareness

Traumatic stress in childhood happens when events which are violent or dangerous overwhelm the child or adolescent's ability to cope. They can include the sudden violent death of someone they love, witnessing or experiencing domestic violence or a serious accident, or having a life-threatening illness. They can also include war or refugee experiences, natural disasters, terrorism, violence at school, neglect, or physical, sexual or psychological abuse.

Reactions will vary but here are some common reactions to be mindful of when working with children of different ages.

In pre-school children:

- Having nightmares, disturbed sleep.
- Fear of being separated from parents or care-givers, clinginess.
- Poor eating.
- Screaming or crying a lot, trembling.

Primary school children:

- Feeling shame or guilt.
- Difficulty concentrating, becoming disruptive.

- Difficulty sleeping, nightmares.
- Being fearful or anxious, withdrawn.

Secondary school teenagers:

- Self-harm and eating disorders.
- Starting to abuse alcohol or drugs, rebelling.
- Feeling alone or depressed and possibly suicidal.
- Flashbacks, emotional numbing, feeling guilty.

Children's understanding of loss also varies according to age. These age ranges are guides, as children will vary in their development, given personal and environmental factors.

- Between 0 and 4 years it is 'emergent' but they can appreciate some of the events around them, more so if they are directly affected by immediate changes in routines and comfort. They may not understand the long-term consequences.
- Between 4 and 7 years, understanding is still limited and largely related to their personal experiences. Children may still struggle to understand loss fully and may develop 'magical thinking' and fantasise about things they have lost.
- Between 7 and 16+ years, understanding is more mature and many clearly have developed appreciation of the loss for themselves and others.

Children and adults may experience a range of emotions related to loss, including shock, distress, anger, denial, guilt and relief. These may be felt in quick succession or over longer periods of time. Most people 'recover' within a few months but, for a few, this may take up to two years or longer, depending on family circumstances and other factors, especially levels of social support.

Points to discuss

What adjustments may you need to consider when working with children of different ages?

What are the rules and guidelines around working with and filming with children?

What do you need to make them aware of if they choose to be identified in your report?

Notes

1 Roger Simpson and William Cote, *Covering Violence: A Guide to Ethical Reporting about Victims and Trauma*, 2nd edn, Columbia University Press, 2006.

2 Sarah McCrum and Lotte Hughes, 'Interviewing Children: A Guide for Journalists and Others,' 2nd edn, 1998, Save the Children, https://resourcecentre. savethechildren.net.

3 Ruth Teichroeb, 'Covering Children and Trauma: A Guide for Journalism Professionals,' Dart Center for Journalism and Trauma, 2006, https://dartcenter. org.

6
The interview

'I think let the interviewee speak, because it's hard enough to talk about, without being interrupted. Listening is the number one thing.'

Holly, who was an eyewitness to the terror attack
on London Bridge in 2017

In this chapter

What to ask, what not to ask and why not.

Focus on news reporters and on live interviewing.

Insight from families about how they would choose to be interviewed.

Overview from Richard Bilton on how he covers sensitive stories.

Vulnerable interviewees

Whether you are interviewing victims and survivors face to face, by phone or Skype; whether your interview is for TV, radio, print or online; whether it is live or recorded; cast away any pre-conceived notions of how a journalist is *meant* to behave. 'Mute your inner hardboiled reporter,' advise US investigative journalist Miles Moffeit and award-winning reporter Kristen Lombardi. 'Break from routine by granting the victim more control over the story process.'[1]

This is not a time to be overly challenging or combative, to demand answers or use trick questions to try to catch them out, to be pushy or persistent or to imply blame. Nor is it a time to be sneaky or unclear as to whether quotes are on or off the record. It is not the place to be sceptical, disbelieving or judgemental, to guard your questions closely or to refuse to give them an idea of how the interview will be used. It is not the situation in which to play devil's advocate, to have a fixed agenda, to insist they revisit the scene for a better visual background to the interview. Nor is it the time to be prescriptive, to over-react to their answers or to take control from them. All of this can be damaging.

Unlike an interview with a politician, police officer or business leader, vulnerable interviewees can be struggling with issues of control, uncertainty, self-blame, worry, trust, memory problems or poor concentration. Because *they* may be disempowered, *you* may acquire a greater sense of control in these interviews and that has to be managed wisely, responsibly and carefully. The journalist Jina Moore refers to it as 'a major power shift.'[2] She adds that, 'Trauma changes the rules. Everything about our practice must reflect that.'

Facing facts

As Gavin Rees points out in 'The Trauma Factor,' 'Sometimes trauma survivors lie, and interviewers may find that a traumatic or dangerous context makes it much harder to work out what is really going on.' He recalls the case of a woman in Kosovo who told a reporter her young sister had been killed by soldiers. When the journalist, who had reported on the death, returned for a follow-up piece, she found the sister very much alive. Her dilemma: should she have delved deeper for more details of the killing at the time, or accept it was difficult to ask probing questions about such a sensitive experience?

Situations in which survivors deliberately lie to manipulate journalists are rare in my experience. Gavin makes the point that, more common, are cases where people's accounts contain inaccuracies because the events were so traumatic, they have trouble remembering them in the right order. He adds that in some cases they lose access to key details you might expect them to recall.

He says that checking facts with a person who is traumatised requires great care. 'How does one query an account without implying that one does not believe it? Ill thought out, overly interrogative styles of interviewing could do real damage where somebody is already pre-disposed to self-blaming,'[3] he explains.

On the whole, as I mentioned in the introduction to this book, when you are doing these interviews you are rarely there to *hold* someone to account, but to *hear* their account and to hear it in the best way you can for them, for you and for your output.

Where to do the interview

Let them help to choose where they would like to be interviewed. They need to feel comfortable and safe and able to open up to you. This may be in the kitchen, the garden, on a park bench, and it may be, as one mum I interviewed chose, in her daughter's bedroom which had been left undisturbed since the 11-year-old had drowned on a family holiday.

By talking through possible locations, people can explain their choices. One TV producer told me how her team worked with a former footballer who had been sexually abused as a boy by his coach. She discovered he had been trapped in rooms by his abuser, so whenever they interviewed him, 'we always had to make sure the doorway was clear,' she told me.

Be aware that revisiting the scene of a traumatic event can trigger disturbing and powerful memories. Some people may choose to do so but it has to be their decision. If they choose to return, let them decide where they prefer to stand or sit. Be aware the environment may have changed. People may have left flowers or tributes and this too may have an impact on your interviewee.

Also be mindful, particularly when recording in outdoor locations, of noise and distractions such as lawnmowers, planes flying overhead, dogs barking, or workmen drilling – guaranteed to happen at the worst possible moment in your interview. Check all phones are on silent before you begin.

It is usually preferable to sit, but I have seen powerful interviews where people have been standing, maybe near to where a fatal crash had happened, and venting their fury and anguish.

Allow people to have someone with them at the location if it makes them feel more secure.

At each step of the interview process, think: how can I give this person some control over the way I am working with them? Involving them in choosing the location is a good place to start.

How to prepare

As ever, do as much preparation as possible and avoid insulting your interviewee with ignorant questions or misconceptions, as they are likely to clam up. If you are asking a teenager about self-harming, eating disorders or suicide, there are charity websites which can inform you about the complexities of these conditions and many more. Read around your subject and remember that survivors can be experts in their subject too, so involve them.

Avoid having a set news agenda or a rigid list of questions, as these are both likely to change as you talk with your interviewee. Keep an open mind, sit with them and give them an idea of the areas you would like to ask them about while accepting that, although the questions may seem simple to ask, they may be difficult for them to answer. Listen to their opinions about your questions.

'Interviewees should understand that they don't have to answer questions they don't want to answer and that they can end the interview at any time. It's important to reiterate this as it can be difficult for traumatised people to trust others,' explains the clinical psychologist Katy Robjant when asked for her advice for journalists covering the refugee crisis.[4]

It is also worth asking people their reason for choosing to talk to you. Their answer may surprise you.

If the interview is for TV, take time to put their mind at rest about the equipment. It can be scary to have a large camera recording you at close range, so acknowledge this and suggest they focus all their attention on looking at you and ignore the camera. Explain you will take your time, it is not live, there is no pressure and they are in control over what they would like to share with you.

How do you feel?

This much-maligned question is one that some survivors say they find inappropriate and distressing. Joy and Roger Membrey's daughter Elisabeth disappeared, believed murdered. Along with other families who became the focus of intense media attention at a time of trauma, the couple took part in a joint project run by the Australian Broadcasting Corporation and the Dart Center in 2014 called *Getting it Right*.

Joy Membrey told them, 'The question I most hate is being asked "How do you feel?" There's no answer to that because you immediately get very upset and angry and would like to swear. You think "Well how in hell do you expect me to feel?" It's just so impersonal.'[5]

However, alongside a journalist's basic six questions: who? what? when? where? why? how? there is often a requirement to find out how people *feel* about what has happened to them, their emotional response.

There are ways of doing this. Across more than thirty years, Professor Stephen Regel has worked with many people trying to deal with the effects of traumatic experiences. 'Asking a cognitively framed *thinking* question can often get a more meaningful *emotionally* framed answer,' he tells me. He suggests asking the following questions: What did you think about when …? What were your first thoughts? When reflecting on events later that day … some weeks later … what came to mind? He explains. 'It is less of a "cattle prod" than the clichéd "How did that make you feel?" question and makes them more reflective, thus giving you a more meaningful response.'

Or you could also ask: I wonder if you can share what the impact of this has been on you and your family? How are you coping with what has happened?

How did you experience that? You sometimes hear interviewers prefacing these questions by saying, 'I can't begin to imagine what you are going through ...'

To re-iterate, never say, 'I know how you feel.'

At the start of your interview, stick with the facts and chronology of what happened: what was going on beforehand, what they then experienced and what happened next. Bear in mind that trauma can re-order memories, so take your time.

The 'when' question

This can be a useful springboard to encourage your interviewee to say more. The network broadcaster Julian Worricker, who gives advice on live interviewing in the *Focus* section of this chapter, regularly carries out sensitive interviews for TV and radio and tells me, 'It is an unchallenging short, open question: *When* did you first hear the news? *When* did you first see the fire? It's a question that encourages story-telling and people never answer it literally.'

Julian was in New York immediately after 9/11, covering events for network radio. He went to meet a woman whose husband had been working in one of the Twin Towers on a floor above where the plane hit. She chose to be interviewed in her garden because there were family members and children in her house. '*When* did you first hear about the attacks?' Julian asked, and she gave him a chronological and measured account of what she knew, when she knew it and what she had done to try to find her husband. There was no happy ending to the story, but the family asked for a copy of the interview as they were compiling memories of him. 'It seemed so little to ask and of course we did as they wished.'

Use open questions, ones which cannot be answered with 'yes' or 'no,' and keep them simple. Remember the confusion and exhaustion they may be feeling, so be gentle but confident and clear. It may help to prompt them with questions such as: what happened next? I wonder if you could tell me a bit more about that?

'Why' questions

Be careful with these, because overly interrogative interviewing can be damaging. 'Why' questions can feel accusatory and imply blame, so think before you use them: Why were you out so late on your own? Why didn't you call the police sooner? Why wasn't he wearing a bike helmet? Why didn't you just leave him? Why didn't you fit smoke alarms? You can, of course, ask difficult questions, but be careful how you couch them and prepare your interviewee for what you would like to ask. Remember in these interviews you are not trying to catch anyone out.

Avoid sceptical *devil's advocate* questions. These can be particularly damaging to survivors of rape and sexual abuse who may have a need to be understood and believed. As Fay Maxted, the CEO of The Survivors Trust, tells me, 'Victims and survivors of sexual violence and sexual abuse often experience toxic emotions of self-blame and guilt, believing that they could have done something to prevent the sexual abuse happening. Child victims may even be told, by an abuser, that it is their fault for tempting them.' She adds that it can take many years for a victim to seek help because of the fear they will not be believed or be seen as complicit.

Melody is a survivor of childhood rape who, as an adult, took her stepfather to court. One of her most momentous days was when twelve strangers, the jury, said *guilty*, in other words, *we believe you*, and that meant everything to her. As a child her abuser had told her no one would believe her, so, even decades later, any unnecessarily sceptical questions from a reporter could have distressed her.

Would you say ...

Sometimes journalists use the technique of suggesting quotes to their interviewee and then reporting them as if they have been spoken: Would you say you are lucky to be alive? Would you say you are shocked and horrified?

Broadcasters can't use this technique, as the quote has to be actually spoken by the interviewee and recorded. Be careful of being suggestive with your questions, bear in mind your interviewee's possible sense of confusion and avoid putting words into their mouths which may hurt them when they read the headlines. Take a look at the Writing chapter and avoid sensationalising your accounts. If you take time to listen to your interviewee and handle them well, their accounts should speak for themselves and often be more powerful for being authentic.

Tell me about him ...

When reporting on a death, it can be appropriate to begin your interview by asking about the person who has died. This is a judgement call, because some families will welcome questions such as: Tell me about him? What was he like? What did he like to do? Others, however, will find that a very difficult question coming at the start of the interview, and can dissolve into tears at the mention of his name. Assess this during your conversation beforehand and don't be afraid to ask your interviewee, gently and tactfully, what they would prefer.

If you need to use specific terms, ask them which they feel comfortable with to describe what has happened. The advice is to avoid euphemisms such as *passed away* or the *incident*, but for some the word *died* or *raped* can feel too harsh.

The power of silence

Listen to what they are telling you, respond to it and do not be afraid of silence. Listening rather than talking is often the key to a successful trauma interview. If you aren't going to listen, 'don't show up,' says Louis Theroux, who describes it is a foundational skill.

'Know when to shut up,' advises current affairs reporter Jane Corbin. 'You just keep quiet. They will give you that gem because they will continue talking and they'll give you the thing that you would never get by constantly asking the questions.'

She and Jon Sopel, the BBC North America editor, were asked for interview tips for the BBC Academy website. 'You will sit agonising, thinking about what are the questions I'm going to ask. The most important thing though is to listen,' explains Jon.[6]

Active listening is non-judgemental. Remember in these interviews you are not there to hold them to account. It includes:

- Appropriate eye contact.
- Short words of encouragement – although this is not always possible in a recorded interview.
- Reacting to what has been said – this shows empathy and understanding, but be careful not to over-react or recoil if they say something which shocks you.
- Asking open questions.
- Clarifying if you have not understood.
- Reflecting back what they have told you – 'what I'm hearing is …'
- Summarising to show you have understood.

Strong emotional reactions

When interviewing someone about a painful emotional experience, they are likely to get upset. Some reporters feel uncomfortable with intense emotions and can be quick to step in, turn off the camera and halt the interview.

However, this may not be what the interviewee wants and can, in effect, be taking control away from them.

'When survivors cry during interviews they are not necessarily reluctant to continue,' explains the renowned psychiatrist Dr Frank Ochberg who educates journalists about trauma. 'Interrupting them may be experienced as patronizing and as denying an opportunity to testify. Remember, if you terminate an interview unilaterally because you find it upsetting or you incorrectly assume that your subject wants to stop, you may be re-victimizing the victim.'[7]

Often they will gather their emotions and wish to carry on and have their say. In my experience people can also apologise for getting upset, so reassure them and never let them feel awkward or embarrassed.

If, however, your interviewee breaks down or has a strong reaction, ask if they need to take a moment. 'You need to give them time to recover,' explains Katy Robjant, who suggests keeping your actions calm and predictable. 'Don't jump up to open a window, fetch water or try to help immediately. Instead, reassure the person that they are safe … and ask what you can do to help. '

Avoid actively wringing emotional responses from your interviewee. Do not provoke tears, but do not be afraid of them and be mindful not to cross professional boundaries and over-empathise.

Equally, do not give yourself a hard time if you become emotional. One seasoned reporter told me how, at the end of a particularly harrowing interview, she, the person she was interviewing and the camera operator were all in floods of tears. It can happen; we are only human and an authentic response is not necessarily unprofessional. Check out the Self-Care chapter if you find yourself responding in this way regularly though.

Also take a look at the 'What if …' section at the end of this chapter. It will give you advice should your interviewee tell you they want to end their life, if they disassociate (zone out) while you are with them or if they have a panic attack.

Finishing the interview

Let your interviewee know you are drawing to a close and be careful not to be abrupt or dismissive. I will often end by telling them I have asked all I need to ask but is there anything at all they would like to add? This simple question gives them the chance to say all they wish to say. It often elicits a useful response, because they can be feeling more relaxed and keen to emphasise their main points.

In trauma interviews, people may relive their pain. Before leaving them, try to bring them back into the present moment. This has to be done sensitively and carefully, so you do not change gear suddenly and appear dismissive of the emotions they are sharing.

It may be that they have started a campaign, so a later question in your interview may be to ask them about it. This has the effect of bringing them into the here and now. Counsellor and former journalist Cathryn Bullimore suggests the simple question: Where are you with this today?

If you are looking after a guest who is doing a live but sensitive TV or radio interview, or if you are a presenter, bear in mind the need to care for your interviewee either side of the broadcast. Apply the good practice of explaining what will happen, preparing them for the questions, involving them and acting on their opinions and being there for them after the broadcast.

Always thank them and give encouraging feedback.

EXTRAS

Gavin Rees runs the European programmes of the Dart Center for Journalism and Trauma. Prior to working for the Centre, he was a news journalist and documentary filmmaker producing content for channels in the US, UK and Japan. He was a lead producer on the BBC docudrama *Hiroshima*, which won an international Emmy in 2006. It told the story of the first use of a nuclear weapon against a civilian population, by interweaving survivor testimony with dramatic reconstruction. Here he expands on sensitive interviewing.

- *Allow yourself to be human*: Interviewing someone about a painful, traumatic situation can be daunting. You might well find the material distressing. Stop, take a breath and reconnect with yourself before rushing in. I find it helpful to imagine myself heading out into wet weather with a good overcoat. The rain might get through in places but I am not going to drown. Sometimes, interviewers think that, if they artificially stifle their own feelings, it will help them be in control during an interview. But there is a paradox in play here: cutting yourself off from your own responses can make it more likely that they hijack you, jack-in-the-box fashion during an interview. Being in touch with your feelings will help you read others'. Just remember that the primary focus during the conversation itself is always on their experience not yours – don't let your own stuff get in the way of that. Later on, when you are back from the interview, could be a good time to process anything that came up.

(Knowing how to put troubling knowledge into perspective is a key craft and self-care skill for any journalist doing trauma work.)

- *Where there is a risk of conflict*: There are times when you might disagree vehemently with what someone is saying. Here, I try to think through what it takes to treat someone with dignity. *Dignity* is sometimes a more useful word than *respect*. If I am talking to a white supremacist who has just been bereaved, nothing is going to make me respect their hateful views on race, but I hope I can find a place where I can listen and acknowledge their loss.

- *Explain the process*: Remember that most people aren't media savvy and don't really understand what the journalist is doing. Trauma itself leaves people feeling disempowered, and so it is doubly important not to compound that and to explain the process. If you need to ask a question that appears off-the-wall, explain why. If you are working with video and need to shoot B-roll of somebody walking or making tea, again it is good to explain why. These small collaborative gestures can do a lot to make people feel more secure.

- *Head-off unwelcome surprises*: Imagine that you are interviewing a survivor of sexual assault who is willing to speak to you; they may not fully understand that you could be using difficult or graphic details or even be interviewing the perpetrator. It is really important to explain this and make sure that you have fully informed consent. Again, think collaboratively and don't be afraid to discuss with them what you are planning to write.

- *Simple questions*: We can invest too much attention and energy in worrying about the kinds of questions that we ask and make them overly complicated. Simple questions work best such as 'what happened?' or 'tell me about X' when asking about a family member who has died. It gives people a space to locate a starting point in which they feel comfortable.

- *Listen*: This is the single most important skill you need to develop as an interviewer. People want to be heard. The better you are at listening, the easier it becomes to spot that important, potentially overlooked detail. But it is not a sit-back and just-let-it-happen process. Give people space to talk about what they are comfortable to discuss, and then pick up on threads that you are interested in knowing more about. That way, you narrow the topic down without cutting across your interviewee's natural train of thought too much.

- *Be careful not to load questions with emotion*: The danger with a question like 'how do you feel?' is that it targets the emotional centres of the brain. If you are unlucky, it can drop somebody straight back into the same, intense visceral feelings that they had during the traumatic incident. People may even dissociate (space-out) or start to become hyper-aroused (i.e. agitated or angry). Questions with lots of feeling words or graphic illustrations in them are likely to get answers that are less balanced and coherent than simpler questions that focus on events. If someone has lost their son to knife crime, it is not a good idea to ask 'What did it feel like when you heard he had been stabbed?' as it is likely to bring the shock of that moment back. 'What has the impact been of his death on you?' is a better question to ask. It encourages somebody to think about their feelings rather than feel them. Similarly, a slightly abstract, round-about question such as, 'If you were to look back at that time, how *now* would you describe the feelings that you had then?' This may give someone that extra distance from the experience that they need to speak with clarity. Be careful not to dig into feelings in an abusive way – people have the right not to talk about traumatic experiences if they don't want to.

- *Think about where you are leaving people*: Conversations about traumatic events in the past can leave people feeling as if they are back in that time and place. With such interviews, it is good practice to spend the last section talking about the present, what the person's life is like now, or their future plans. This reduces the risk of leaving someone in a place where they are still churning over the most painful parts of their narrative.
- *Know your limits*: Journalists sometimes get into trouble when, motivated by a strong desire to take someone's pain away, they promise things that they can't deliver, like friendship or a solution to a problem. Having ill-thought-out boundaries can get you into all kinds of messy and morally compromising situations.
- *No formula*: What might work in one situation may not in another, so there are very few hard and fast universals. You need to cut your cloth according to the situation.

FOCUS on journalists

> *Network radio and TV presenter Julian Worricker started out as a local radio reporter. The BBC network shows he has presented include* Five Live Breakfast *alongside Victoria Derbyshire,* You and Yours *for Radio Four, the current affairs programme* Worricker on Sunday, *as well as presenting for TV News and the BBC World Service. Julian is also a BBC Academy trainer in interviewing. Here he offers his advice to journalists on how to handle 'live' sensitive interviews.*

Being empathetic and genuine are Julian's starting points. 'The listener or viewer can spot a fake a mile off. So, in this situation, the "I know exactly how you must be feeling" approach rarely works and if it does, it doesn't deserve to,' he tells me.

Be assured but not pushy and be politely clear about what you want and look them in the eye as you make your request. 'Once the interview is underway short open questions work best. That's true almost all the time anyway but especially here. In an emotionally charged situation, the temptation to add to a straightforward question is acute, resist it.'

He suggests a slower pace and a measured tone. 'Don't be afraid of gaps or pauses. The viewer expects a halting delivery from the interviewee because of the subject matter so go with it and don't rush it.'

If an interviewee breaks down on air and cries, he suggests asking if they are okay to carry on or if they want a moment to compose themselves. 'The effect that gentle enquiry nearly always has on the interviewee is that he or she steels themselves to say more. They've agreed to talk, they want to give their side of the story and they don't want to miss that chance.'

Above all he advises presenters to be human. 'If someone walks away mid-interview because they can't carry on, talk directly to the listener, "as you can see this is a deeply upsetting time for X, if he or she wants to talk more later I'll bring that to you."'

> Simon Hare began his journalistic career as a newspaper reporter before joining the BBC as a news reporter for local radio and then regional TV. He currently reports and produces current affairs documentaries. He won a Royal Television Society award for his work on the Philpott case in which the parents of six children were convicted of killing them in a house fire.

As a rule, Simon doesn't structure his questions in advance of a sensitive interview but will talk to people beforehand to get an idea of what they would like to say. 'I get them to explain in their own words and I tend to react. The simple things like what's happened, what was the person like? You're trying to humanise things,' Simon tells me.

Listen rather than talk. 'There may be things they don't want to talk about, or there may be legal restrictions and obviously respect that. Tell them it's not a "live" interview because people don't understand the grammar of television or what we need or how we go about getting it.'

Simon worked on a large-scale sex abuse story involving more than a hundred complainants at a former psychiatric hospital. 'I am conscious that every time you do an interview with a victim of sexual abuse, particularly when it may have occurred a long time ago in their childhood and they have horrible memories of it, you are really pushing to the fore of their consciousness something unpleasant. You have a responsibility in how you do that.'

Rather than interview many victims time and time again, Simon chose instead to tell their stories through the woman who became the group spokesperson. 'She had been raped and drugged and had found other victims and brought them together.'

She was able to speak publicly and although she said the experience was cathartic, Simon didn't underestimate his responsibility when interviewing her. 'We're not psychologists, we're not counsellors and we're not trained and we're asking them to relive horrific moments in their lives.'

Early in his dealings with her, Simon learned the harm that 'devil's advocate' questions can do. 'She got a bit angry with me and I realised that she felt I didn't believe her. That absolute need to be believed is important. Also, only do interviews if you are going to use them, and be conscious, especially with victims of sexual abuse, that when you leave you've probably left them in an upset state. Check they are all right and that they've got somebody with them afterwards.'

> Rose Aston's career as a journalist has been spent in magazines and in BBC local radio where she is currently a Managing Editor. When she was a news reporter she was sent to East Germany to cover the story of George, a soldier who was captured at Dunkirk and had spent the rest of World War II as a prisoner of war.

Rose explains it was the anniversary of thousands of prisoners of war being marched across Europe in 1945. 'Many of the prisoners fell down and died of exhaustion. The survivors ate horses that had fallen down and died of exhaustion. It was nightmarish. George was going back to a village he had stumbled on where the Americans had turned up and told them they were free. He had maintained friendships in the village,' Rose tells me.

Many of the veterans had shared their stories many times. 'They told me how resourceful they were in the camp and adopted this slightly "chirpy chappy" way of telling it. There is a truth in that but it's not the whole story and I felt my job was to get George slightly outside that performance mode. But I didn't want to dig too deeply into areas that I wouldn't then be able to deal with, as I'm not a counsellor.'

She and George went for a long walk and after a couple of hours he stopped and was staring at the landscape. It was the actual road he'd had to march on. 'He just stopped and I left it quiet for a long while and then I simply asked him, what was it like George? I could well up now just remembering this. He told me all about the degradation and fear. A whole load of stuff came up and he cried. Although it's what you want on tape you are left with this responsibility of what to do now. I've got this guy in his eighties in tears standing on the side of a road in eastern Germany fifty years after the most traumatic event of his life.'

Rose's response was to take her time, to listen to George and to move the conversation gently from the past into the present without being dismissive in any way. As they walked back they chatted about where they were staying and what the hotel was like. Much later, she says, they all had a riotous night in the pub so all was well.

INSIGHT from interviewees

Nicky's son Jack died in hospital when he was 6 years old. The doctor and nurse involved in his care were both convicted of manslaughter through gross negligence. It was an unusual case which attracted national attention. As her story unfolded over several years, Nicky gave many interviews to journalists and shares her insight into the process.

Jack's death turned her family's life upside down, Nicky tells me. 'We will never ever get over the fact of losing him. What hurt most and what I struggle with is the fact that had he been treated correctly that day, Jack would still have been here. It has had a massive impact.'

When doing sensitive interviews, Nicky asks reporters to bear in mind that people like her are not used to cameras and recordings, or to the overpowering emotions they are going through. 'You want them to have some sort of empathy and not just ask questions. Be human rather than being a robot. Just be you and know what you are talking about. Know my little boy's name and how old he was, the things that are personal to me. I think it's very important.'

She also warns against reporters implying blame or criticism when interviewing her. 'If someone asked why I didn't take him to hospital straight away, these things went through my head and it would get my back up. They don't need to be critical, they just need to ask the questions in a sympathetic way to get the information they want. It's important to be really sensitive when it comes to things like this.'

Sharon's daughter Louise was cycling to work and was waiting at traffic lights alongside a lorry. As Louise pulled forward, the lorry turned left. It was not indicating and Louise was crushed beneath it. After a three-day trial, the truck driver was convicted of death by careless driving. After the verdict, Sharon gave interviews to reporters. She wanted to make people aware of the life-changing impact Louise's death had had on her family.

Louise was Sharon's only child and her sense of loss is profound. 'Initially it was disbelief and then just the horror of what happened and it is really very difficult to take it in. It was total numbness and then just real shock and loss.'

Sharon preferred reporters who wished to interview her to be honest about what would happen and how the material would be used. When information about Louise was lifted from social media sites it felt like an invasion of privacy. 'They'd not even contacted me. They were just running this story and they lifted the clips from Facebook and I just felt they'd invaded my space,' she tells me, through tears.

When interviewing people who are distressed, shows of emotion such as tears are likely. Sharon felt the camera should keep running if she cried. 'Your instant reaction is your truest one and maybe, if this is being used as a tool to show people the impact this has, then leave it in, even though I look awful. It's instantaneous, not rehearsed and you see it how it is. You are bound to be upset, that's going to live with me for the rest of my life, but I don't want people to be embarrassed if I do get upset because I'll be fine. I'm bound to be upset because it's a constant reminder of what I've not got.'

Rose works with many families whose loved ones have been murdered or killed and is herself a bereaved mother. Here she offers further insight about being interviewing sensitively.

She explains it is important to allow the family to talk about the person they have lost. 'Give them the opportunity to say how much they loved that person and how devastated they are at the loss of that person.'

She adds that it is important to give families control, so tell them they can stop at any point and they can tell you if you are asking a question insensitively or inappropriately. Because they are traumatised, Rose says they may not remember things very well so it may help to give them an idea of the questions.

Rose urges reporters who have to do sensitive interviews to be comfortable with death, dying, bereavement and grief. 'I think that's a top priority. You can't do this job if my crying and getting upset is going to upset you because then you are going to upset me even more. You need to be comfortable with me crying and being very angry. When families display anger, they're usually not angry with you personally, they're just angry with everything for taking their loved one away.'

Rose shares her insight about how best to behave in the face of tears. 'It's actually very powerful for me as a bereaved mother to actually just sit there quietly. Just take your time, sit there and be comfortable with them. We're not comfortable with silences, we have this desperate need to jump in and say something and often what you say is totally inappropriate.'

Faith who is also a bereaved mother adds this for reporters to consider.

Although some people prefer to begin an interview by talking about the person they have lost, Faith found this question particularly difficult. 'When they start off asking me about Joshua, I struggle because I get so emotional. I used to think to myself, why can't they ask me the other questions they want to know first of all and then, at the end, ask me what Joshua was like.'

She explains that this allows her head to be clear for most of the interview. 'I can answer the relevant questions first of all and then I can talk about my Josh and know that it doesn't matter if I get upset.'

Holly, who spoke in previous chapters about being an eyewitness to the terror attack on London Bridge, offers this about being interviewed by reporters.

Holly says that the interviews she did which worked best in the wake of the attack were ones in which there were very few questions and where she was allowed to keep talking. 'It's because it is all a memory and if you get interrupted in your train of thought you can forget something that may be a key point. So I think let the interviewee speak because it's hard enough to talk about without being interrupted. Listening is the number one thing,' she tells me.

> *Rachel gave many media interviews when her daughter needed a bed at an eating disorder unit. The only bed available was hundreds of miles from home. It was a situation Rachel described as being 'one of the worst scenarios you could imagine being in.' Here she offers her observations about being interviewed.*

Rachel did several 'live' interviews for both local and network radio programmes, and stresses the need to give people like her positive feedback. In one 'down the line' interview she gave, the phone simply went dead once she had finished on air. No thanks, no feedback, no reassurance. 'Positive feedback when you've been interviewed is really important. Not just saying that was really good, but saying you got this across well, or this worked well, that's important when you feel vulnerable.'

The most rewarding experiences for her were live radio interviews with few interruptions. 'He wasn't bombarding me and picking me up on everything. I had time to articulate what I wanted to say without feeling I was going to be pulled apart.'

This made her feel empowered, but a TV interview with many more questions was a struggle. 'I'm thinking through what I just said and maybe, as a journalist, you can handle that because that's what you do, but if you're just an ordinary member of the public who's not used to doing this, I need one question with time to think about my answer.'

> *A mother whose daughter was murdered prefers to remain anonymous but gave me the following insight into being interviewed by national newspaper reporters and TV journalists.*

When being interviewed, she preferred questions about her daughter. 'Remembering her character, her personality, what she had achieved in her short life, the things she liked to do and her main interests.' The questions she didn't like in the interview were talking about her killers. 'We didn't feel they deserved any air time, or our time in thinking about them. It brought back painful memories and betrayal and none of these we wanted to remember.'

She goes on to explain how it feels to be interviewed at such a time. 'Reporters must remember when interviewing murder victims' families they are going through a traumatic time, through the most horrific circumstances anyone could imagine. They have lost someone really precious to them and some of the questions which are asked seem very cold and uncaring. It is very difficult talking in front of a camera with a microphone. You are very nervous when going through a traumatic time, it is often very difficult to think of the answers quickly and sometimes the words don't come out in the correct order.'

HOW I COVER SENSITIVE STORIES: RICHARD BILTON

'Good journalists don't just disappear.'

Richard began his career as a local radio reporter before becoming a TV reporter for the BBC in the East Midlands region where he says, 'You do the learning that you take with you wherever you go.' He went on to become a network news correspondent, then environment correspondent and after that, social affairs correspondent.

Richard was the BBC's Special Correspondent for the *News at Six* and *News at Ten*. In 2007, he began reporting for *Panorama*, the BBC's investigative current affairs documentary programme.

He reported from New York in the aftermath of 9/11 and has covered wars in Iraq, Lebanon and Sri Lanka. He covered the disappearance of Madeleine McCann in 2007, the Soham murders in 2002, the kidnapping of Shannon Matthews in 2008, and the Grenfell Tower disaster in June 2017. He has produced a wide variety of films, from sham marriages to preventable disease in children, to teenage drug dealers and child labour in Brazil.

'I've interacted with lots of big news stories or crossed paths with people who were going through terrible times. I've interviewed people in really horrendous situations,' he tells me.

Telling stories through the people they affect

Richard believes telling stories through the people affected is enormously important. As journalists, he says, we are trying to explain something in a way that will reach out of the screen so people at home will feel connected. 'Emotion is one of the primary ways that television functions. People who've lived or seen something or been through something, they are the way that we can best explain the story to a large audience.'

In 2016, Richard was sent to cover the Orlando shootings in Florida where a security guard had killed fifty people. 'I interviewed some of the people who were in the nightclub and they were so powerfully evocative and emotional. Just listening to people who talked about what they'd been through, that's the way you can help people understand the horror of an event like that.'

He also covered the Grenfell Tower fire in London, filming with families newly and profoundly affected. 'What we were trying to do in that story was show people the horror of Grenfell. The reality that all these lives just got smashed up. If you're with someone when that happens there is no more powerful way of showing it. Immediately, all of the viewers will put themselves in the place of that person,' he explains.

He stresses that in doing this sensitive work, 'reporters have an enormous duty of care which is right at the front of everything we do.'

Staying in touch

'Good journalists don't just disappear,' says Richard, who takes the time to keep in touch with his interviewees. 'They have your number or your card, they can ring you, talk through what they're worried about and they can veto. You're crashing into people's lives, you're broadcasting it to millions of people, they have to have the final voice,' he explains.

If at all possible, Richard will also take time to run through his cut story with his interviewees before it is broadcast. He does it for two reasons: first he thinks it must be terrifying to sit in front of a TV screen not knowing how you are going to be portrayed, and he can take that fear away from people who are emotionally vulnerable. Secondly, if there is any small error, it can be put right before the piece is broadcast.

Even when he is up against it with a late edit for the six or ten o'clock news, 'I'd ring and try to go through it with them because then everybody wins. You're being true to your word and they see that their trust was rightly placed.'

'Part of that honesty will be staying in touch with them so that they're not plunged into a world they don't understand, and then you disappear leaving them worried.'

Making your approach

If you're covering a big national or international breaking story, like the disappearance of Madeleine McCann, there is enormous pressure on the reporter. In 2007, the 3-year-old disappeared from her holiday apartment at the Praia da Luz resort in the Algarve region of Portugal. Madeleine would become the world's most famous missing person.

'You are up against competitors on a story that is important to the nation and you are there to deliver. People will want exclusives and they want you to get the big interviews and, of course, the people who suffered the most are at the heart of the story and you need to get near them.' Significantly, he adds that the pressure should not change the way you behave.

Richard's approach when covering these stories is to be open and straightforward. He explains that when he is making a sensitive documentary over many months, he can be maintaining a professional relationship with someone whom he may interview several times. 'I think you should be really honest with them so that they understand the relationship; that you are a journalist and that you are not their friend. You will look after them and you have a duty of care. You are there because you want to talk to them about what they've been through and you want to do it sensitively.'

He says it is common that when people start to talk to him about what has happened to them they can't stop. 'You have to bear in mind that people are going through grief and this whole crazy set of emotions. You're trying to do your job but people are just trying to understand what's happened in their world and they will just talk for hours and hours.'

Managing expectations

Over time, Richard says he has learnt the best approach is to be really straight: this is why we're doing the interview; these are the questions I'm going to ask you; we won't harm or hurt you; I'll run it past you; I'll stay in touch with you.

'They should know when they sit down with you why they're doing it and where it's being broadcast. You also give them a sense of the impact that's likely to come.' He says that if the interview is likely to generate headlines and create attention for them, the ruthless approach would be to play that down, 'Apart from being manipulative, cynical and unpleasant, that's just bad form for everybody.'

He adds, 'Try to get yourself a bit in their shoes, be really sensitive. You need to know the inside track on their story. I've spoken to reporters who've blundered in to very sensitive interviews and there is nothing worse than making mistakes on something as close to the heart as somebody who's lost someone or been through something terrible.'

Knowing when to stop

Six days after the Orlando shootings, Richard travelled to Philadelphia to interview a woman who was speaking about the attack for the first time. She had been trapped in a toilet cubicle, with dead people on top of her while the shooter was outside killing people.

As she spoke about it, Richard became uncomfortable. Experience taught him that her reactions were verging on a breakdown, so he called a halt. 'On the one hand it was very powerful but she wasn't telling me as an interviewer, she was reliving it. I thought it was unhealthy so I stopped the interview. I'm convinced that was the right thing to do because I've done enough interviews to realise the difference between somebody who is telling me something that they know very well and they're in control, to somebody who is reliving something all over again and being harmed by it.'

He adds, 'This woman was shaking. She still had wounds in her leg. She was making herself incredibly upset and that isn't what television is for. I was now observing a breakdown rather than harvesting information as a journalist.'

Again, Richard stayed in touch with his interviewee, who told him later she was grateful he had stopped the recording.

'We're there to get the information from people and broadcast it or write it down so that people understand the story and what people went through, but we are not there to harm people. You are not there so that when you move on in two weeks and you're doing a different story in a different country, they shouldn't be re-living what you did. You can't just go around destroying lives and then wandering away.'

Putting people at ease

Most weeks, Richard will be doing a sensitive interview and he takes time to explain the process and reassure. 'I think it's part of our job that we should run through who we are, what we do, what's going to be edited later on, I'm going to ask you some questions but you can stop at any stage, nobody will mind, you're in control, not me. I think the cameramen who work with me regularly get tired of the speech but it's really important.'

He says that once the interview gets going, people often settle down. What can be nerve-racking for them is a TV world they have never come across before. It is this initial stage where you have to work your hardest, explains Richard, 'I think you should spend as much time as possible on that early section. I will always try and go and meet people beforehand so that they get a sense of me and that this isn't shiny TV but a normal bloke who is going to ask them questions that they don't necessarily need to answer.'

Journalists tend to have well-developed soft skills and it's important to be human and friendly, he says.

Interviewing and interacting

Lots of nodding and eye contact during the interview will help to encourage people to talk but can also give them confidence in what they are telling you. 'What people often do is abandon an answer because they think they got it wrong and look a bit sheepish and embarrassed. I would say no, that's good, carry on. It just encourages them and you want them to feel like they're in a safe place where they can talk about things. Use your eyes. Human beings are very expressive without saying anything.'

In TV and radio interviews, reporters tend to avoid making encouraging noises, as they will be heard on the recording, but sometimes Richard breaks that rule so the interview feels it is more like a genuine interaction.

He does not shy away from asking difficult questions but always warns his vulnerable interviewees beforehand. 'As a journalist you should always think about what the viewer would want you to ask in that situation.' Reassuringly, in his lengthy reporting career, he cannot recall a single interviewee who recoiled or became angry with him for asking a difficult question.

An example was when he had to put to Madeleine's parents Kate and Gerry McCann the toughest of questions, because the Portuguese police had made them suspects.

He warned them that because of the rumours in the press, he would have to ask the question. 'I didn't accuse them of anything but they needed to answer it because it was out there, the viewer will want you to say it.' He stresses though that free-wheeling and going off on tangents yourself with unfounded questions or accusations in sensitive interviews is not acceptable.

Filming sensitively

Filming sequences and shots with people who are emotionally vulnerable can be challenging. 'I would work hard in advance to think about what I want them to do. Be guided by them. Once you are with people, they will often want you to see every picture, go through every book or look at their room. But if they're so raw that you're going to offend them then just don't go there for a sequence, would be my view.'

He offers fundamental advice to reporters who are new to filming with families suffering distress or trauma. 'If your starting point is: I don't want to upset you, I don't want to add to your woes, this is what I'm going to do, this is the kit we're going to use and this is how it's going to function and then I'm going to stay in touch with you, you won't go far wrong.'

Writing and framing your reports

Tell your story straight, is Richard's advice, 'If people are very emotional or it's a sensitive topic, you do not need to be building that up. You are doing everybody a disservice if you do that. Our job as journalists is just to explain things.'

Avoid being over the top, melodramatic or over-emotional. Keep your writing straightforward, or, says Richard, 'it may look like you are trying to sell this and that's the very last thing that you should be doing.'

He cautions against being seduced by the emotion at the expense of putting your report into context. 'Without the context, the emotion makes no sense at all so you're putting the cart before the horse.' Keep your writing nice and tight, no flowery language and no sentences that are not required, he adds.

He will also tend to use longer clips of his interviewees in his pieces as they are the people who have experienced what has happened. In his documentary about the Orlando shootings, the interviewees were so powerful that they sustained the whole programme.

Key advice

Prepare as best you can, be honest with interviewees. Put them at their ease and, having laid the groundwork, you should be able to do a proper interview. Be sensitive to the fact that this is not an equal situation: you are doing your job then going home, their lives have potentially been ripped apart.

Bear in mind also that the viewers' sympathies will be with them and not you. They want you to treat these people well. That ought not to be the reason you treat them well, but it is important to be aware how your attitude or behaviour is coming across.

It isn't complicated, adds Richard, it's about being human and doing your job properly.

WHAT IF ...?

Suicidal thoughts

There have been occasions when distressed interviewees have told reporters they feel like ending their life. In the UK, the charity Samaritans gives guidance to journalists who find themselves in this situation. 'In most cases, if an interviewee expresses that they have suicidal thoughts, you can signpost them to Samaritans' 24-hour free helpline. This is the advice we give journalists if they have concerns about a case study they are working with,' Lorna Fraser of their Media Advisory Service tells me. 'They could also speak to the person about other support they have around them, if there is anyone they can call immediately for help. If there is a significant or urgent concern, they should call 999.'

For Samaritans' tips on reporting suicide, see the Writing chapter.

'Zoning out'

Dissociation – where a person disconnects from their thoughts, feelings and memories – can be used as a coping mechanism to escape traumatic thoughts. 'If an interviewee is experiencing dissociation, you may notice them becoming confused and detached, experiencing memory difficulties and sudden changes in mood,' explains the BBC's Occupational Psychologist, Susannah Robertson-Hart. Here is her advice:

'Grounding' is a really useful technique that helps keep someone in the present and helps them regain connection with their physical body and is often used as a way of coping with flashbacks or dissociation. It helps reorient the individual to the here-and-now and can be very helpful in managing overwhelming feelings or intense anxiety. There are a number of different techniques for grounding which generally involve helping someone to get back in touch with their body. The 5-4-3-2-1 method is widely used – this involves asking the person to think about 5 things they can see, 4 things they can hear, 3 things they can touch, 2 things they can smell or like the smell of, and 1 slow, deep breath. This may end the period of dissociation or at least make it more manageable.

Panic attacks

It is possible an interviewee may experience a panic attack during an interview, if they are triggered by something. 'You may notice their breathing become very quick; they might start sweating and complain of feeling weak or dizzy and appear to have lost control. Panic attacks can be very scary for all concerned. It's important to stay with someone who is experiencing an attack and help them to "ride it out,"' Susannah explains. Grounding techniques – as described above – can be really useful during a panic attack, as can breathing exercises. 'If the person is breathing very quickly – encourage them to breathe in slowly, deeply and gently through the nose for a count of five and then breathe out slowly, deeply and gently through the mouth. Count with them and reassure them that the symptoms will pass and that you'll stay with them,' advises Susannah. Stay quiet and calm and avoid crowding them.

Bear in mind, though, that the symptoms are similar to a heart attack, in which case call the emergency services.

Notes

1   Miles Moffeit and Kristen Lombardi, 'Ethics and Practice: Interviewing Victims,' 19 January 2012, https:/dartcenter.org/content/ethics-and-practice-interviewing-victims.

2   Jina Moore, 'Five Ideas on Meaningful Consent in Trauma Journalism,' 14 July 2011, www.jinamoore.com.

3   Gavin Rees, 'The Trauma Factor: Reporting on Violence and Tragedy,' *Journalism: New Challenges*, 2013, https://microsites.bournemouth.ac.uk.

4   Katy Robjant, 'Reporting on Refugees: Tips on Covering the Crisis,' 26 February 2016, https://dartcenter.org/resources/reporting-refugees-tips-covering-crisis.

5 Cait McMahon, Matthew Ricketson and Gary Tippet, 'Getting it Right: Ethical Reporting on People Affected by Trauma,' 25 March 2014, https://dartcenter.org.

6 Jane Corbin and Jon Sopel, 'TV Interview Tips,' BBC Academy, www.bbc.co.uk.

7 Frank M. Ochberg MD, 'A Primer on Covering Victims,' Harvard University, 1996, *Nieman Reports*, Vol. L, No. 3, www.giftfromwithin.org.

7
The filming

'I definitely needed to know why they were doing it ... Someone who's been a victim of abuse, they've already had too many people making them do things without explanation and it wasn't pleasant.'

Melody, a survivor of childhood rape, speaking about being filmed for TV

In this chapter

How to film sensitively.

Focus on video journalists and camera operators who film with vulnerable interviewees.

Insight from families who have been filmed at difficult times.

Overview from Helen Long on how she covers sensitive stories.

The power of pictures

When recalling a major news story, it is often the images which spring to mind first: the planes crashing into the Twin Towers of the World Trade Center in New York in 2001, Grenfell Tower engulfed in flames in London in 2017, or Nilüfer Demir's photograph of the Turkish soldier holding a lifeless 3-year-old boy on a beach, during the Syrian refugee crisis in 2015.

Even in day-to-day TV news, powerful or poignant pictures can define your piece, so always have an eye for shots which will help to convey the story. Filming sequences with, for example, a grieving family can be challenging as you are limited as to what you can reasonably ask someone to do for the camera, given their emotional state.

In my experience, people expect to be filmed for an interview because that is what they have agreed to do. However, they rarely expect they will also have to be filmed *doing things* in order that the reporter can tell their story, by scripting over the pictures. It is often alien to them and can feel like they are being made to perform. When filming, more than ever, you need to make sure people understand and feel involved, secure and in control.

Some families allow the camera access to intimate moments and meaningful locations. They choose to be filmed at the graveside, or the roadside of a fatal crash, or the lakeside of a drowning, or in the bedroom left untouched. However, any suggestions have to be broached carefully, and never try to persuade them. People can be tolerant of our strange filming requests and generous with their time, because they want to do their best for the person who has died. Never abuse this, and be aware that revisiting these locations can trigger distressing memories.

'Consider what you are asking people. Sometimes it just takes time,' says US documentary photographer John Happel, who asked five fellow immersive photographers how they gained trust with their subjects. He reflects on how important it can be to be sensitive to a person's privacy and comfort levels. He also says that being transparent about what you are doing can give back some control to people. The documentary photographer Anthony Karen told him, 'Humanity should always come first … What better way to help a person carry on as they normally would and be comfortable with you than to be yourself and to open up a bit.'[1]

It can often work best to do the interview *before* filming your sequences because the pressure is off and you will hopefully have made them feel comfortable with you. If you are covering a bereavement, the family are likely to have photographs and video footage of the person. These are often evocative and, by using them, you can also curtail the number of filmed sequences you may need for your piece.

Getting shots can be tricky, but always bear in mind how they will sit with your script. If you film people walking in the park and they are chatting and smiling, this may look inappropriate if your script will describe how they are struggling to come to terms with what has happened. You may have to explain this to them carefully and tactfully.

As mentioned in the Relationship chapter, it can be hard for people outside broadcasting to equate the time it takes to film sequences with the eventual duration of your report. You may need to manage this expectation, by explaining why the pictures are essential for you to tell their story well. People tend to understand this more clearly once the piece has aired and they can appreciate why you needed the shots. Some families have told me how frustrating it can be to take part in many hours of filming, only to see a few minutes of the footage used. Avoid over-filming, remember the exhausting effects of trauma and distress and allow breaks.

As ever in this work, *explain, involve but don't overwhelm*. They do not need to know the finer points of a white balance, but people may need to know, in simple terms, why you are taking the same shot from several different angles and why they are being asked to repeat an action.

Prep the crew

It is not always possible, but try to discuss the plan with the camera operator before the shoot. It avoids talking through the mechanics in front of your interviewee. They may be able to use less obtrusive kit if given enough notice. In this job, more than ever, the reporter and crew are a team and both need to approach the job with the same courtesy and consideration. Pre-planning can help to avoid over-shooting. Always check the kit is in working order. This is not the job on which to have technical problems.

Avoid rolling up outside the house in a satellite truck. Families say they prefer discretion when they have agreed to share their sensitive stories. When you arrive, introduce yourself and the camera operator and allow the person you are interviewing to lead you round their home and help choose the best place for the interview. You may need to compromise on the shot if they have a strong preference. It may also not be possible to rig up exquisite lighting.

Preferably bring your own power sources rather than plugging into theirs. Always check before moving furniture about and make sure you put everything back as you found it. They may seem like small details, but they matter.

Allow for breaks when filming, as it can be draining for people.

Jargon

In broadcasting, we use jargon to describe the shots we may need such as cutaways, set-ups or noddies. Although it is a language you and the crew are familiar with, it can sound alarming to your interviewee, so use simple and understandable descriptions. Also resist the temptation to objectify your interviewee, consulting each other about the shots as they are sitting in front of you looking bemused. This is more common than you may think, so take care to avoid it.

Always be clear when you are recording. If you are filming on your phone for an online piece, it may not be apparent to your interviewee, so you need to tell them.

Personal space

Be mindful of your interviewee's personal space when filming and try not to encroach on it. This can be particularly important when fixing a personal microphone onto their clothing. Consider the male/female dynamic in the room and the story you are covering.

A rape survivor may understandably feel uncomfortable with a man clipping the microphone onto her clothing. If you are an all-male team, you may have to use the stick microphone instead. In this situation, avoid filming in an enclosed space and always keep a clear pathway to the exit. As ever, talk it through and involve them. It is important for people to see you are being sensitive, that it matters and that you want to hear about their needs and opinions.

Disability

The National Center on Disability and Journalism's top tip when filming with people with disabilities is 'ask the expert – the person you are interviewing.'[2] They also point out the importance of placing yourself and the camera at eye level if the person you are filming is in a wheelchair. Avoid leaning on someone's wheelchair and if you offer to assist, wait until your offer is accepted and ask how to proceed.

If you are filming someone with hearing loss, face them and don't cover your mouth when you speak. When filming with someone who is visually impaired, identify yourself and the camera operator. Remember guide dogs are working, so avoid fussing them. Shake hands with your interviewee. People with prosthetics or limited hand motion usually shake hands, explain the National Center on Disability and Journalism.

If people can't see you, it is even more important to sit with them, explain what's happening and encourage them to talk to you and check they feel comfortable and consulted at each step of the process.

If you are filming with someone who has difficulty speaking, take your time and listen attentively. I have found it can be effective sometimes to film these interviews as a two-shot. The viewer can then see the interaction, as you respond to what the person is trying to tell you and reflect it back to them.

In a two-shot, a young boy at a children's hospice, who struggled to articulate, was able to express to me that he enjoyed moving to music. My response, reflecting back his words, was, 'So you like dancing, that sounds like fun!' The carers then decided to turn up the radio and have a spontaneous wheelchair disco. He was able to have his say and the dancing made delightful shots.

Filming at the scene

Capturing shots at an ongoing disaster is clearly different from the often more controlled environment of regular reporting. As Simpson and Cote explain, 'The best photojournalists pursue violence as a way to convey truths to the world about the horrors they see.' But they add that there can be a dilemma for crews and news organisations about what shots should be shown, particularly as they can be streamed live. 'Photography raises the issue of intrusion on people suffering unexpected and devastating events.'[3]

Tips for filming at the scene:

- If you are among the first to arrive, you may face hostile reactions, so stay focused and calm.
- A camera will not protect you from harm, so leave the scene if it becomes too dangerous.
- Be polite, sensitive and respectful of witnesses, explaining who you are. Never match anger with anger.
- Think about the pictures you are capturing. 'You will record many bloody images during a tragedy. Ask yourself whether these are important enough for historical purposes or too graphic for your readers or viewers,' say Joe Hight and Frank Smyth in their tips for photojournalists working at the site of a tragedy.[4]

They add that you should do all you can to avoid violating someone's private grieving. 'That doesn't mean that you shouldn't record photos of emotion at public scenes. However, do not intrude upon someone's private property or disturb victims during their grieving process.'

Always put your safety first. Donna DeCesare worked as a documentary photographer for more than thirty years focusing on civil conflict, natural disaster and gang members and their families throughout Latin America and the US. Her advice is to be mindful and focused. She describes photojournalism as an embedded form of journalism which requires the photographer to get close emotionally and physically. 'Your relationship to people and being human with people, letting them be curious about who you are as well – that keeps you safe.' She explains that, because you build relationships with people, they will look out for you.[5]

Sometimes in news features and documentaries, you can film reconstructions of events to tell your story. Make it clear they are re-enactments, always prepare your contributors and involve them if appropriate.

Imagery is particularly powerful so think about protecting your own emotions too. See the Self-Care chapter.

EXTRAS: anonymous filming

Neil Evans has been filming and editing stories for thirty years and currently works for the BBC. He has filmed sensitive assignments across the globe, from the Bosnian conflict in Serbia to the war in Rwanda, plus many traumatic stories closer to home in the UK. He acts as a trainer and mentor to young camera operators.

'I have found filming people who have gone through trauma requires a considerable amount of understanding, patience and above all empathy. Looking at life through a viewfinder often pulls you away from reality and I've found that just speaking to your contributors prior to filming can offer a more realistic perspective on how you approach your story,' he tells me. Here he offers tips when filming someone who wishes to remain anonymous.

- It is vital that when recording someone who does not want to be identified their whole environment is taken into consideration: Are there photographs on the wall? Can you see anything through the window that would give their location away; a church, sign, place of interest? Are there any unusual sounds like railways, church bells, or planes going overhead, perhaps indicating an airport nearby?
- Make sure the contributor cannot be identified by avoiding any distinguishing shots of rings, tattoos, unusual hairstyles.
- Throw your interviewee out of focus by filming items like plants in the foreground.
- Use your reporter as a focal point by filming them from behind your contributor.
- Use lighting creatively and film shadows.
- If you are using a silhouette, make sure the interviewee's face is totally blacked out in the edit and can't be lightened.
- Let your contributor look at the shots and check if they want their voice disguising.
- Try to use your surroundings to make the story interesting – shots of war-torn areas if that's what the story is about. The more shots you have to overlay the interview the better.

FOCUS on journalists

Jason N. Parkinson started out working in computer games before training as a journalist and feature writer. He also trained in editing and camera work and is a freelance video journalist who covers political protests, social issues, housing, education, immigration stories and terrorist attacks around the world. He works largely for Associated Press.

The minute he hears something big is happening, often via Twitter, Jason will head off with his camera in hand. 'I hear there's breaking news and within thirty seconds my bag's packed and I'm out the door. I'm on the phone to say I'm on the way and I aim in roughly the right direction, hoping the thing isn't shut down too much,' he tells me.

'Twitter is a good place to get information, so find out which hashtags are the most popular. Keep checking each one and work out which is best with the most information coming through,' explains Jason.

Preparation is paramount. 'When you come home from a job the first thing you do is plug in your batteries. Keep your laptop charged, keep your phone charged and keep all the camera batteries charged because in half an hour you may get another call. I keep everything ready to go, including an extra microphone and headphones because the audio is just as important as the images you're capturing.'

The night of the London Bridge terrorist attack, in June 2017, Jason had been out with friends and he says never head out on a job if you've had a drink. 'Even more so in a situation like that where you've got to have your wits about you, you just don't do it.'

When covering incidents such as the Manchester Arena bombing, be mindful of your safety. 'You're going into a place where everyone else is being told to go away because it's dangerous. You don't know what you're walking into.'

Take a moment to assess the situation. 'Be very aware of your environment and anything or anybody that looks out of the ordinary. Look at people, check the expressions on their faces and their mood and the sense you get from them. You start making a mental picture, so if something untoward happens you're going to be more prepared.'

Most of Jason's assignments are tense. 'Your adrenaline level is telling you this is a fearful situation and telling you to flee. It is quite easy to feel panicked, especially in riot situations, and you'll start to feel your hands shaking or a bit wobbly but a few deep breaths and everything starts to calm down. Step out, give yourself a few seconds and you'll feel much better and more in control.'

When approaching people at the scene, be calm and polite, talk loudly enough so they can hear you, but don't appear heavy or forceful. 'If their response to you seems friendly, ask if they'd like to tell you what happened and approach in that way, so it's their decision if they'd like to do it or not. Have a few minutes' chat with them.'

Video journalists can sometimes become targets for people's anger. 'Don't sling your weight around like it's your right to film, that's the last thing anybody wants in that situation. People can be aggressive towards you, so remain cool and rationalise and reason with them, don't argue back. Explain you've got a job to do. People calm down quite quickly when they understand.'

'Be vigilant and be aware it's a hyper-tense scene so people's reactions and emotions are going to be all over the place. Respect that because the most important thing is those people, not getting your story to a news desk.'

> BBC Home Affairs correspondent Dominic Casciani explains how he went about filming sequences with Nicola. Her teenage son had been radicalised and died close to the border between Syria and Iraq. In the Writing chapter, Dominic gives an overview of how he covers sensitive stories. Here he describes how he filmed with Nicola, to help tell her story.

Dominic advises talking through the filming process and explaining what is involved and what to expect. 'You shouldn't turn it into a right song and dance but you've got to make them feel comfortable with it because if you work in TV, you basically rock up and there's you and a cameraman and he may be half thinking about another job he's got to do later in the day,' he tells me.

Filming can be disruptive for people with lighting to set up, furniture to move around and strangers in their home. 'I think it's critical that you sit down with your colleagues who are going to be involved in the filming process and talk through how you are going to do it.'

It is important to check what people feel comfortable with and be careful not to impose on them. 'Nicola wanted to be filmed in her kitchen, but it was quite small, so that influenced the way we chose our kit for that day. There was a particular cameraman I wanted to work with, a guy who's fantastic at the craft but enormously empathetic and puts people at their ease. He used a small HD camera which was unobtrusive.'

To tell the story you have to film sequences and, in Nicola's case, she volunteered to show them her son's social media account from the time he had been out in Syria. 'She had an entire copy of it and that was extraordinary because it really helped us tell the story of his final weeks in Syria and we talked to her about reconstructing various elements of that.'

Nicola told Dominic about a park where she used to go walking with her son and they filmed her there, looking at her phone. In post-production they then overlaid the text exchanges between them. 'That really helped us drive the story-telling because it took away from the black and white world of terrorism but rooted it very much in the family. Families go walking and here is a mum out in a beauty spot she used to go to with her son and her son has gone off and joined IS. Nicola was able to get the message out that she was just an ordinary mum and what happened to her could happen to anybody else.'

Jemma Cox worked as a newspaper photographer before moving to the BBC as a camera operator. She worked regionally as a video journalist and is currently a network camerawoman.

Feeling apprehensive when you have to film emotional stories is natural because you cannot know how people may react. 'For the first year or two I would have the fear in my stomach of what am I going to do? How am I going to cope with this? How are they going to cope with the camera? I was nervous as well about saying the right thing and not upsetting or offending them,' Jemma tells me.

Preparation is essential, especially if you are working alone as a video journalist. 'Make sure your kit is ready to roll because you don't want to be worrying about it. It's unfair on your guest if it's a really sensitive story and you've suddenly got to rush out to get batteries.'

Before going into a home, check your tripod isn't muddy from a previous shoot, and keep lighting to a minimum if possible, as it can be intimidating. 'If you've got all your stuff in order you're not going to make life difficult, dirty the carpet or use their power. They might not want you to plug in your lights or traipse wires everywhere so be mindful of people's houses.'

As a VJ (video journalist), Jemma would advise going into homes without your kit initially, then taking time to talk to your interviewees and get a sense of how best to proceed. 'Acknowledge why you are there and give your sympathies and explain what you want to do. Have a look round, ask where they would like to do the interview and where they'll feel more comfortable so you'll know if you need to bring in extra lights, rather than turning up at their door with a shedload of kit which you might not necessarily need.'

It is important to compromise and accommodate people's requests. Jemma had set up to do an interview with a man whose nephew had been murdered. The uncle then said he wanted to do the interview sitting alongside another member of the family. 'We had to move them to a different place and the lighting was difficult, but you have to work round it because it's a difficult time for them and you'll get more out of them if they're comfortable.'

Avoid jargon and explain what you would like them to do, so they aren't overwhelmed with terminology they don't understand. 'I think most people have been through grief but probably not on the scale they have and you have to put yourself in their position and think what would it be like if I had a film crew in my house, how would it feel? Take time and let it breathe rather than thinking you've got to get this done and edited.'

Avoid cluttered backgrounds when filming an emotional interview because it will distract. When getting your pictures afterwards, involve your interviewee. 'If they've lost a relative, was there something they did together, anything that is relevant to what the story is about? They have to be comfortable, you don't want them thinking they have to act or do something they wouldn't normally do,' explains Jemma.

She filmed with a father whose son had taken his own life and who chose to walk through a park for the shoot. 'They'd always gone to this park and done lots of things together and he was talking about his memories of his son. It was easy to shoot because there were so many things I could cut away to but it was really relaxed for him, just letting him talk.'

If you are there as a crew, avoid asking people lots of questions which they are likely to be asked again in the interview. 'Also remember they're not politicians or people who have been media-trained and this could be the first time they've had a camera pointed at them. They've been through something really difficult and you're expecting them to open up about it. Try to find that ground where you can be conversational without being in their face and always respect what they have been through.'

> Richard Faulkner is a veteran news cameraman who has filmed hundreds of sensitive stories across a forty-year career on the road. He has filmed sequences with countless families who have suffered trauma yet admits he still has to brace himself to work with them.

After all these years Richard tells me he still finds it awkward. 'I'm very conscious of their grief and conscious I don't want to upset them. I'm going into their home feeling I shouldn't really be there, but I know it's my job and I've got to be there.'

Once there he works to gain their confidence. 'I'm gentle in my approach and I'm constantly aware that they're grieving so I do things delicately. I think it's common sense to some degree but you cannot be a bull in a china shop. You've just got to be gentle.'

He can sense the shift as they start to loosen up and talk to him. 'I think you can feel that bond coming on a little bit as you chat to them. You need that because after the interview you're going to need to do the set-up shots and you might have to instruct them.'

Richard is conscious not to over-shoot or put them through too much filming. 'I would shoot minimally knowing that the least disturbance is probably better.'

Often on a warm day, it can work well to interview people outdoors in their garden, but this may not always work for a sensitive story. 'I think privacy is important because they don't want to have neighbours listening over a fence and the chances are they're going to get emotional. When you are indoors pretty lighting isn't necessarily a prime concern either, you may have to compromise.'

Asking permission is important when adjusting furniture for shots and particularly when filming personal items such as a photograph. 'You can take a shot of it on the mantelpiece in a frame but there might be reflections coming off the glass. You might need to take the photograph out of the frame and some people understandably might be reluctant to let you do that. But it's worth asking and hopefully by that time you've won a bit of their trust, they'll allow you to do it because you want a clean picture without reflections.'

Richard is mindful never to put pressure on the people he is filming and to be constantly polite and tactful when asking them to do things for the camera. He will also explain some of the process of filming. 'I'll say they might need to do something a few times because I need to film it from different angles. I would be careful not to slip into jargon.'

Filming someone who does not wish to be identified, such as a rape or abuse survivor, can be challenging. 'There are various ways from a total blackout, to filming their shadow on a wall. You can shine a bright light close to their face and that gives a silhouette outline shadow of the interviewee and I think that can work quite well.'

Richard's preferred way to shoot anonymously is to have an object in the foreground such as a plant or flowers and keep the object in sharp focus. 'The interviewee is slightly in the distance and fuzzy or out of focus so you can't identify them. Another alternative is to film from behind the interviewee looking at the reporter's face, but I don't think you can sustain a whole interview with just that shot.'

Be conscious of the jigsaw effect when filming anonymously. 'If you were taking a shot of the eye, then the nose, then the mouth it's not beyond the bounds of technology today to stitch the picture together to make a face if somebody was really keen to try and identify that person.'

> *Interviews for online news can often be filmed on smartphones. Caroline Lowbridge, who told earlier (in Chapter 3) how she approaches through social media, explains how she shot a sensitive interview on her phone.*

Caroline was covering the story of a man who ran a construction company and had won the Black Businessman of the Year award. His company gave opportunities to young people from difficult backgrounds and Caroline wanted to interview some of them, filming them using her smartphone on a stand.

'One of them ended up telling me this really emotional story about how his best friend had been stabbed to death in front of him when he was 14. It was a room full of builders and they had no idea this had happened to this lad. I looked round and all these big men had tears in their eyes and it was a really emotional story. I thought if I'd had a proper camera crew he wouldn't have told that story. He hadn't told it to anyone before and I think the phone was less intimidating.'

INSIGHT from interviewees

Melody is a survivor of childhood rape. She shared insight into how she wished to be treated by journalists in the Relationship chapter. Melody has worked with many people who have suffered sexual abuse and gives advice about what to bear in mind when filming with them.

In common with many people who agree to be interviewed, Melody was surprised the crew would need to film sequences with her, in order to tell her story. She was filmed packing her suitcase to go on holiday after the trial had finished. This she found to be rewarding. 'It actually made me look at things differently. This is me stepping into my future, a future of my own design. So that was exceedingly helpful and I hadn't expected that,' she tells me.

Crucially, because of the abuse she had suffered, Melody needed the crew to involve and explain the process to her. 'I definitely needed to know why they were doing it because, without context, it would have meant nothing to me. I would have been wondering why are you doing this? It's about having rapport and having that communication level of: this is why we're doing something, rather than just do it and we'll explain later.'

Melody goes on to give powerful insight into why involving her was so important. 'Someone who's been a victim of abuse, they've already had too many people making them do things without explanation and it wasn't pleasant. Therefore, by having things explained to me, checking I was comfortable with it and asking if there was anything I would prefer, I felt I was part of the team. That helped absolutely tremendously. It made me feel a part of the process rather than a rabbit in the headlights, spotlight of the subject.'

Melody was also asked to be filmed walking outdoors. 'They took on board that I didn't feel entirely safe out in the open world. So they suggested if it would make me feel safer, to bring my dog with me. That element of feeling safer really had a massive impact.'

Holly was an eyewitness in the 2017 London Bridge terror attack, narrowly escaping with her life. In Chapter 3, she shared her insight into how best to be approached. In the days that followed the attack, she was filmed by various camera crews and she described what helped.

The day after the attack, Holly was filmed at her home in London and having the process explained to her was essential. 'I just remember thinking how lovely the cameraman was because he came into my home and said right this is what we're going to do, are you happy for us to film here, it's only going to be a head shot, so it's only your face we're going to see. We can stop filming at any time, it's not "live."'

Holly found it helped to know exactly what was going to happen and advises reporters and camera operators to steer clear of using technical terms in front of interviewees.

When filming people at the scene of an attack, Holly also advises being mindful of how they may look. 'When I finally saw myself in the mirror I was horrified. I had make-up everywhere, but the shocking thing was I had blood all over me and it wasn't my blood. Some people had been sick. Try and think of it from their point of view. How's that going to make them feel the next day if they've been on national TV?'

> In the Interview chapter, Rachel shared her insight to help reporters prepare to work with vulnerable interviewees. Rachel's daughter has anorexia, but the only hospital bed available for her was 300 hundred miles from her home. Here Rachel offers insight for journalists when filming.

When she agreed to be part of a network documentary, Rachel's kitchen became filled with strangers: cameraman, sound man, producer, director, presenter, lighting man. 'I couldn't believe how many people there would be,' she tells me. She says that before they arrived, she needed to be told who each person was and what they were there coming to do because otherwise it felt intimidating. 'Having that knowledge is important, so that when six people pile into your house, you are expecting it and you're not overwhelmed by them.'

Be careful about using jargon when filming. Terms like noddies, cut-aways and set-ups can be alarming for people who are feeling vulnerable and unsure of themselves. 'It made me feel stupid and a bit fearful hearing these terms and wondering what they meant,' explains Rachel.

Rachel was also wired up with a personal microphone to record her voice but no one explained she might need to turn it off, when going to the toilet for instance. 'I'm still mortified. Things like that do matter because it's embarrassing,' she rightly points out.

> Faith also shared her insight in the Preparation and Relationship chapters. Her teenage son Joshua died after being knocked off his bike by a car as he cycled to school. Here Faith explains what helped her when reporters needed to film with her.

Taking the time to film with a crew was exhausting. 'I liked it when the filming was broken up into segments because it gave me a breather in between. We did a certain amount in the house, then we went down to the skate park, so it was broken up and that was easier to deal with,' Faith tells me.

'Whenever I was interviewed or anything was done I was absolutely completely shattered afterwards because it is emotionally draining. Break it up and have a cup of tea in between and say right let's do this bit next, so bite-sized pieces.'

HOW I COVER SENSITIVE STORIES: HELEN LONG

'Humility is your starting point.'

Helen has more than twenty years' experience of covering war and disaster as a senior news journalist and field producer for Reuters. She is currently the Operations Manager, Europe, Middle East and Africa for Reuters Video News.

As well as reporting on people suffering the effects of trauma, Helen focused her attention on helping journalists who were struggling with the effects of covering traumatic stories and introduced a global peer support network to Reuters. She has delivered stress and trauma workshops around the world.

Helen learnt how to interview people who were traumatised long before she became a journalist. She worked on a seminal landmine project that examined the socio-economic impact of anti-personnel mines. Her research involved travelling to the most heavily mined countries – Cambodia, Afghanistan, Mozambique, Bosnia-Herzegovina – and interviewing landmine victims and refugees.

'I was confronted with people who were mute from trauma in countries where they had no concept of PTSD. People who had just been blown up, people who had just been bereaved,' she tells me. 'So I learnt and developed the techniques in the course of those two years.'

It struck her that when she then did her post-grad in journalism at Cardiff University, the issue of how to approach sensitive subjects was never raised, 'It was all about how to be in charge of the interview, how to control it, how to run it. It was quite aggressive actually, nothing about the emotional landscape of the interview itself.'

Key techniques

'Humility is the most important thing for me,' Helen says. Years of working with disempowered interviewees overseas and acknowledging the unequal relationship has ingrained this approach. 'It is absolutely fundamentally important and has served me well. Whether it's interviewing refugees in Afghanistan, in Greece or interviewing people here who have been bereaved, just being humble and polite is the basis on which to forge that initial relationship from which you build the rapport and the trust. That's the real key to getting the best out of somebody. They have to trust you in order to open up and feel, "I can tell my story, my truth to this person."'

A hard lesson learned

One of Helen's worst experiences as a young reporter was being sent to get a highly sensitive story under intense pressure. The experience lives with her to this day. Helen was up against it with a piece to edit, yet was dispatched to get a quick vox pop with any survivors of Rwandan genocide she could find in a demonstration which was winding up in central London.

'It was just awful,' she recalls. She found a young demonstrator who was the sole survivor of his family. Mistake number one, she says, was covering such a story under time pressure; mistake number two was inevitably being unprepared. 'I carried out what I would call a smash and grab interview. I got him to talk about his story, this awful genocide and what happened to him and to my eternal shame and horror he began to cry. I was completely at a loss at what to do. I was under time pressure and I had to walk away from this guy who was just in floods of tears.'

Her reaction was fury that she had been forced to grab the story but also anger at herself because she feels she should have said no.

Take your time

Helen fully accepts, however, that it is hard when you are a young journalist starting out and you are trying to manage the expectations of both your editor and your vulnerable interviewee.

'The expansion of the digital universe has opened up all these new and exciting spaces which, as journalists, we are now required to fill and tell stories in all sorts of different ways. It crushes time and space but time is a journalist's basic unit of currency; without that we cannot do our stories justice.'

She adds that the tension will increase which is why it is so important for journalists to push back when they need to. 'Certainly on these kinds of stories you have to prioritise time. You have to get to know people, you have to build trust. You can't do that in two minutes.'

Preparation is key and that takes time too. 'You have to do your homework, you have to understand something of the person and their trauma whatever it is, so that when you go in, you are as prepared as you can be.'

Time also allows spaces, says Helen, 'It's in those spaces that your interviewee will often say the most extraordinary things.'

Giving control

When working on sensitive stories, Helen describes the relationship as more of a partnership. 'Certainly when there is trauma in the story, it is very consensual. It is about giving people a say and a voice, their own agency, control if you like.'

So at each step of the process, she will map out what she wants to do and check in with her interviewee. 'It is really important, especially when you are dealing with traumatic material, to reinforce to the person that they can stop at any time and they are in charge. This is their emotion, their loss, their pain. It is so important not to disrespect that.'

She acknowledges that the reporter will have deadlines and professional obligations. 'But if you push people, it will destroy the interview in a heartbeat. So you have to go at their pace. In that sense, they are the one in charge, and that is right and the key thing is to signal that to them.'

The power of pictures

Helen's work has involved reporting on refugees. In a camp, she will initially keep her cameraman in the background and spend some time on her own, getting to know people and finding a translator. The translator will effectively be doing the interview. 'It's absolutely vital that you find the right person who speaks good enough English, but more importantly, is an open empathetic person themselves.'

As a reporter, she says it is important to spot the human moments for your cameraman to film. If she was filming with a refugee family she would always ask permission to film the children. It is worth it because those shots are effective in telling the story. 'Having close-ups of the baby playing in the sand, or munching or yawning, it's those little human moments.'

'I want the audience to connect with them as people first and foremost. Rather than just dismiss them as "oh they're refugees, they're probably economic migrants" but to actually think "that's a young family, I've got a young child, that could be my child, that could be me." That's the ultimate objective really.'

Reporting from the scene

Reporting from the scene of an atrocity can be a tough call for reporters and there are judgement calls to be made. Crucially, Helen says, it is important to approach adults and not children and to get their consent and acknowledge what has happened, 'Are you okay? This must have been terrible.'

As young families were leaving the Manchester Arena after an Ariana Grande concert in May 2017, a suicide bomber carried out a terror attack which killed twenty-two people. Some of them were children and hundreds more were injured.

A team was dispatched to the scene from Reuters, arriving in the early hours of the morning. 'They said it was like a zombie apocalypse. You had lots of distressed predominantly teenage girls wandering around the streets, but they did not go near them. We're so strict about that and it is really important,' explains Helen. 'There were lots of reporters going round saying can you give me your photographs without any kind of care or attention and that was just wrong.'

Again, she says, it is about taking time, especially when you are dealing with people who are in shock, and establishing some kind of rapport, 'The way in which shock operates, people don't process emotion. So if you talk to them at a hundred miles an hour or you're asking lots of different questions, they will just stare at you in mute blankness because that's how shock affects people's bodies and their minds.'

Simple questions are key here, she says, as well as allowing them time to respond and making sure the person has heard and understood you. People in shock fall into two categories, she explains, 'They either want to talk and talk or they go mute and silent as they are trying to process.'

She described how, in the aftermath of the Grenfell fire, people were walking around wailing and clearly distraught. 'I would never approach someone in that level of distress because it's unethical. At the end of the day, as journalists even though we've got our professional detachments, we are human beings and we don't want to sustain a moral injury ourselves. You can easily do that when you report in the aftermath of something like Grenfell. You have to be very clear about where the ethical boundaries are.'

Sensitive interviewing

Ask very open and simple questions, is Helen's advice, as is explaining to your interviewee why you want to talk to them and preparing them for what you may like to ask.

Helen describes how she interviewed a woman who was a survivor of the Edgware Road tube station attack in the 7/7 London bombings in 2005, in which fifty-two people lost their lives and many hundreds more were injured. She was covering the first anniversary of the attack.

She set the expectations, explained what she would like to ask, checked the woman was comfortable with it and asked if there was anything in particular she would like to say. She also spelt out some of the basics, 'Explaining that it's not "live," don't worry about the camera, we can do it as many times as possible if needs be.'

In the interview itself, Helen first asked for a sense of what life was like before the attack. 'This one event had completely changed every single survivor's life. Even those who didn't lose limbs and there were many who did, but those who suffered psychological trauma. This lady hadn't been able to ride on the tube since that day.'

Helen did the interview in a park. 'We walked and talked during the interview because I thought it would put her at ease, well away from triggers because I was listening out for that and green spaces, trees, because that's very calming. Make sure you pick your location properly, location is key.'

Helen suggests starting with general warm-up questions to put people, who are often nervous, at ease and to get them used to talking. '"Tell me about that morning, before the bombing, what were you doing?" That puts them back where they were and then you follow up by asking, "So tell me, when did you know?"'

Be delicate in your questioning and keenly aware of body language and signals, Helen advises. Some people are willing to talk openly but there are others whom you can easily re-traumatise if you push too far, and you don't want to do that. 'Be very astute and be watching, most language is non-verbal, 70 per cent is body language. So you've got to be looking for that.'

Key advice

Make time. Make enough time. Be humble. It's a privilege to hear people's stories and for them to open and share their pain. Never abuse that, never.

Notes

1 John Happel, 'Five Immersive Photographers Share Their Experiences on Gaining Trust,' 19 April 2018, Nieman Storyboard, https://niemanstoryboard.org.

2 National Center on Disability and Journalism, 'Tips for Interviewing People with Disabilities,' https://ncdj.org.

3 Roger Simpson and William Cote, *Covering Violence: A Guide to Ethical Reporting about Victims and Trauma*, 2nd edn, Columbia University Press, 2006, pp. 142 and 144.

4 Joe Hight and Frank Smyth, 'Tragedies and Journalists,' 17 February 2009, https://dartcenter.org/content/tragedies-journalists.

5 Annie Hylton, 'Safety and Self-Care Strategies for Every Beat,' 9 November 2015, https://dartcenter.org.

8
The writing

'Accuracy, accuracy, accuracy!'

Joseph Pulitzer

In this chapter

Considerations when writing and framing sensitive pieces.

Extras on terms and phrases to use and not to use.

Focus on writing tips from Louis Theroux, Lucy Williamson and Jina Moore.

Insight into the impact of our words on our interviewees.

Overview from Dominic Casciani on how he covers sensitive stories.

Facing facts

When writing your story, keep it simple. 'After a disaster or tragedy, stories do not need to be sensationalised or embellished. Rely on good solid factual journalism and a healthy dose of sensitivity,' advises Mark Brayne, in his guide for journalists who are covering trauma.[1]

Accuracy is crucial. At a time of intense vulnerability, a person trusts and confides in a reporter. They feel understood and that the reporter will take care of their account. Then they discover they could not even get their name or basic details right. 'It wasn't a meaningful moment at all. It was just the journalist trying to get a series of quotes for something they had to do for work,' explains Gavin Rees. 'It breaks the contract and it undermines the value of the trust that had previously been earned between the journalist and the contributor.'

'The burden of responsibility on the journalist to get it right should be immense. The bereaved need to feel that the emotional cost of this intrusion is worthwhile and productive,' says Dr Sallyanne Duncan, who evaluated more than four hundred 'death knock' stories in UK newspapers to examine how they were written.[2]

The teaching video *Getting It Right* refers to the *second wound*. This is inflicted by the further 'collateral damage that hasty, thoughtless and inaccurate journalism can do to trauma survivors or people who have lost loved ones to violence and tragedy.' Jim Ward contributed to the video. He survived a gas blast that killed two workmates at Longford, Victoria. He says, 'Accuracy in reporting a trauma victim's circumstances is paramount. I distinctly remember reading a report about the two dead men and one's name was misspelt. Straight away I was thinking about his sister and how she would feel.'[3]

As Mark Brayne adds, 'Research now suggests that even if people are only rarely clinically re-traumatised in the longer term by poor coverage of their story, many are profoundly distressed by the way they've been reported and especially by even small inaccuracies.' So do not be afraid to go back to them and double-check. It is better to keep ringing back to clarify than to broadcast or publish something that is wrong. If families make a formal complaint, the sympathy won't be with the journalist.

Stages of a story

There is a cycle to reporting and writing about a disaster: Are you covering the initial stage of impact, shock and bewilderment? Do you need to clarify dramatic rumours? Are you then focusing on *brave* rescuers, *hero* survivors and is this helpful? Soon afterwards, it switches again: Who is responsible for the disaster or the response to it? Weeks later, sometimes sooner, are you moving on to the next story and forgetting the victims and communities who may be trying to recover?

In her memoir, *Becoming*, Michelle Obama talks of the many visits she and Barack made to people caught up in disasters. 'When one or both of us traveled somewhere in the wake of a tragedy, it was often to remind Americans not to look too quickly past the pain of others.' Tellingly she adds, 'Grief and resilience live together. I learned this not just once as First Lady but many times over.'[4]

The raw emotion at the start is only half the story. As you revisit people and communities, you can reflect ways in which they re-build their lives, try to heal and come to terms with what has happened. Some may remain angry or bitter. The Follow-ups chapter has more on this.

Mind your language

When writing your piece, avoid labels and stereotypes. 'When tragedy hits a community, journalists may find ourselves shoehorning complex sequences of events into set narratives and defaulting to stock characters – the grieving widow, feckless parent who cannot control a delinquent child, the brave rescuer etc.,' says Gavin Rees in 'The Trauma Factor.' While accepting that this form of shorthand can be useful and can engage an audience, he adds that, equally, it may 'obscure crucial details and traduce the experience of victims and survivors.'[5]

This can be particularly relevant in headlines and the short sequences and soundbites used to sell your story. As a reporter, these can be out of your immediate control, but try to keep a check on what sub-editors, producers or presenters are saying or writing. If you object to their take on the story, warn them their words are likely to offend your interviewee, risk distressing them further and that they are likely to complain. Be ready with alternative suggestions.

Be careful with labels as, time and again in the *Insight* sections in this book, people object to them: Holly disliked being called a *hero* for helping others caught in the terror attack on London Bridge; Nicky, whose son Jack died in hospital, objected to him being labelled *Downs boy* in newspaper headlines; Suleman Nagdi asks journalists to avoid labelling a person with their religion, such as a *Muslim boy*, if it is not relevant to the story.

The charity Child Bereavement UK warns of the distress subjective language can cause when reporting the feelings of an interviewee. They ask journalists to avoid sensationalising with projected adverbs or adjectives which the interviewee has not used, such as 'horror-stricken.'

Dave Cullen spent a decade researching and writing *Columbine*, his account of the 1999 shooting in Littleton, Colorado. In his article, 'A Reporter's Lessons from Past Shootings,' he explains how, in writing the book, he became aware of how he and other reporters, who covered the story as breaking news, got it wrong. His over-arching advice is to qualify your witnesses carefully, don't jump to conclusions about a suspect's character or motive, treat survivors humanely, and 'excise the word "snapped" (as in, "that was when the killer snapped") from your vocabulary. "Snapped" perpetuates the mistaken notion that people go off suddenly. The vast majority of shooters plan their attack in advance,'[6] he explains.

Be careful too with the language of blame because, however unintentionally, certain phrases can hurt. Rose Dixon, who works with many families bereaved through murder or manslaughter, says many object to the phrase *she was in the wrong place at the wrong time* because it implies the victim was partly at fault.

Parents have also told me they dislike the word *closure* as they never have closure. Think carefully before you write your piece or script.

Journalism versus voyeurism

'The best journalists know how to spin a good yarn and often audiences appreciate stories full of details. But in trauma journalism, details can turn against the story and the people in it,' Jina Moore explains, and warns against journalism slipping into voyeurism, exploiting victims and sensationalising violence.

Read through your copy carefully and imagine if it was being written about you or a close family member. Would you alter the wording? Are graphic descriptions necessary? Could what you are writing harm anyone in the story? Are you covering all angles carefully to tell a fully rounded story?

'We have a responsibility to survivors of trauma to treat them well and handle their stories ethically and we have a responsibility to our communities to give them reliable information and sometimes … to give them hope and help restore their sense of power,' explains Jina.[7]

Quotes

Emotive quotes, expressing reactions to a sad or tragic event, can be central to your piece. They can be powerful because they are authentic and personal. As Sallyanne Duncan adds, having researched the many newspaper articles about deaths, 'The presentational style may appear sentimentalised but this form of reporting reflects the pain and suffering of the bereaved and the language of the quotes is the language they have chosen to express their feelings.'

Reflect quotes accurately, both in the words used and the tone and context in which they were expressed. Writing carefully about people's trauma is important work and can be rewarding, says Kevin Kawamoto. He has written about best practice in trauma reporting, based on insights from award-winning newspaper articles. 'Producing an engaging, well-crafted and sensitive news story about crime victims, survivors and their loved ones is not only good for the reputation of the news organisation and its employees, but it is also good for their communities,'[8] he explains.

When putting your package together for broadcast, it can help to include some of your interview questions. These can show the audience you are trying to be careful and sensitive in the way you are interacting with people. Viewers and listeners can be quick to object if they feel you are not treating your interviewee sensitively.

EXTRAS

Writing about suicide

Extra care needs to be taken when framing and writing stories about suicide. Not only may they be particularly sensitive, the way they are reported can influence the risk of imitational suicidal behaviour among vulnerable people.[9]

Take a close look at the Ethics chapter for more on the rules around reporting suicide.

The respected charity Samaritans produces media guidelines and provides pre-print advice for journalists. Here are Samaritans' top ten tips to help journalists when writing or scripting their reports:

- Leave out technical details about the method of suicide such as describing the type of ligature used or the number and types of pills taken in an overdose. Never suggest that a method is quick, easy, painless or certain to result in death.
- Language matters. Avoid dramatic headlines and terms such as 'suicide epidemic' or 'hot spot.'
- Include references to support groups and places where suicidal people can get help – it really does make a difference.
- Treat social media with particular caution and refrain from mentioning websites or networks that promote or glamorise suicide.
- Avoid dramatic or sensationalist pictures or video. Refrain from including content from suicide notes.
- Young people are especially vulnerable to negative suicide coverage. Do not give undue prominence to photographs of a young person who has died and avoid repeated use of images such as galleries.
- Try not to give a story undue prominence, for example with a front cover splash or posting live updates on social media.
- Don't brush over the complex realities of suicide and its impact on those left behind. People bereaved by suicide are often vulnerable and more likely to take their own lives.
- Speculation about the 'trigger' for suicide, even from close family members, should be avoided.
- Use statistics with caution. Check with Samaritans or the relevant national statistic agency to make sure you have the most recent data and are comparing like with like.

When scripting a piece about suicide, Samaritans offer these suggestions:

Do use phrases like:

- A suicide.
- Die by/death by suicide.
- Take one's own life.
- A suicide attempt.
- A completed suicide.
- Person at risk of suicide.

Avoid phrases like:

- Commit/committed suicide (this refers back to when it was illegal).
- A *successful* or *unsuccessful* suicide.
- Cry for help.
- Suicide victim.
- Suicide *epidemic, craze* or *hotspot.*
- Suicide-prone.

There is further advice at www.samaritans.org.

Writing about sexual violence and sexual abuse

When writing and framing a report about sexual violence, take care not to over-simplify or make assumptions about survivors and abusers. They come from all walks of life, all ages and all sexual orientations.

Domestic violence, against women and men, can include verbal abuse, threats, intimidation, manipulative behaviour, physical and sexual assault, rape or homicide.

Sexual violence can be physical or psychological and be against men, women or children. Rape is known to be one of the most deeply traumatic experiences. Rape is not *sex* and a pattern of abuse is not an *affair.*

Framing your story

Be clear. Use accurate facts and statistics to put your piece in context and look at the broader impact. How has it affected the family and the community? 'Help the audience see beyond criminal justice and understand that sexual violence is also a public health and social justice issue,' suggests the National Sexual Violence Resource Center (NSVRC).[10]

Be informed. Be wary of the many myths and judgemental opinions around sexual violence and abuse. These include what a woman was wearing, whether she had been drinking; or men may be judged for not fighting off an attacker. Fay Maxted, CEO of The Survivors Trust charity, tells me, 'These myths create a toxic social environment that victims and survivors struggle with daily, which is why it is so important for journalists to be aware of the facts and issues around sexual violence and abuse.'

Be careful, too, with assumptions about the abuser. As the German American journalist and trauma educator Stefanie Friedhoff explains in her articles on domestic violence, 'It is typical for abusers to show a kind face to the world while terrorizing their intimate partners.'[11]

Salacious? Consider the level of detail you are using. 'Too much can become gratuitous, too little can weaken the survivor's case,' explains the Dart Center in its tip sheet for reporting on sexual violence.[12]

Anonymity. Check you are not unwittingly revealing someone's identity through the details of your report. 'All victims of sexual offences, including children, are automatically guaranteed anonymity for life from the moment they make an allegation that they are the victim of a sexual offence.'[13] Take care that your report does not compromise any legal proceedings. Take a look at the Ethics chapter for more on this.

Getting help. Reports about child sex abuse can trigger strong reactions in survivors. Try to include a helpline, website or support group information and consider trigger warnings on social media posts.

Giving hope. If possible, include positive elements in your piece. 'Highlight resilience and healing among survivors to avoid perpetuating the myth that sexual violence irrevocably ruins the lives of those who experience it,' suggests the NSVRC guidance.

Writing your story

Blame. Read your copy carefully to check you are not implying the victim is to blame or is complicit in some way, or that you are not down-playing the role of the abuser. In her investigation into the impact media coverage of sex abuse inquiries has on victims, the Australian journalist Tory Shepherd refers to an article which said a *child had sex with an adult*, as opposed to an adult raping a child. The phrase *had sex with* suggests the child had consented, even though this is not possible because they are a minor.[14] She also recommends, 'Don't focus on "stranger danger". Most assaults are perpetrated by a person known to the victim.'

Victim or survivor? Many people ask to be referred to as survivors not victims, but this may not always be the case. Some may feel it is premature to be called a survivor, so check with them which they prefer.

Abbreviations. When Tory Shepherd spoke to survivors for her investigation, some felt words like 'pedo' or 'perp' were dismissive or flippant. They also said it was important to distinguish between paedophiles, rapists and child abusers.

'Historical.' In its media guidance the charity NAPAC, which supports adult survivors of childhood abuse in the UK, points out that rapes, murders and robberies are not referred to as historical. 'Survivors may be living with the physical and mental consequences of abuse every day. There is nothing *historical* about it for them.'

'Child pornography.' This term along with *child porn* or *kiddie porn* can normalise and diminish the sexual violation of children. 'Children by definition cannot consent to their own abuse,' say NAPAC. Use instead *child abuse images* or *indecent images of children*, they suggest.

Affair or fling. Use instead *child sexual exploitation*.

Child prostitute. This, say NAPAC, is an outdated term which can blame a child who has been exploited by adults for profit. They suggest referring to a *sexually exploited child*.

Accuracy. Write and frame your piece accurately. 'Inaccurate or manipulative reporting may lead to survivors being portrayed in the media as unreliable,' explain NAPAC.

There is further advice at https://napac.org.uk.

In concluding her report, Tory Shepherd reflects the words of Anne Longfield, the Children's Commissioner for England: 'The single most important thing a journalist can do when reporting child sexual abuse is to think about the impact the article could have on that particular survivor or others who may have experienced sexual abuse.'

Writing about human trafficking

The Irina Project is based at the University of North Carolina School of Media and Journalism. It monitors how the media reports sex trafficking locally, nationally and globally and offers guidance to reporters on making contact with survivors, interviewing them and writing about them.[15]

The researchers collaborated with survivor leaders to develop tips for journalists. Written by Minh Dang of Survivor Alliance, they include advice when writing your piece:

- Use accurate descriptions of your interviewee, avoiding *child prostitute, underage prostitute* and *illegal immigrant*. Ask your interviewee which terms they feel most comfortable with.

- Do not take statements out of context.
- Consider re-framing the story – survivors are more than case studies. Ask them what they most want people to know and avoid sensationalising. 'While human trafficking is horrifying and disgusting, we need the general public to move beyond their shock and to understand the issue,' explains Minh.
- Track down the original source of statistics. If you cannot validate them, don't use them.
- Do not conflate human trafficking with prostitution. Human trafficking is about humans forcing other humans into slavery and profiting financially and emotionally from others' labour in many different industries. They do not get to keep their wages.
- Avoid using cliché images such as a girl in chains, a person with a barcode on them, a kid in a brothel, says Minh, as this contributes to the stereotype about human trafficking.

There is further advice at www.theirinaproject.org and www.survivoralliance.org.

Writing about mental health

The charities Mind and Rethink Mental Illness produced guidance for reporters on working sensitively and responsibly as part of a campaign called Time to Change. It explains that, when done well, stories about mental illness can raise awareness, challenge attitudes and help to dispel myths.

They offer the following advice when framing and writing your stories:

- Is it relevant to the story that the person has a mental illness?
- Don't speculate about their mental health being a factor in the story unless you know this is 100 per cent true.
- Don't provide 'on air' diagnosis or encourage 'experts' to do so.
- Is it appropriate to mention their mental illness in a headline?
- Are your sources reliable, or have neighbours or eyewitnesses made assumptions about someone's mental health status?
- Use facts, put it in context and remember people with severe mental illness are more likely to be victims than perpetrators of violent crime.
- Consider consulting people as experts on their own conditions.

They also suggest commonly misused words and phrases to avoid and alternatives to use. These include avoiding *unhinged, maniac, loony* or *mad* and saying instead *a person with a mental health problem*. Avoid terms such as *the mentally ill, a victim, the afflicted, a person suffering from, a sufferer*; instead use the phrase *people with mental health problems*.

When referring to people being treated in a psychiatric hospital, avoid *prisoners* or *inmates*; instead refer to them as *mental health patients* or *patients*. Avoid saying they have been *released*; instead say they have been *discharged*. Also avoid the expression *happy pills*; use instead *antidepressants*, *medication* or *prescription drugs*.

Other common language mistakes: somebody who is *angry* is not *psychotic*, a person who is *down* or *unhappy* is not the same as someone experiencing *clinical depression*, and *schizophrenic* or *bipolar* should not be used to mean *a split personality* or *two minds*.

Consider the pictures you are using to tell your stories, maybe through a graphics sequence. 'Very often we see an image of a person holding their head in their hands. All manner of mental health stories, about anything from talking treatments to scientific research, are illustrated by a "headclutcher" photo.' Mind offered alternative shots for editors to use through their Get the Picture campaign.

There is further advice at www.time-to-change.org.uk.

Writing about eating disorders

The charity Beat offers helpful tips for reporters working with people who have eating disorders. They explain that they often judge themselves very harshly and constantly compare themselves negatively with others. They often talk about being 'triggered': how their eating disorder behaviour can be stimulated, encouraged or reinforced by certain words, images or situations.

The following are features of media reporting that the majority of people affected would find triggering:

- Any mention of the lowest weight a person was at is unhelpful as it plays to the competitive nature of their disorder by offering a target to aim for. Similarly detailing exactly how much weight someone lost or gained can trigger people to compare themselves negatively.
- Mention of amounts eaten. Saying for instance that someone 'lived on half an apple a day' or how much they consumed in a binge could act as encouragement to restrict, binge or purge.
- Photographs of emaciated body parts are triggering, such as ribcages, concave stomachs, collarbones and spines.
- Describing ways in which people avoided eating or hid their illness can be seen by others as inspiration for ways of maintaining their own eating disorder.

Avoid inaccuracies such as referring to an eating disorder as a 'slimmer's disease,' a phase or fad or some celebrity copycat. Avoid calling someone an eating disorder victim, an anorexic or bulimic, or trivialising by referring to them as 'flirting with an eating disorder.'

They add that eating disorders are not lifestyle choices – they are not choices at all – and stories about them should be treated in the same way as for other illnesses.

There is further advice at www.beateatingdisorders.org.uk.

Writing about disability

The disability equality charity Scope campaigns on behalf of disabled people and has produced tips for journalists on language to use and avoid in their reports.

Words and phrases to avoid:

- The disabled, victim, sufferer.
- The deaf, the blind.
- Retard, slow, simple.
- Wheelchair bound or confined to a wheelchair.

Preferred phrases:

- Disabled person, person with a disability.
- Deaf person, hard of hearing person, blind person, visually impaired person.
- Person with a learning disability.
- A wheelchair user.

They add that everyone talks about their disability in a different way and recommend asking your interviewee, 'how should I refer to your impairment?'

When framing and writing stories, avoid making assumptions: not everyone in a wheelchair is paralysed and many disabled people drive, go to the gym, play football and have a night out, just like everyone else. Most find being called *brave* or *inspirational* patronising, say Scope, but, if in doubt, check with your interviewee.

You can find out more at www.scope.org.uk.

FOCUS on journalists

As well as presenting his documentaries, Louis Theroux writes all his own scripts. Here he hands on tips to consider from his experience of story-telling.

'You have to be aware that your contributors are almost certain to see the film, so imagine them seeing it,' Louis tells me. 'The story is your story to tell and it's your responsibility to tell the truth.'

Sometimes there is a balance to be struck between terminology and sensitivity. 'The fact that somebody is uncomfortable with terms you use shouldn't always be prohibitive but it is definitely something you should keep in mind. In these kinds of stories you're talking to decent people who are trying their best to recover from something or deal with something and I think where possible there's nothing to be gained from upsetting them unnecessarily. So be aware that they'll see it.'

Be careful with the words you choose when referring to people, particularly the term 'victim.' 'When I did a story about Jimmy Savile and the people he'd offended against, I would check with them before I started the interview what term they preferred; whether they were okay with the term victim or if they preferred another term.'

Where possible he will try to extract positives. It means that when he is writing his scripts he finds he has to guard against overdoing words like 'strength,' 'courage' and phrases such as 'I couldn't help admiring.'

'This may be specific to my kind of story-telling. Clearly there are many other ways of doing things but in my story-telling I'm trying to show ways in which there is room for hope in situations that appear dark and there are human connections that take place in situations that seem absolutely bleak. So even someone who is dying in hospital, the eloquence they show or the bravery or their ability to connect in extremis, I see all of those as things to be validated and where possible in the script, I do try to acknowledge that.'

This approach compensates for covering often difficult emotional stories. 'It's giving everyday people the space to exhibit a kind of heroism in dealing with what they deal with and I try to honour that in the script.'

> When Lucy Williamson took up her post as BBC Paris correspondent she found herself relentlessly covering terrorist attacks. Here she offers advice on scripting and structuring pieces for TV reports.

Watch the pictures. 'Watch your opening sequence again and again, really watch it and think about what comes up for you,' Lucy tells me.

Be clear in your own mind what you are trying to get across. 'Know what you want to say in the piece and what you think about the story and what you are trying to tell the audience. Think what is the way in to telling that story? What's the "once upon a time" of this news piece?'

There is a particular art to writing TV news scripts. 'Keep it really short and always underwrite for TV. It is about pictures so never describe what you see on the screen. The pictures do a lot of the work for you so let them do that work. Write something that adds to them, something that boosts the pictures and gives them another element and that makes someone watching the picture see it in a different way.'

In her report, if Lucy needed to make a wider point about France or about a terror attack, it had to fit with the pictures and she had to keep her scripting succinct. 'You have to pack a lot into a few words so you have to distil what you're trying to say. You also have to write to the pictures, you can't just slap words on like a layer of paint.'

When structuring TV news pieces, break the mould. 'Don't be hidebound by the official structure of what you should do because the best packages work when you mix it up and let the strongest material lead the piece. Don't be afraid of breaking rules and be creative.'

> *Jina Moore was the East Africa Bureau Chief for the* New York Times *and has specialised in gender-based violence. Here she shares advice when writing and framing sensitive newspaper reports.*

Just as interview techniques are turned on their head when working with trauma survivors, it can be similar when relaying information to readers. 'Usually we're taught in print writing to get a little bit of colour to set the scene and the instinct tends to be that people try to set the scene of the violation. The effect that has when you encounter it on a page can be alienating and sensationalistic,' Jina tells me.

It struck her when she was reading a story about a rape in Congo. 'It was textbook perfect and if you didn't think about the meaning you would have got gold star honours at journalism school because it had active verbs, action took place over time, it was colourful, descriptive and dramatic.'

The article was describing a woman sitting on a bench in a public place mimicking the violation that had happened to her. 'She had been raped with the barrel of a gun or stick. So it was just totally horrifying to read and you just go, what the hell is happening here? That's when I realised the training for writing doesn't serve us very well when we're trying to write ethically and compassionately about victims of violence.'

She advises against leading your report with a description of the violence, in the same way as, in an interview, you wouldn't begin by asking someone to describe the rape. 'The operating principle I try and figure out when I'm writing is how to make people feel morally uncomfortable with the situation you are describing because we should be horrified that there was this woman raped in this fashion, but ethically comfortable with *how* you write it.'

Failing to do this can leave readers wondering about your ethics and practice. 'Some of it is about not using all the lurid details because when you read them on the page they amount to sensationalism even if that wasn't your experience when doing the interview. Some of it is about bringing in, depending on the story, context from experts who can say what this woman went through is really very normal.'

INSIGHT from interviewees

> *Roderick is black and gay and when he was imprisoned in Texas for burglary and drug possession he was nicknamed 'Coco,' repeatedly raped and sold as a sex slave by prison gangs. A jury dismissed his civil lawsuit against prison officials who, the court heard, had ignored his screams for help. But Roderick says his case meant he could tell the world what happened to him, highlight the prevalence of prison rape and campaign against trafficking and sexual violence in prison. He has told his story through US talk shows, through newspapers, radio and TV programmes, books and articles. Here he explains what he needed from journalists who were writing and framing his story and his message.*

Roderick welcomes speaking to journalists to tell his story because he wants people to understand what can happen in prison. 'My interactions with journalists have been from a more positive standpoint but I don't think they understand all of the issues that we face. I think they should be more educated around the issues and be able to convey how important the story of trafficking and sexual slavery actually is,' Roderick tells me.

He values journalists who do their research before speaking to him. 'I find it very important that people convey my story to the public in a way that makes people feel sorry for me but also makes people feel a sense of outrage, a sense that what happened to me was an injustice and should not be part of our society or community.'

By telling his story, it enabled people in authority to be held to account. 'The media is a form of protection without actually being a protector.'

When framing his story, he was keen for journalists to give a rounded picture. 'It was important to me that they were interested in showing how I feel now, where I am in my therapeutic recovery, the devastation surrounding what I went through and what I do and how I cope.'

He prefers them to use his experience as a means to telling the wider story. 'They should focus on the event in our lives, how we were victimised and move on to where we sought help, what agencies provide protection, the legal enforcement of the law and then tell their audience where we are today.'

Roderick has a clear motivation for sharing his story through the media. 'There are a lot of people who suffer in silence. There are a lot of people who live with the effects of this on a daily basis. If you've got people still living in darkness, there has to be some kind of light shed on the subject so people know what to look for and that comes from you being the reporter, the medium that expresses and shows where people are more vulnerable and where they exist.'

Facts and evidence were crucial when telling Roderick's story and he valued reporters who detailed the grievances and complaints he had made whilst in prison. 'The story has to be believed because people just don't believe these things happen in our society at all. The way that articles have been written with in-depth research means a lot of my experiences have been documented and people all over the world are familiar with what happened to me.'

He gets frustrated when articles focus on his individual story rather than highlighting the wider problems of sexual slavery and challenges reporters to get digging. 'Where's the investigative spirit, the undercover investigators going inside these prisons? It's one thing to highlight a story that's already known but go in and bring the story out.'

The following are snapshots of experiences families share about how the writing and framing of their stories may impact on them.

Avoid labelling people. Nicky, whose 6-year-old son Jack died in hospital, objected to headlines which appeared on reports about Jack's inquest. 'I didn't like "Downs Boy" headlines. He was a little boy; yes, he had Downs Syndrome. They put it in all the papers and I found it insulting. He was a little boy, his name was Jack,' Nicky tells me.

Holly, who was caught up in the terror attack on London Bridge, found it uncomfortable to be labelled a hero. 'I just did what anybody else would have done. Of course, everyone in that situation would like to think that they would help but everybody reacts differently. It can be quite embarrassing to brand your interviewee a certain way because at the end of the day I'm still alive and there are people who weren't. You have this thing called survivor's guilt.'

Alice was diagnosed with anorexia when she was 12. As a student she agreed to do interviews to raise awareness of her condition and its complexity and the need to fund mental health care. She stresses the importance of reporters avoiding mentioning anything at all to do with weights, heights, BMI or calories. 'These can cause real problems for people with eating disorders or those who are vulnerable,' she tells me. Asking for photographs of when she was thin is also disturbing for her and many like her.

Rose, who works with families bereaved through murder or manslaughter, says many struggle when they discover that once they have given their story, they cannot take it back and it can be resurrected years later. 'The family don't want that, but they are powerless to stop it,' she tells me.

Rose describes the distress it can cause when families trust a reporter with their story and the context or facts are changed. Rose has personal experience of this from when she agreed to a magazine article about the death of her daughter Avril who was 22. 'The lady read it to me over the phone and it was what I'd actually said, and I was happy with it. But when the magazine came out, I was mortified. I just wanted to run away and hide, I really was so distressed. It had been changed and bits had been added in that I hadn't said. I was so angry with her. She said it was the editor who changed it, but I wasn't told the editor would be able to do that.'

HOW I COVER SENSITIVE STORIES: DOMINIC CASCIANI

'Don't let them down.'

Dominic's first experience of covering a sensitive story was at university when he was a journalism student. A fellow student took his own life. 'I rang his mum and asked if she wanted to talk about it and she did want to talk about it because she wanted to warn other students about the mental health issues her son had experienced,' he tells me.

It meant that when he began as a newspaper reporter for the *Grimsby Evening Telegraph* in 1995, a patch he describes as a busy, hard news area with a lot of depressing stories at the time, he wasn't too scared of making contact with families when something grim had happened.

He moved from there into the BBC, writing for an early version of the news website. 'They were trying to recruit lots of people with newspaper experience because they needed good writers who could deliver crisp copy,' he explains.

As BBC Home Affairs correspondent, Dominic is part of a team which specialises in coverage of terrorism. His exclusive interview 'An Extremist in the Family' won him Interview of the Year in the 2017 Sandford St Martin Awards.

Conquering nerves

If you want to be a reporter you have to get over the fact that there are times when you're going to be nervous, says Dominic. 'When students see people doing lots of daring interviews on TV news and asking lots of tough questions, they shouldn't kid themselves that the reporters who're asking those tough questions aren't sometimes nervous about asking them, particularly in very sensitive circumstances.'

His advice is to think carefully about your motivation in asking them, how you are going to ask them and what the precise wording may be. 'Then just ask away and see what happens and respond immediately to the circumstances in front of you rather than keeping to a script.'

Early reporting of sad stories

As a local newspaper reporter, Dominic was often dispatched to knock on the doors of families who had been newly bereaved. 'I was nervous for my first one. It was a horrible accident where a man had been killed on the motorway and we had his name and had to find out what had happened. I went to see his family and his poor wife was in bits, she'd literally heard hours earlier that he'd been killed.'

He explained to the wife that there would be a piece in the evening paper because people would want to know why the motorway was closed. 'She got all that and she told the story. The whole thing was devastating and he was by all accounts a top bloke.'

An early lesson was noting the response Dominic got from the wife when he asked her about the circumstances of her husband's death. 'She really didn't want to go there, and I very quickly twigged that was a bad question to ask because that was clearly me prying into an intensely private moment. It is the kind of question in years hence I've never directly asked unless it's pretty clear it's something that somebody wants to talk about.'

You have to ask yourself if the precise details of the death are editorially relevant, he says. 'It's obvious you need to know the circumstances such as a horrible murder, when they are key to the evidence, but other circumstances you probably don't need to know and neither do the public and you should exercise some self-control.'

Dominic still applies this rule when covering terrorism-related stories. 'I meet people day in day out who have gone through absolutely extraordinary and difficult circumstances and professionally it's my job to report those events in their lives, reporting bereavements is one of them.'

'Act like a normal human being as well as a reporter, someone who understands pain,' Dominic advises. 'You're not sitting there drumming your fingers looking for the perfect quote or trying to push someone to say something they're not prepared to say in that moment and also give them a sense of what's going to happen.'

Chasing an exclusive interview

As part of a news team responsible for the coverage of terrorism, Dominic felt there was a need to understand what was happening in British Muslim communities in relation to Syria because it was clear many young people were getting caught up in it.

The team wanted to hear from a family whose child had been radicalised and gone to fight. 'What we found, unsurprisingly, was that people didn't want to talk. I think for a lot of families there was a real sense of shame, of shock and embarrassment. I think a lot of families were in complete denial about what their children were doing.'

He put out messages to many people within Muslim communities, telling them it was really important for people to hear these stories from ordinary Muslim families, to start changing some of the narrative around the security threat and radicalisations. He explained that ordinary people needed to understand how a young person gets groomed into extremist politics then takes the fateful step to get involved in foreign conflict.

Eventually, Dominic was put in touch with Nicola whose teenage son Rasheed had been radicalised, had travelled to Syria and was killed just over the border in Iraq. 'We had a bit of an email exchange where it became clear the family did want to talk and they were trying to find a journalist they could trust, who could work with them in a considered way.'

Dominic explains that Nicola appreciated it would be a national story so she wanted some sort of control over how it was told. 'What she wanted was to talk about every single step and what had happened to her son and how he'd been groomed and brainwashed into joining IS. What she didn't want was a story that was going to be reduced down to: another kid has joined the extremist group IS and got blown up fighting on the border between Syria and Iraq.'

Nurturing trust

Dominic took his time and had a series of meetings to talk about options. The first time they met, Nicola poured out a lot of detail. 'I made it clear in that first meeting it was just us talking. It was completely off the record and I wouldn't do anything with the information she was giving me at this stage until she was confident she had a clear view of who she wanted to work with.'

He also helped to manage her expectations by spelling out which aspects of her account would make it a national story, which aspects would work best for TV and which for radio or online, so she could have some understanding of the process of journalism.

They agreed to work towards running the story on the anniversary of her son's death. It helped that Nicola wanted to launch a self-help group for other families in an attempt to find something positive out of her loss.

Dominic took time to explain how the material would be used and that much of it may have to be left out. He explained that this is the nature of TV news but that sometimes it has greater impact because the reports are short and focus on the emotions.

At the other end of the spectrum, Dominic explained he would be writing an online special of 5,000 words with video, but even that wouldn't include all the details.

The award-winning interview

'It is really important to know what you're talking about before you actually start the tape rolling or open that notepad. You've got to have a clear view in your mind about what questions you are going ask and a sense of where those questions are going to go,' says Dominic, adding that sometimes key details can emerge unexpectedly so it is vital to take your time and listen.

'It just came out of the blue. It was this remarkable story which was a theory about how he had said goodbye to her. He had used all his savings to buy her this small diamond necklace. It was such an extraordinary gift that he had bought for her before going to Syria. It was only after discovering he'd gone, that it occurred to her that it had been his way of saying goodbye.'

It was such a powerful line that Dominic used it to promote the story. 'It came out of allowing the conversation to take its course, but at the same time, never losing focus. You've got to be thinking there is a new piece of information coming out there and I need to bottom that. I need to go back and clarify it so I'm getting all the facets of the story.'

Unusually for TV, the interview with Nicola ran for a lengthy two hours, and Dominic advises allowing people time to talk, even though much of what is said will not be broadcast. He explains that not only have you given them a commitment to hear their story, but also when you have edited the interview you will be telling the story in its complete form, and it will be compelling.

Telling the story

Writing his online special report about Nicola's story took time and care, 'You've got truthfully to seek out the contours of the story and make sure that you cover all those contours and you draw that map of the person's life.' This is from Dominic's award-winning feature:

> Rasheed was full of energy. Football and karate weren't enough for this growing young man. He got seriously into the adrenaline-fuelled world of free running – urban acrobatics in which walls, bus shelters and park benches become the apparatus. And he was good at it. Nicola dutifully watched her son front flip, back flip and side flip his way round Birmingham and drove him to A&E every time something went wrong. 'The joke

was that I would have taken him to Accident and Emergency so many times that he had an annual membership,' she laughs. 'Very much a risk taker. It's great when utilised in a good way – but when it's not it can take you down a bad path.'

'An Extremist in the Family,' Dominic
Casciani, 2016, www.bbc.co.uk

'When dealing with a story about some enormous human tragedy, it's so focused on human loss that the entire audience should be able to relate to it in some shape or form, so you've got to capture it correctly,' explains Dominic.

When writing, he suggests restraining your language and stating the facts. 'Just write in a very human simple way. You need to get rid of all the hyperbole. You don't need to build the story up because it's fairly obvious to the audience that what's happened is shocking or horrific so you don't need that kind of language. Let the words and events speak for themselves.'

He finds the most extraordinary stories tend to write themselves. 'If you take the time to listen to your interviewee and get a sense of the situation they've been through, just write it all down and let it flow.'

With his long-form online piece, he called in a friend and trusted editor to read it through. 'He read it over a weekend and we thrashed out a few bits which didn't work and dropped a couple of sections. You've got to bring in someone you really trust because you feel a real sense of ownership over the story and you shouldn't feel precious about it.'

Key advice

When dealing with somebody who's gone through a tragedy and they've put their trust in you to tell their story, you've got to work really hard not to let them down. If you do, you'll also be letting yourself down because of the promises you've made to them.

*Dominic describes how he filmed sequences for his
award-winning piece in the Filming chapter.*

Notes

1 Mark Brayne, 'Trauma and Journalism: A Guide for Journalists, Editors and Managers,' 2007, Dart Center for Journalism and Trauma, https://dartcenter.org (last accessed 26 January 2019).

2 Sallyanne Duncan, 'Sadly Missed: The Death Knock News Story as a Personal Narrative of Grief,' 2012, https://journals.sagepub.com.

3 Cait McMahon, Matthew Ricketson and Gary Tippet, 'Getting It Right: Ethical Reporting on Traumatised People,' 25 March 2014, https://dartcenter.org.

4 Michelle Obama, *Becoming*, Viking, 2018, p. 343.

5 Gavin Rees, 'The Trauma Factor: Reporting on Violence and Tragedy,' *Journalism: New Challenges*, Bournemouth University Media School, 2013, Ch. 25, https://microsites.bournemouth.ac.uk.

6 Dave Cullen, 'A Reporter's Lessons from Past Shootings,' 9 January 2011, https://dartcenter.org (last accessed 26 January 2019).

7 Jina Moore, 'Covering Trauma: A Training Guide,' 2011, https://www.sfcg.org.

8 Kevin Kawamoto, 'Best Practices in Trauma Reporting,' 2005, Dart Center for Journalism and Trauma.

9 Samaritans, 'Media Guidelines for Reporting Suicide,' www.samaritans.org.

10 NSVRC, 'Reporting on Sexual Violence: Tips for Journalists,' www.nsvrc.org.

11 Stefanie Friedhoff, 'The Basics: What Every Reporter Needs to Know about IPV,' 19 January 2012, https://datercenter.org (last accessed 26 January 2019).

12 Dart Center Europe tip sheet, 'Reporting on Sexual Violence,' 15 July 2011, https://dartcenter.org.

13 IPSO, 'Guidance on Reporting Sexual Offences,' www.ipso.co.uk.

14 Tory Shepherd, 'An Analysis of How Media Coverage of Child Sex Abuse Inquiries Affects Victims,' 2014, The Winston Churchill Memorial Trust of Australia, www.churchilltrust.com.au.

15 Minh Dang, 'Putting the Human in Human Trafficking Reporting: Tips for Interviewing Survivors,' The Irina Project, www.theirinaproject.org.

9
The follow-ups

'The physical injuries heal pretty quickly but you've got to live with the nightmares of what happened to you on that day ... the dead girl on my shoulder and looking at her face and survival guilt as well.'

Jeff was the last child to be rescued from the Aberfan disaster in 1966

In this chapter

Considerations when revisiting sensitive stories.

Focus on how journalists followed up their news reports.

Insight into what helps interviewees to talk about a past traumatic event.

Overview from Judith Moritz on how she covers sensitive stories.

Trauma Awareness: Post-Traumatic Stress Disorder and post-traumatic growth.

Recounting and reliving

When you are interviewing people years or even decades after they have suffered a traumatic event, avoid the assumption that they have got over it. Continue to treat them with sensitivity.

Rose Dixon's daughter Avril died suddenly nearly thirty years ago, yet when she recalls the traumatic time in an interview, the effect on Rose is profound. 'If I talk to you about walking into a mortuary and seeing my beautiful 22-year-old daughter lying on a marble slab, I can actually see the mortuary as I'm looking at you and I can smell the mortuary. I feel cold and shivery because the mortuary was very cold, and I think it is so important for people to understand. As soon as the family starts talking about their loved one, it's like it has just happened at that moment in time and they're really into the pain and trauma,' she tells me.

When you revisit people, you are often trying to report a sense of them re-building their lives: How have they fared? What issues still linger? How do they choose to remember the tragedy and the person or people who died? How are they recovering physically or emotionally from an assault? Is there a sense of hope and resilience?

They may be demanding answers, campaigning or fighting to change a policy, but they can still be hurting and, in asking them to revisit events, you can be opening emotional wounds. Tread carefully and follow the good practice out-lined in previous chapters.

'I think what reporters need to realise is that those feelings don't go away. It doesn't get any easier,' explains Nicky whose 6-year-old son Jack died in hos-pital. She still gives interviews several years after Jack's death. 'That doesn't mean they've not got to be delicate with me, not got to have any empathy. That still needs to be there whether it's early stages or years down the line.'

Asking about sexual violence

Be particularly mindful when working with people recounting being sexu-ally violated. This can cause extreme distress, with survivors potentially re-experiencing the emotions they felt when being assaulted. Be careful not to compound this in the way you work with them.

In 2014 Nadia Murad was abducted with other Yazidi women when their home village in northern Iraq was attacked by ISIS. Her mother and six brothers were killed and she was raped and beaten repeatedly before eventually escap-ing. 'My story, told honestly and matter-of-factly, is the best weapon I have against terrorism and I plan on using it until those terrorists are put on trial,' she says in her autobiography *The Last Girl: My Story of Captivity and My Fight against the Islamic State*.[1]

But she reveals how hard it is to keep recounting what happened. 'It never gets easier to tell your story. Each time you speak it, you relive it,' she explains. 'I am transported back to those moments and all their terror. Other Yazidis are pulled back into these memories too.'

For a UK Channel 5 documentary called *Raped: My Story*, ten people spoke publicly for the first time about what had happened to them. Directly to cam-era, they told their stories of being raped, and described their experiences of the legal process. Fay Maxted, CEO of The Survivors Trust charity, was closely involved in the programme made by Lambent Productions. 'The survivors were incredibly brave in offering to waive their anonymity in this way and in talking so openly about their experiences,' Fay tells me, and explains how the producers were determined to make sure no one would be harmed through their involvement in the documentary. 'This entailed ensuring the psychological welfare of the participants was safeguarded at all times. The impact of the process of filming and broadcasting was considered in detail for each of the survivors who wished to participate, including the impact of their case not being included in the final documentary.' She adds that the documentary is now used in training settings for the police and other professionals.

Fay emphasises the need to be clear, when you plan your interview. 'Be aware that the survivor may not have fully considered the impact on them of publishing their experiences, particularly if they opt out of anonymity,' she explains. 'Ensure the survivor has given informed consent, with an understanding of what will be included, where and for how long the piece will be available. It is good practice to allow them to see the final copy before it is published and to be able to withdraw any or all of their comments if they wish to at any time,' she says.

When the Australian journalist Tory Shepherd investigated the media's reporting of child sex abuse inquiries, she spoke with many survivors. 'One of the best outcomes is when journalists stay involved throughout the process, let interviewees know when the story is likely to run and do a thorough follow up. Otherwise it can seem like someone taking advantage for a one-day story, then dropping the subject,' she found.[2]

When reporting on-the-day news, it is not always possible to have this level of involvement. Do take time, however, to contact and talk to your interviewee, particularly after your piece has aired or been published.

Occasionally, some reporters have told me how interviewees have become dependent on them. This can happen when you work together closely over a lengthy period of time. In these cases, manage expectations carefully, avoid acting as their intermediary with the authorities, and establish your boundaries, tactfully but clearly, early in the relationship.

Covering anniversaries

Anniversaries of tragic events can be complex and particularly painful times for survivors. News organisations are able to prepare in advance, unlike with a breaking story. Handled with care, their coverage can give a sense of how people are coping, commemorate their losses and clarify events surrounding what happened.

Try not to over-simplify the event. People will each have reacted differently, and one or two people cannot speak for a whole community. As Pam Dix, of the charity Disaster Action, whose brother was killed in the bombing of Pan Am Flight 103 over Lockerbie in 1988, explains, 'Recalling and remembering and memorialising are incredibly important to people affected by incidents.' She suggests journalists should report generally on the event and use some personal voices, 'but not to say this voice or that voice is representative of *the* Survivors or *the* Bereaved.'

Anne Eyre is a survivor of the Hillsborough disaster of 1989 and explains how it feels when anniversaries loom. 'You start to get anxious because you want to face it on the one hand and you want to run away on the other.'

There is no excuse for a 'door knock' or impromptu approach on these stories. Interviewees need to be carefully prepared and briefed well before an anniversary, not just contacted the day before. 'Being blindsided on the day is never good,' explains Anne, and both women stress the importance of doing your research. 'Some of the most obvious things like: "How do you and your husband feel about this?" Where the answer turns out to be: "Well actually it was my husband who was killed!" Can't you just look something up? Get a little bit of the groundwork done,' adds Pam.[3]

When approaching, interviewing and filming with people in these situations, it is important to apply all the good practice from the previous chapters. If you have taken the time, intermittently, to keep in touch with a family since covering their breaking story, this contact will pay dividends both professionally and personally for you and for them when the anniversaries come round.

Covering court cases and inquests

These can happen months and even years after a crime or death. I believe journalists covering a trial should give the victim, or the victim's family, a chance to have their say after a guilty verdict. The court case will, by its very nature, focus on the accused. Through the media, the family may have the chance to express publicly how the crime has impacted on them.

At trials and inquests, you may catch up with old faces from other news outlets, on the press bench or in the court precincts. You often check facts and spellings together and can chat about the case. But be mindful of how you may appear to the family you are hoping to interview. They are likely to be sitting close by in the public gallery and may be feeling vulnerable, fearful or angry. The switch from banter to concern can seem false when you make your approach to them. This also applies if you have already filmed a background piece with the family. They will rightly expect you to appreciate how gruelling they are finding the experience of the trial or inquest.

Make sure you know the legalities of who you can and cannot interview during a trial and never compromise legal proceedings.

Sometimes, families can be surprised to see you at an inquest, but you are allowed to go and have a legal right to report them. Be mindful that inquests, like court cases, can be profoundly distressing for families. Take care that what you publish is neither insensitive nor unnecessarily graphic and that it is reported accurately. Remember that, when covering a suicide, you may not report the method in detail. (See the Ethics and Writing chapters.)

In the IPSO guidance on reporting deaths and inquests, it states that if families ask journalists to stop asking questions or photographing them, they should stop.[4]

Be aware that these are difficult times for your interviewees. 'For the reporter, anniversaries and other occasions like court cases, where the bereaved person is likely to be strongly reminded of their loved one, will be highly sensitized times to approach the relatives,' Sallyanne Duncan points out.[5]

Approaching at court cases and inquests

Approaching family members for an interview when they are attending a trial or inquest is clearly different from speaking to them in their home. In the *Insight* section of this chapter, Sharon spells out how families at court are struggling with yet more distress. It can be profoundly disturbing for them to hear in unvarnished detail how someone they loved met their death, especially when they can see the person who may be to blame.

They are trying to follow what is happening, they are in unfamiliar business-like surroundings and they can be working hard to keep a lid on their emotions. Be careful, if you do speak with them, not to press emotional buttons and unleash what they are trying hard to contain. Approach them with compassion and 'a professional friendliness,' as Sharon suggests. After a guilty verdict, outside the court, they may wish to give full vent to their emotions.

It's generally preferable to make your approach sensitively, before the end of the trial, rather than *en masse*, outside court after the verdict.

One tip I would hand on about approaching families at court, via their police family liaison officer or police press officer, or through their lawyer at an inquest, is this: rather than asking them to check if the family are giving interviews, ask them instead if you may have a quiet word with the family. This allows you to make a human connection and to reassure the family that filming with them would be a low key process. A press officer is likely to ask them if they want to do TV media interviews which, to a family, may seem daunting and off-putting.

Added stress

As you cover people's ongoing quest for justice or answers, never underestimate the added distress for bereaved families of each twist and turn. In the wake of traumatic events, such as a terrorist shooting abroad, they have to contend with a range of stressors. As Stephen Regel points out in his book *Post-Traumatic Stress: The Facts*, 'The flow of information can be inconsistent, and affected people have to deal with information that is highly graphic and traumatic, such as coroners' reports.' He adds it may affect their finances, family relationships and their jobs. 'Preoccupation with the traumatic event can also naturally, and sometimes seriously, disrupt normal parenting patterns. This in turn can contribute to confusion and distress in surviving children and, at worst, to truancy and antisocial and criminal behaviour.'[6]

Even if you are covering their unfolding stories years down the line, apply the same sensitivity. I followed the story of a mother whose young daughter had drowned, on a sailing holiday in Greece. It took the mother thirteen years of fighting through the Greek and British courts to get some kind of justice for what had happened to her child. Her grief, though less raw, was as palpable in her final interview as it had been in her first.

FOCUS on journalists

As BBC North of England correspondent, Judith Moritz regularly covers court cases, inquests and inquiries which follow in the wake of tragic events. They are also often attended by the families of victims. Judith gives an overview of her work at the end of this chapter.

Having sat on many press benches at trials and inquests, Judith adds her observations. 'In our press bench mentality there are lots of hacks sitting together and seeing it as a place of work and for people who are yards away it is nothing like a place of work. They're there because they're having a major life experience. Be sensitive to that, be aware of that and tailor your behaviour accordingly,' Judith tells me.

The close proximity can offer an opportunity to talk to families. 'I've covered court cases that have lasted for several weeks. All the journalists will always go at the beginning and they'll always go at the end but there may be a stretch of time in the middle where it's a little bit quieter. The families will go every day so that can be a good opportunity to speak to people.'

Use your common sense when choosing to make an approach. 'If it's someone who's lost a loved one through murder or through a tragedy like Hillsborough, some families welcome that approach and others don't. There are ways of checking that it's going to be okay without blundering straight in.'

Be aware of the evidence they'll be sitting through on a particular day. 'Are they listening to something which is new to them or upsetting and graphic in the courtroom? Pick your moment sensitively so you're not wading in at the wrong time.'

Dress appropriately when covering court cases and inquests. 'There's how you look on screen and how you dress within the courtroom and generally if you're being respectful the two go hand in hand.'

It is inappropriate to wear jeans or appear scruffy in court. 'You might have to stand up and address the judge which is rare but not impossible. If you're going on screen afterwards wear a jacket, cover up and don't look flamboyant or inappropriate, wear something respectful.'

Your outfit shouldn't distract the audience from listening to the story. 'You are part of the story but you are not the story as a reporter. You need to wear something which is not controversial or loud and no slogans.'

When covering an inquest, be aware that the family are there to find out how that person died. 'If they're going to speak publicly, one of their motivating factors will be that they want the public to know the truth about their loved one. So if you are approaching a bereaved relative for an interview around the time of an inquest you must make sure that they have the chance to talk about that person: What were they like? What will you remember about them? Have you got any photographs or video? That will just help people to understand that this was a real human being that they're badly missing.'

Judith covered the case of a child who had anorexia and took her own life. 'The family in that case wanted to speak so people could understand the pain and distress anorexia causes. They wanted people to see the gravity of it, but they also wanted people to see the full picture of their child and what she'd been like.'

If you are not used to going into courtrooms and inquest hearings it can feel foreboding and difficult and complicated. 'If you just take a step back, it is a formal way of doing it but it is a way of telling somebody's story and you need to get to that.' There is more from Judith, about how she covers sensitive stories, at the end of this chapter

> The reporter and documentary maker Simon Hare won a Royal Television Society award for his coverage of the Philpott case. In 2013, the parents of six children were convicted of killing them in a house fire.

When the children died in the fire no one knew their parents were to blame and Simon was sent to the scene along with many reporters. 'I've only been attacked twice in my life as a journalist and that day of the fire was one of them. There was a lot of anger and a lot of pain and people lash out at reporters.'

Building a relationship with people over time and treating them well, paid off. 'It's like Aesop's fable with the sun and the wind trying to get the coat off the guy. If you treat people gently, if you're friendly and warm with them you are more likely to get an interview rather than being aggressive or pestering people.'

To cover the Philpott case over the following months, Simon worked closely with the community. The eventual trial lasted a month and the pressure was intense. 'Everyone is getting backgrounders ready to run at the end of the case, should there be a guilty verdict. Obviously it's incredibly important that you don't interview someone before they've given evidence. That's something that isn't emphasised enough.'

Covering such a trial can be gruelling, with many demands to deliver material to different news outlets. 'Long term it's exhausting, you have to structure your coverage. The demand was huge and you're also trying to compile stuff to run at the end. The whole case dominated my life for a year.'

Some reporters were paying for interviews. 'You can't compete with money being thrown at them so you're not going to get every interview, you just need enough to tell the story.'

At the end of the trial when the parents were convicted, Simon's programme was aired and it finished with a montage about the six children. 'It was such a horrific story and we'd told how the kids died, what role the parents had played in it and how the police had solved it. I felt we needed a reminder at the end that it was six kids.'

The montage showed photos of each of the children with a description of what each child was like, mixed with short clips from people within the community. 'Although this was a big story that journalists got excited about and the police solved, six kids lost their lives and it was showing who they were; one wanted to be a fireman, one a footballer, another loved her pet rabbit.'

Simon followed the story closely and when the children's gravestones were put in place in the cemetery the relatives allowed him to film it. 'One of the women, who had been there when I'd been attacked, thanked me for how I had dealt with them.'

Simon still keeps in touch with some of the family members. 'You're not a friend but you're a trusted ally and people say, "you're the only one I can trust" but I've earned that.'

When writing about the case, Simon was careful to keep it simple. 'Don't be too shmaltzy or over-dramatic or sickly. After the Philpott programme we got lots of emails, texts and tweets saying it was brilliant and what they liked about it was that it wasn't sensationalist. It was clear, very measured and very calm and had the montage at the end. For the audience to contact us and say that, that was worth more than anything really.'

As a video journalist Navtej Johal can be under pressure to deliver daily news pieces but works to maintain ongoing contact with his sensitive sources.

If your opening premise in securing an interview is that you are going to handle people sensitively then you have to carry that through. 'That means staying in touch with the interviewee but not pestering them. Every few months, just check in and ask how they're doing,' Navtej tells me.

He will maintain contact in whichever way suits his interviewee. 'Some of them like using Facebook messenger and I'll drop them a message now and again. Some of them follow me on Twitter so I might DM them as well but normally I find text or email is the best way, rather than going on social media.'

In one case he covered an inquest into a woman who died and the doctor had been partly at fault. 'The father remained very angry at the end of the inquest so I stayed in touch with him finding out what steps he was taking legally. With him it's a case of checking how things are going and how he's coping and not pushing it.'

Some interviewees need more input than others. 'There might be the odd occasion where they want to meet up or they might want a longer phone call and again I would say I know everyone's busy but try and make time for that. The more you delay it the more likely they are to take the story elsewhere because they feel you don't care anymore.'

Some stories involve a one-off relationship, but many tragic stories will run. 'In those ones, put the effort in and it doesn't need to be a lot, it can be just every few months asking how they are.'

INSIGHT from interviewees

On the morning of 21 October 1966, coal slurry slid down the mountain above the Welsh village of Aberfan. It engulfed buildings including the junior school killing 116 children and 28 adults. It was a catastrophic disaster which has captured international media attention ever since with countless anniversary stories across more than fifty years. Jeff was 8 and trapped inside the school, becoming the last child to be rescued. Here he shares insight into the impact on him and his community when the world's media descends and he offers sound advice to reporters when covering the anniversaries of tragedies.

Every time Jeff sees footage of a disaster anywhere in the world he is transported back to the classroom where he lay trapped more than fifty years ago. The traumatic memory is so vivid he can instantly smell the coal. 'Out of my class of thirty-four, only four of us survived. So I was buried under the debris that came down from the tip as well as the roof. The only reason I survived and didn't perish on that day was because I had a pocket of air to breathe until the rescuers came and dug me out.'

Jeff describes the huge impact his experience has had on him. 'The physical injuries heal pretty quickly but you've got to live with the nightmares of what happened to you on that day, in my case the dead girl on my shoulder and looking at her face and survival guilt as well.'

With colossal media attention focused on Aberfan over the years, Jeff has chosen to share his story with reporters and admits that, on the whole, the process of doing so has been cathartic. 'I think by speaking about it, I've tried to encourage others to speak about what happened to them too because that helps us in our recovery,' he tells me.

Advice he would give to reporters is to always make an appointment. When covering an anniversary there is no excuse for turning up on spec. 'I feel quite angry really because I'm a busy person but just to turn up out of the blue and want an interview with you is totally unacceptable.'

He also advises journalists to do their research because if you're covering the anniversary of an event, there is no reason for not knowing the facts. Ignorance can prompt hurtful questions. 'If you ask silly basic questions you won't get a good story out of people. How many people died? When did it happen? Was it on a Friday? It's stupid basic stuff that they should know.'

Jeff described how one reporter asked a woman if she had lost a child. 'She had lost two children. It was totally inappropriate and upsets people,' explains Jeff.

Every tenth anniversary heralds huge media focus on Jeff's home village. 'You get invaded by people from the BBC, ITV, Sky and all sorts of press and international press and it heightens that sense of anxiety. A lot of people want to do their grieving in isolation, others are able to engage.'

Attitude is key. 'What's important is you don't have people saying I'm a superstar on a major network and then think the world is going to fall about you because it doesn't. It's about the people themselves, not the person who's doing the interview,' explains Jeff.

Being pushy won't work and Jeff says the best reporters are the ones who make a connection then stay in touch and build up a relationship. 'Make sure you keep in contact after you've done the interview because people want support. You've opened up a lot of wounds and they need reassurance from you that you are interested in them as individuals, not just getting the story and then moving on.'

Jeff explains that some people can feel violated if they open up to reporters, never to hear from them again. 'One lady was open and frank about how it had affected her. She had lost children in the disaster but after the interview she felt like she'd been raped because she had been open about it all and as soon as they went, it was over for them.' He adds that a good reporter would go back and ask if everything was okay, maintain a link with the community and show an interest in the person. 'A bad reporter would just disappear and you never see them again.'

When interviewing people at the anniversary of a disaster, Jeff says it's vital to ask questions softly, show empathy, put people at ease and have an understanding of how that person may be feeling. 'Talk around the subject, ask how it affected them, what were the short- and medium-term consequences. Most communities want to move on rather than look back, so I wouldn't dwell on the past. You can ask the impact of what happened to them on the day but also ask them what their outlook is for the future.'

Although it gets easier as time passes, it is still very difficult for people to talk about. A special service is held at the cemetery in Aberfan on the morning of 21 October but Jeff explains how hard it still is for him to walk past all the graves. 'They are people of my age eight, nine and ten years and I don't see the graves, I see the children.'

> *Sharon spent three days in court hearing the details of how her only child Louise was dragged under the wheels of a lorry and killed. The driver was convicted of causing her death by careless driving. Here, Sharon explains to reporters how it feels to be sitting through a trial and how best to talk to families during court cases or inquests.*

Court cases revolve around the accused person with little reference to the impact his actions have had on the victim's family. Sharon agreed to be interviewed to make people aware of how devastated she was by her daughter's death. Although she chose to speak to reporters, she explains they needed to make allowances for her because conversations at court are very different from conversations at home.

'When you get to court, it's a whole new raft of emotions: anger, grief. You don't want to break down, you want to know what's going on and to be as alert as possible,' Sharon tells me.

'I was spoken to with professional friendliness and in a business-like way because if reporters start getting a bit over-zealous and over-sympathetic then what you're trying to hold together suddenly starts to crumble. I appreciated there was just enough sympathy to show that they were genuinely sorry for the situation but asking questions in a respectful way and guiding you through without being over-gushing or over-sympathetic.'

After the verdict, outside the court families may then wish to vent their reactions and emotions more fully.

She explains that reporters will get more cooperation if they work with families rather than firing questions. 'Treat them as a person, as an equal and don't treat them as a commodity to get something out of, we're not. We're very vulnerable, we want to help, we want to work with you but be mindful of the situation we are in and don't be intrusive.'

> Rose works with many families supporting them through murder trials. If the reporter has not worked with the family prior to the court case, she suggests approaching them through a third party such as the police family liaison officer.

Rose explains why a family may not wish to be approached directly by a court reporter. 'They will have listened to a lot of traumatic material. They've probably sat through minute detail of the injuries that their loved one has suffered. They will have had to sit through the defence almost trying to say it was the victim's fault and that the killer isn't a bad person. It's so traumatic for them, that being approached by the media at that point is probably not a good idea.'

She also makes the observation that reporters sit at their own press bench, with a privileged view of the proceedings, whereas the victim's family has to sit in the public gallery often alongside the family of the alleged killer.

HOW I COVER SENSITIVE STORIES: JUDITH MORITZ

'Basic courtesy goes a long way.'

While studying for her English degree, Judith did a raft of work experience in newsrooms and was selected as a BBC news trainee.

As the BBC's North of England correspondent, Judith works across all network news programmes reporting for TV and radio. On any given day, she can report for the six and ten o'clock news, the Radio Four *Today* programme, 5 Live and the news summaries on Radio Two. She also provides copy and digital video for the news online website.

As a general news correspondent she is often covering a variety of highly sensitive stories. Judith was heavily involved in coverage of the Manchester Arena bombing in 2017. She also worked with families of the Hillsborough football stadium disaster in which ninety-six people were killed.

She covered the Rochdale grooming scandal, which led to convictions in 2012. Forty-seven under-age girls were identified as being victims of child sexual exploitation.

Hearing from the people affected

Telling stories through the people they affect is vital, says Judith. 'The job of the correspondent is to make a connection as directly as you can between the viewer, the listener and the person about whom the story centres,' she tells me. 'There is room elsewhere for policy journalism and pieces which deal with theoretical matters. But if I'm telling a story about a human situation then I have to hear directly from the people who are personally affected. That is how the audience are best placed to understand the impact, the importance of it.'

Treat them well

You are a human being and they are a human being and you forget that at your peril, Judith explains. 'It is common courtesy and common decency to treat someone as you would want to be treated if, God forbid, you were in that situation yourself. So I always approach every interview with that sort of perspective.'

'I also think the audience will sound you out quickly if you come across as falling short of that or talking to somebody in an unsympathetic or overly voyeuristic or probing or pushy way.'

Although it is essential that you do not exacerbate their suffering, it is also important to ask the questions that need to be asked. 'Be tough in questioning if that's required but treating people with decency and courtesy and making sure they have the room to speak about a very difficult experience, if you do that properly then that has its own power.'

Be mindful of giving people time and space to tell their stories. 'I spoke to a man who had lost four of his grandchildren in a house fire and that was a very emotional interview which took a long time. But that was because it was so important for me to allow him to pace himself,' explains Judith.

Approaching people at difficult times

Judith explains that there cannot be a standardised way of approaching people because everybody is different and that in itself is important to remember. 'Before you speak to that person you need to just think for a moment about how they're likely to receive the approach. Are you talking to somebody who's lost a child? Are you talking to someone who is likely to be struggling to make a quick or rational decision? What sort of experiences have they had? I tailor my approach depending very much on who it is that I'm trying to do the interview with.'

Judith made many approaches to families in the wake of the Manchester Arena bombing. 'I think it's just the real basics, treat somebody else how you would expect to be treated,' she tells me, adding you have to expect that it may take time to secure the interview. 'It's not necessarily something that you're going to be able to get on the first day of the attack happening. People take a while to feel able to speak publicly in some cases.'

To secure interviews, she worked closely with the police and also, where children had died, she contacted their schools to ask if they would approach the family on her behalf. 'We wrote letters as a respectful way of making an approach, so the family could then read it and respond in their own time. We checked with the police whether it was all right to approach families and when it wasn't, we didn't.'

'I never made an assumption that someone would want to speak for the sake of it. People have to have a reason for going public. When you lose a relative in the eye of the storm of that sort of disaster, in such a public way with so much media attention, you have to decide either to make yourself public or request to be left alone entirely. Of all the Manchester families, some did the former and some did the latter.'

When they chose to speak to her, Judith tried to clarify their agenda and find out what they wanted to get across so they felt accommodated. 'Make sure before you do an interview of that sort of sensitivity that you're not giving interviewees a false idea of what's going to come of it. I would always be honest and open with anybody in that situation about where the interview is going to be used, how it's going to be used, how much coverage it's likely to have, which programmes it'll go on.'

She adds, 'I think there's a duty of care if you're going to speak to somebody who's had that level of public attention attached to bereavement. There was world attention attached to the interviews and if you never contact them again, I think that's irresponsible.'

Interviewing sensitively

Judith will take time to talk through any areas which may be particularly difficult to go into, so her interviewees feel more comfortable. She doesn't have her questions ready in advance, preferring instead to see where the conversation leads. 'I have in my mind an idea about where I want the interview to go and I might have an idea about certain topics I need to cover. I might arrange it chronologically or it may be more complicated. The person may dart around in their recollection so the interview will find its form depending on the conversation we're having and the answers I get.'

As Judith explains, it is important to adapt. 'It's a courtesy to listen fully and not interrupt and not give the appearance that you're not interested in the interviewee's story. But if you listen properly, it will also do you a service because it will help you to form the next question.'

'There is a skill in knowing when, in an interview, to ask a question that is going to be difficult to deal with and just making sure you don't chuck it in at the beginning. Keep an eye on the person you are interviewing whilst it's underway: Are they okay? Do they need to take some time out? Do they need to have a break? Make sure that they understand that it's okay and they're not there to be examined and grilled. Recognise and respect that it's a big effort for them to tell their story and give them the time and courtesy that that demands.'

She defines difficult questions as ones which are likely to provoke extra emotion; questions which ask them to relive what happened such as remembering the night they found out about the attack, or about losing their relative, or about going to look for them. 'That might provide you with some very powerful testimony but you have to ask the question carefully or you're going to prolong the upset. It is sensitive handling in such a way that enables you to ask that question at the right moment so you get the best answer.'

Filming with people who have been sexually abused

Judith says that when she works with people who were abused as children, she always allows time. 'You never rush somebody that you're interviewing in that situation.'

She described an interview with a man who was in his seventies who had been sexually abused by a politician. 'The abuse was more than fifty years ago but he was extremely emotional. It was a very painful thing to speak about. I would always advise everybody to take a little bit of time to speak to the interviewee before you begin.'

'Be completely clear with them when you are recording and when you are not recording,' she adds.

In this particular case, it was clear to Judith that the man wanted to tell his story and it was cathartic to do so. But it was important for him to tell his whole story chronologically, because that was how he had organised it in his mind. Judith's job was to take time to listen and not rush him. 'I probably spent over an hour doing the interview. We used far less and I explained that to him.'

In agreeing to the interview, the man wanted to remain anonymous, as did a young girl Judith interviewed when covering the teenage grooming case in Rochdale. 'With victims of sexual abuse you are required by law to anonymise them unless they have given written consent to waive their anonymity,' explains Judith. In both cases, she made sure that they, or the person they were with, looked at the shots on the camera to reassure them they could not be identified.

Prepare as much as you can

Do as much preparation as possible. 'Find out as much as you can before the interview about the person you're going to be speaking to and about the person they've lost. There may not be much information available but, if you haven't done your research first of all, you can look stupid. Worse than that, you may find yourself being insensitive about something that you hadn't realised.'

She suggests checking the date to see if it may be the birthday of the person they have lost, in which case the family may prefer to be left alone that day. Checking facts such as how names are spelt is crucial. 'It may seem like a small detail but to that family it's a really big deal. Also ask permission to use photographs because there's a lot of material that is digitally available now which you can lift off the internet, but courtesy goes a long way.'

Covering the Hillsborough inquests

Judith has reported many inquests but the Hillsborough hearings stand apart because they were, she says, 'uniquely enormous.' They lasted two years up to 2016 and covered the deaths of ninety-six men, women and children killed in the football stadium crush in 1989. The original inquest verdicts had been quashed.

'One of the things which the families found difficult about the first set of inquests in 1990 was that the individual victims who had died were presented to the court by number,' explains Judith. This time around, every effort was made to reflect the individuals who had died so, for the first time in a British inquest, the process began with pen portraits about them. 'Ninety-six individual accounts were read out to the court by each family about the pop music they liked, the clothes they liked to wear, what they did at school, what their characters were like. Those people came alive to the court and to the public through that process.'

It was a vast process for journalists to report and reflect. To do so, Judith offered each family the opportunity to read their pen portrait to camera. Not everybody agreed, but many chose to do so, and their accounts were then put online.

Key advice

It is about respect. Treat somebody as you would hope to be treated, and listen. Always listen.

Trauma Awareness

Exposure to traumatic events, such as natural disasters, transportation accidents, terror attacks and sexual assault, has the potential to have a lasting psychological impact on survivors. In many cases, they will improve over time but some people go on to develop the more disabling

Post-Traumatic Stress Disorder (PTSD). This is when reactions, which are often normal after exposure to traumatic events, become more intense in frequency, intensity and duration.

PTSD can occur weeks or months after the event and, if untreated, can last for many years. It is often considered to be 'complex' trauma, especially for those who have experienced repeated or prolonged trauma through neglect, abuse, or having been a victim of torture or held hostage, rather than a single event, such as an assault or road accident. However, current research indicates that a 'complex presentation' can also occur after single events.

Greater sensitivity is needed if your interviewee experienced the trauma as a child, the trauma involved a bereavement, or they may not have spoken about the experience for many years.

What may they be going through?

- Anxiety, fear and panic attacks.
- Numbness, emotional blunting and detachment.
- Avoidance of any reminders of the original trauma.
- Depression.
- Guilt and shame.
- Destructive behaviours such as alcohol or drug abuse.
- Disturbed sleep and nightmares.
- Re-experiencing the event through 'flashbacks' – this will present as the person feeling as though the event was happening again, e.g. experiencing smells or taste associated with the experience.
- Irritability and anger.
- Poor concentration.

These symptoms can worsen over time and their distress can be prolonged if they are caught up in litigation such as claiming compensation or going through the protracted experiences of multiple inquests, formal reviews or inquiries, e.g. Grenfell or Hillsborough.

Bear in mind when interviewing someone some time after the event that their memories may often be linked to strong negative emotions which may emerge in the interview.

Avoid using the term PTSD unless it is relevant to the story, the person has been diagnosed by a medical professional and they are happy for you to use it.

Some people may have experienced positive changes after exposure to trauma and loss. This is often referred to as post-traumatic growth and is usually characterised by the following changes:

- Relationships are enhanced in some way – valuing friends and family more, feeling increased compassion and kindness for others.
- Changing one's view of oneself – having a greater sense of personal resilience, wisdom and strength coupled with a greater acceptance of vulnerabilities and strengths.
- Changes in life philosophy – shifts in understanding of what really matters, finding a fresh appreciation of each new day, possible changes in spiritual beliefs.

Points for discussion

What do you need to be mindful of when covering stories such as ongoing medical negligence cases, industrial accident claims, inquests, inquiries or court cases when people are involved in lengthy legal action?

What are the sensitivities around asking someone to remember, recall or relive a traumatic event?

In your follow-up stories, why may it be important to report positive outcomes of a traumatic event?

Notes

1   Nadia Murad and Jenna Krajeski, *The Last Girl*, Virago, 2018.

2   Tory Shepherd, 'An Analysis of How Media Coverage of Child Sex Abuse Inquiries Affects Victims,' 2014, The Winston Churchill Memorial Trust of Australia, www.churchilltrust.com.au (last accessed 7 February 2019).

3   Gavin Rees, Anne Eyre and Pamela Dix, 'Interview Excerpt on Covering Tragic Anniversaries,' 21 October 2016, https://dartcenter.org (last accessed 25 January 2019).

4   IPSO, 'Guidance on Reporting Deaths and Inquests,' 2018, p. 3, www.ipso.co.uk (last accessed 25 January 2019).

5   Sallyanne Duncan, 'Sadly Missed: The Death Knock News Story as a Personal Narrative of Grief,' 2012, https://journals.sagepub.com.

6   S. Regel and S. Joseph, *Post-Traumatic Stress: The Facts*, 2nd edn, Oxford University Press, 2017, pp. 49, 50.

10

The self-care

Cait McMahon

The Dart Center for Journalism and Trauma is an internationally respected organisation. It is a project of the Columbia University Journalism School. It is part think-tank, part training organisation, which collaborates with an international network of journalists, filmmakers and trauma specialists who are dedicated to promoting best practice in reporting tragedy and violence. You will find a rich seam of tips, articles and advice on its website, https://dartcenter.org.

Dr Cait McMahon is a psychologist and the founding managing director of Dart Center Asia Pacific. Her interest in journalism and trauma began when she worked as staff counsellor at *The Age* newspaper in Melbourne. Her subsequent PhD focused on Australian trauma-reporting journalists, post-traumatic stress and post-traumatic growth. Cait has received a Medal of the Order of Australia (OAM), one of Australia's highest civil accolades, for her work with journalists and trauma. Here she advises reporters how best to look after themselves and each other when covering emotionally sensitive stories.

> I remember an incident that took place about two weeks after the tsunami 26 December 2004. I had been in one of the worst-hit areas, where the stench of death hung over everything like low-hanging smog. When I returned home, family members told me I looked ashen, my eyes were in sockets an inch deep and I was moody. I had seen so much death that it was becoming unbearable.
>
> When I returned to the office, I told some of my colleagues what I was feeling. Some consoled me, but most were too over-worked to pay much attention to my whining. But a remark from a senior pro remains fresh. 'What is this nonsense about seeing dead bodies? All of us have seen them. I saw 13 dead bodies once,' he barked. The words were searing, because they came from someone I respected very much.
>
> But all of them were wrong. In fact, by creating an environment where a poorly held up façade dictated that no emotions (especially those of pain and sorrow) are allowed, we made it a living hell for most of us. This was

especially true for reporters like me who had voluntarily (or otherwise) taken to covering the war (Sri Lankan civil war).

Trauma does affect journalists. It impacts their physical and emotional wellbeing, as well as their work. I learnt that late in my career, and hope and pray the new generation does not have to wait that long.

Amantha Perera, freelancer, Sri Lanka, https://dartcenter.
org/content/trauma-in-course-duty

Potential reactions for journalists post-trauma exposure

Trauma exposure may stir up many reactions in people that are not at a clinical or diagnostic level. We have become aware of the impacts of Post-Traumatic Stress Disorder as an adverse trauma response, but most journalists don't experience this. Many do however experience several other responses that can get in the way of being able to live life to the full. Being self-aware and learning to identify your default reactions is an important start in applying self-care strategies. Whilst we may react differently in diverse situations, by and large we have default reactions that we revert to under extreme stress or in the face of trauma – one person may get a little tick in their left eye and tend to not want to talk to people. Another may get tense shoulders and become angry. Identifying your own reactions is the first step in knowing when you need to increase your self-care.

A way to remember how humans may be impacted after trauma exposure is to say that we all 'BEEP' under extreme stress or trauma exposure. That is, the reactions to these pressures impact our **B**ehaviour, **E**motions, **E**xistential thinking and our **P**hysicality.

It is best to identify your default reactions early, before they manifest as something overwhelming. So, this means applying a time for a daily 'check-in' on how we are doing to monitor our wellbeing and identify the indicators that tell us whether we need to increase our self-care that day. Usually a reaction that is out of the ordinary of our usual way of being is an indicator that all is not well.

Behavioural

Changes in behaviour of trauma-affected persons have been well documented in the general population (Green et al., 2005; Pat-Horenczyk et al., 2007), but also in journalists exposed to adverse events (McMahon, 2016). It is important to learn about your own potential behaviour changes and ask yourself if you experience any of these changes when extremely stressed or trauma-exposed:

Do I withdraw?
Do I talk excessively?

Do I go out and get drunk more often?

Do I miss deadlines?

Can't concentrate?

Do I avoid places, people, things?

Do I become more argumentative than usual?

Do I become involved in risk-taking or self-destructive behaviours more than usual?

Am I having sleep difficulties?

Emotional

The impact on our emotions is probably one of the first reactions we notice and is also probably the most researched. Impact following trauma exposure on journalists' emotions has been well documented (e.g. Backholm and Björkqvist, 2012 a, b; McMahon, 2001). Check in with yourself and ask:

Do I become more teary?

Do I become sadder?

Do I fly into fits of rage?

Do I become angrier?

Do I feel more vulnerable?

Do I feel over-elated or a bit manic?

Do I feel more guilt or shame than usual?

Am I more jumpy or agitated at the moment?

Existential

Trauma exposure may shatter a person's understanding about how the world operates – that it is a safe and benevolent place (Janoff-Bulman, 2004). The world, post-trauma, may feel unsafe. For journalists, covering tragedy has been found to compromise one's existential being (Muller, 2010). Ask yourself:

Do I start questioning my professional capability?

Do I experience 'compassion fatigue' (where I don't care about people's pain and suffering any longer)?

Do I say 'why me' / 'I am hopeless' / 'I can't do this' – doubting myself more than usual?

Do I ask why would God/Allah/Yahweh/the universe allow this? do this to me? do this to others?

Do I question the mission of journalism or my commitment to it?

Do I feel that my values are being compromised?

Physical

Complaints such as stomach upsets, back-aches, headaches, sleeplessness, to name a few, have been identified in journalists following trauma exposure (Feinstein, 2012; Hatanaka et al., 2010; McMahon, 2001).

If you are feeling physically unwell, and you have recently been exposed to an event that has been shocking or tragic, your physical reactions may be associated with the trauma exposure – or may not. If you are feeling debilitated physically it is always best to get checked by a doctor, but maybe find one who has some understanding of how the psychological and physical work together in the face of trauma.

During trauma exposure, or immediately after, it is not unusual to feel:

Nauseous.
A need to use the toilet quickly.
Shaky.
Teary.
Slightly 'fuzzy.'
A little dissociative.

(This list is not exhaustive.)

Preparing before trauma exposure

It is suggested that preparing yourself physically and mentally before a potentially traumatic assignment is the best technique, following the B, D, A – Before, During and After – reporting principle.

Before assignment

Prepare your professional skills. Make sure you are clear (as much as possible) about what you are going to report on. What professional skills do you need to have at the ready? What tools of trade do you need to take with you?

Organise social support. If you know beforehand that this will be a potentially traumatic story, organise beforehand with a mentor or buddy that you can defuse with when you return.

Create inoculation files. If you are fearful of doing a particular story, for example an Australian bushfire, speak in depth with a colleague who has reported on one. Ask them to inform you of what it is like – what does intense smoke smell like, what is the sound of a roaring fire, what does intense radiant heat from a large fire feel like, what is the distress of the victims like, and so forth. Once you have all your information, imagine in your mind's eye reporting in such a situation and coping well with it. You can revisit this imagery as many times as you like before you actually report on such an event. Try this technique for as many events as possible that you may be fearful of – it helps to prepare the brain.

Create 'nano' breaks on your phone. Allowing the brain and body to have very small breaks from trauma exposure may assist in lowering the overall 'dose' of exposure. Before going on assignment, prepare your phone with small distractions such as soothing music, brief guided meditation, jokes and humorous clips, cat, dog or nature pictures. These two- or three-minute opportunities for 'nano' breaks help lower your physiological arousal (rapid heartbeat).

Practise mindfulness meditation or yoga. Both of these techniques have been proven to be helpful with post-trauma impacts. Have them practised and part of your 'recovery kit bag' before taking on potentially traumatic assignments.

During assignment

If you feel overwhelmed during an assignment:

Distract yourself. Focus on your professional skills. Ask yourself: What do I need to write the next sentence? What is the pivotal part of the story that I still need to get? What question will I ask next? You can revisit your feelings of being overwhelmed later when you defuse with a colleague or mentor (this is important).

Grounding techniques. Look around you and focus on how many green things (or any colour) you can see around you. Drink some ice-cold water. Stomp your feet to feel the ground. Anything to bring you back into your body and refocus on your task at hand.

Broadcaster's breathing. 3 / 5 / 8 – take a deep, slow breath in for the count of 3, hold the breath for the count of 5, and slowly exhale for the count of 8. Try this three times. It helps to settle the sympathetic nervous system when you feel agitated or overwhelmed (www.psychologytoday.com/au/blog/neuraptitude/201602/the-science-slow-deep-breathing).

After assignment

Social support and supporting others. One of the most important aspects of trauma recovery is social support and staying connected to people who understand you. Good social support from peers, managers and friends has been found to be a strong buffer against post-trauma impacts in high risk professions such as first responders (McFarlane and Bryant, 2007; Skogstad et al., 2013), and lack of positive social support has been identified as a trauma risk factor for journalists (Beam and Spratt, 2009; Hatanaka et al., 2010; Newman et al., 2003; Weidmann et al., 2008). Seek out people you trust, who you feel understand you, and that you look up to. Confide in them and offer social support to others.

Check in also with your buddies. Ask them how they are doing. Trust your ability to care for your friends. Giving social support to others enhances your resilience as much as receiving it.

> Oh, I do think that the difficult assignments that I've got through the best are the ones where I've had good relationships with the people that I'm working with. I do think that it's easier … I actually think it's much, much easier to cope … if you actually shoot and cut the film and can talk to the journalist about the way it's going. Because a lot of the camera operators do the editing as well now … so I think that both of you being completely part of the experience is … it's empowering. (Oscar – pseudonym)
> (McMahon, 2016, p. 211)

Exercise, rest and reflection. Doing some form of vigorous exercise such as swimming, running, or cycling can assist with what is called hyperarousal after trauma (jumpy and agitated feelings) and also assists with sleep (www.sciencedirect.com/science/article/abs/pii/S1755296615000022).

These things help the body to recalibrate back to its equilibrium after it has been exposed to trauma or extreme stress. There is certainly some currency in the British Army's old adage of 'three hots and a cot' – three hot meals and a bed, to recover from distressing assignments.

Take time at the end of each day for at least five minutes of reflecting back on the day to help process what you have been through. Ask yourself: what is one lesson I have learnt today, what is one thing I did very well, and one thing I would do differently? Journalists take lots of time reflecting on other people's lives but not their own. Trauma may not have an immediate impact, but the accumulation can build up. Witnessing potentially traumatic events is like filming such situations – if you don't process the tape and just throw it in a drawer, eventually the unprocessed tapes will spill out over the floor. They need to be viewed, edited and processed and put in their proper place. Take time to do this for yourself each day.

Professional help. If you are from a culture that accesses professional mental health practitioners, then if you feel overwhelmed to the point that you are not coping, or see a buddy in such a situation, by all means access a trauma-trained health professional. Interview the professional about their expertise and find out if they know how to deal with trauma exposure.

If you are from a culture that does not have access to mental health experts, then it is imperative to use the healing traditions from your culture – speak to an elder, use prayer, meditation, exercise, and speak to your colleagues.

Positive trauma experiences – post-traumatic growth

It is important to recognise that trauma may change us in a negative way if we are deeply impacted. However it can change us in a positive way too. In the words of an Australian war correspondent:

> I would do it all again, the good and the bad. I could not imagine myself without the richness of what I have seen. It has run wires through my thinking and my body. I could not isolate or unpick it, even if I tried. It is part of me now. (Hilary – pseudonym)
>
> (McMahon, 2016, p. 220)

References and useful resources

Babson, K., Heinz, A., Ramirez, G., Puckett, M., Irons, J., Bonn-Miller, M., and Wood-ward, S. (2015). The interactive role of exercise and sleep on veteran recovery from symptoms of PTSD. *Mental Health and Physical Activity*, 8, 15–20.

Backholm, K., & Björkqvist, K. (2012a). The mediating effect of depression between exposure to potentially traumatic events and PTSD in news journalists. *European Journal of Psychotraumatology*, 3(1), (online), https://www.tandfonline.com/doi/full/10.3402/ejpt.v3i0.18388

Backholm, K., & Björkqvist, K. (2012b). Journalists' emotional reactions after work-ing with the Jokela school shooting incident. *Media, War & Conflict*, 5, 175–190.

Beam, R., and Spratt, M. (2009). Job satisfaction, morale and journalists' reactions to violence and trauma. *Journalism Practice*, 3(4), 421–438.

Feinstein, A. (2012). Mexican journalists: an investigation of their emotional health. *Journal of Traumatic Stress*, 25(4), 480–483.

Green, B., Krupnick, K., Stockton, P., Goodman, L., Corcoran, C., and Petty, R. (2005). Effects of adolescent trauma exposure on risky behavior in college women. *Psychiatry*, 68, 363–378.

Hatanaka, M., Matsui, Y., Ando, K., Inoue, K., Fukuoka, Y., Koshiro, E., and Itamura, H. (2010). Traumatic stress in Japanese broadcast journalists. *Journal of Traumatic Stress*, 23(1), 173–177.

Janoff-Bulman, R. (2004). Posttraumatic growth: three explanatory models. *Psychological Inquiry*, 15(1), 30–34.

MacKinnon, M. (2016). The science of slow, deep breathing. *Psychology Today*, www.psychologytoday.com/au/blog/neuraptitude/201602/the-science-slow-deep-breathing (accessed 22 December 2018).

McFarlane, A., and Bryant, R. (2007). Post-traumatic stress disorder in occupational settings: anticipating and managing the risk. *Occupational Medicine*, 57, 404–410.

McMahon, C. (2001). Covering disaster: a pilot study into secondary trauma for print media journalists reporting on disaster. *Australian Journal of Emergency Management*, 16(2).

McMahon, C. (2016). Posttraumatic stress and posttraumatic growth amongst trauma reporting Australian journalists. Unpublished PhD thesis. Swinburne University, Hawthorn, Australia.

Muller, D. (2010). Ethics and trauma: lessons from media coverage of Black Saturday. *Australian Journal of Rural Health*, 18(1), 5–10.

Newman, E., Simpson, R., and Handschuh, D. (2003). Trauma exposure and post-traumatic stress disorder among photojournalists. *Visual Communication Quarterly*, 58(1), 4–13.

Pat-Horenczyk, R., Peled, O., Miron, T., Brom, D., Villa, Y., and Chemtob, C. (2007). Risk-taking behaviors among Israeli adolescents exposed to recurrent terrorism. *American Journal of Psychiatry*, 164, 66–72.

Perara, A. (2013). Reporting death's like a cricket match. Dart Center Asia Pacific, https://dartcenter.org/content/trauma-in-course-duty (accessed 2 January 2019).

Skogstad, M., Skorstad, M., Lie, A., Conradi, H.S., Heir, T., and Weisæth, L. (2013). Work-related post-traumatic stress disorder. *Occupational Medicine*, 63(3), 175–182.

Weidmann, A., Fehm, L., and Fydrich, T. (2008). Covering the tsunami disaster: subsequent post-traumatic and depressive symptoms and associated social factors. *Stress and Health*, 24, 129–135, www.sciencedirect.com/science/article/abs/pii/S1755296615000022.

11
The ethics

Sallyanne Duncan

Dr Sallyanne Duncan is a senior lecturer at the University of Strathclyde, Glasgow, specialising in journalism ethics. She researches media reporting of trauma, death, bereavement, mental health and suicide. Her PhD was an analysis of press reporting of the 'death knock.' She has written a book, *Reporting Bad News: Negotiating the Boundaries between Intrusion and Fair Representation in Media Coverage of Death*, with Jackie Newton of Liverpool John Moores University. She has also published several journal articles and book chapters on death and trauma and is currently working on a book on ethics for journalists. Additionally, she revised professional guidelines on media reporting of mental health and suicide for the National Union of Journalists, has submitted evidence based on her research to the Leveson Inquiry, and gave evidence to the National Assembly of Wales's suicide prevention inquiry on media reporting of suicide.

Introduction

Journalists undertake traumatic reporting work with vulnerable people – as sources, as those who appear in their stories, and in a wider context as their audience – so it is vital that they comprehend their professional standards and behave ethically. Practically speaking, ethics is about trying to do the 'right' thing in difficult circumstances. Journalists do this by assessing a situation, making decisions about how they report a story, and critically reflecting on their actions afterwards. Making ethical decisions often centres on where to draw the line. They do that by applying rules, considering their duties and responsibilities, thinking of the consequences of their actions, and by striving to be a virtuous or good journalist. Generally, they are bound by professional standards, which often originate in codes of ethics, conduct or practice and are regulated by independent professional bodies. There are more than 310 journalism codes worldwide, some in countries with limited freedom of expression. Although they differ according to the particular governance, culture and society within their countries, they tend to be based on four ethical pillars:

truth telling and accuracy; minimising harm; independence, fairness and impartiality; and being accountable.

What are the key regulatory bodies we need to be aware of and consult when covering sensitive stories?

There are two systems of media regulation in the UK – self-regulation, which applies to most of the print media and their online editions; and statutory, which relates to broadcasters, their online versions and their on-demand services. Both advise journalists through a code of practice or guidelines, informing them what they should do in given situations. Regarding print journalism, there are currently two main regulators. These are the Independent Press Standards Organisation (IPSO), of which most regional and national newspapers are members. This is a non-Royal Charter system set up by the national and regional press after the Leveson Inquiry. The other, the Independent Monitor for the Press (IMPRESS), has Royal Charter recognition and its members are mostly micro-publishers or local news sites. Some publications like the *Guardian* and the *Financial Times* chose to regulate themselves using their own codes and complaints procedures instead of joining IPSO or IMPRESS. The Office of Communications, the UK's broadcasting, telecommunications and postal regulatory body, known as Ofcom, regulates BBC news and current affairs content, as well as ITN who produce ITV news, Channel 4 News and 5 News, through its Broadcasting Code. Additionally, BBC journalists adhere to their company's Editorial Guidelines, which set out their values and standards. The National Union of Journalists also has a code of conduct but their ability to regulate is limited because it only applies to their members. However, such trade union codes do provide an alternative perspective. Freelance journalists should adhere to the regulatory system that applies to the sector that has hired them. All journalists, including freelancers, should familiarise themselves with the relevant codes.

Can you summarise the rules on privacy and intrusion?

Journalists have to balance the public interest in freedom of expression with people's legitimate expectations of privacy. BBC Editorial Guidelines state: 'We must justify intrusions into an individual's private life without consent by demonstrating that the intrusion is outweighed by the public interest' (Section 7.2.3, n.d.). However, they also have to consider minimising harm to vulnerable people, either those involved in the stories or amongst the audience. Here, codes tend to cover the broad areas of respect for a person's privacy, regard for any potential harm caused by the reporting, and consideration of the consequences of publishing. Treating people with dignity and appreciation rather than merely as a means to get a story is also important. This is particularly pertinent to ordinary citizens, who may find themselves thrust into the media spotlight because of a tragedy that has befallen their family. IPSO's Editors' Code of Practice and the Ofcom Broadcasting Code are useful examples of how codes deal with privacy and intrusion.

The Editors' Code stresses that everyone is entitled to a private and family life, and respect for their home, health and correspondence, including digital communications. It also states that it is unacceptable to photograph individuals, without their consent, in public or private places where they have a reasonable expectation of privacy (IPSO, 2017, Clause 2). Ofcom recognises that expectations of privacy can vary depending on the situation, but it also acknowledges that some situations are so private that recording, even in a public place, could be an infringement (Section 8: Privacy, 2017). The degree of their expectation depends on the circumstances, leading to grey areas that editors have to work through. Should news organisations show pictures of bleeding, shocked commuters after an explosion at a railway terminus? Should they interview teenagers fleeing from a terrorist attack at a concert? These moments are private in nature but in a public place. Ofcom acknowledges that there may be a strong public interest to justify intrusion when covering tragic breaking news, meaning news teams might struggle to judge whether and how much recording is valid, especially when live streaming.

Consent is another contentious issue. Normally, print/online journalists do not seek or explain explicit informed consent as they assume it is given implicitly when the traumatised person agrees to an interview. Where intrusion occurs without consent, the Editors' Code expects editors to be able to justify it. For Ofcom, privacy infringements must be warranted. Broadcasters need to demonstrate why an infringement is justified, e.g., the public interest outweighs the right to privacy (see Ofcom, Broadcasting Code, Section 8.1, 'Meaning of "warranted"') news. Broadcasters also have to seek consent for transmitting the content unless breaching a person's privacy is warranted. Whilst the intrusion is usually carried out by individual reporters on the editor's behalf, responsibility for invading a person's privacy lies with both. Therefore, reporters cannot hide behind the claim that they were only doing their job. However, the press has some protection as the Editors' Code states that people must take responsibility when they make information about themselves publicly available. Thus, even though a person might consider some information about them to be private, a journalist can use it if it is already in the public domain without it being seen as invading someone's privacy. For example, notes of condolence left at the site of a tragedy like the Grenfell Tower fire may be considered private messages to the bereaved by those who left them but because they are on display in a public place they are deemed to be publicly available for use by journalists. Consent, therefore, is a more accepted, explicit practice in broadcasting than in print/online journalism.

Intrusion is a more subtle issue because what the journalist would consider to be good practice in doing their job – contacting the people at the centre of the story who know about the situation – can be seen as intrusive by traumatised people at a time when they are dealing with 'the raw edges of bereavement' (Dant, 1998). Ofcom suggest that even if they have agreed to be interviewed, broadcast news teams should judge for themselves whether asking grieving relatives for interviews is intrusive and infringes their privacy. The Editors' Code advises journalists to act with sympathy and discretion when approaching those suffering from grief or shock (IPSO, 2017, Clause 4). It reinforces this with a clause on harassment (IPSO, 2018, Clause 3), stating that journalists must identify themselves and who they represent. This is particularly important if they wish to enter a non-public area of a hospital or similar institution. It also informs them they should not persist in questioning, telephoning, pursuing or photographing individuals once they have been asked to stop. But this throws up grey areas of what is meant by sympathy, discretion and sensitivity. When do they cross the line from good journalism practice to insensitive intrusion? For the inexperienced reporter, deciphering these terms can cause indecision about how far to go. Consequently, they might try to please their editor by adopting a 'gung-ho' attitude to get the story rather than taking account of the family's suffering and addressing one of the pillars of ethical journalism, minimising harm. Individual reporters and editors are left to interpret these concerns themselves. To do so, they draw on their humanity, previous experience, professional standards and rulings from complaints to regulatory bodies. Inexperienced staff should also talk to their editors or senior colleagues. Additionally, they can seek help from regulatory bodies. IPSO encourages journalists to contact them for pre-publication advice, particularly regarding the reporting of deaths.

Why are the rules important?

Two reasons: those at the centre of the story have the right to be protected at a time of personal loss and tragedy; and, journalists need to know how to behave ethically. However, these two reasons can result in tension so having rules helps both the bereaved and the journalist know where they stand. Journalists generally want to see themselves as decent and honest rather than as exploiting people, but the nature of reporting bad news necessitates them engaging in exploitative practices (Duncan and Newton, 2017). Let's look at the journalist's job when reporting trauma. They intrude when the situation is at its most intense, at private times such as within hours of a death or at the funeral. They ask probing and personal questions. Sometimes they discuss the family's private business with people who barely know them, like neighbours or work colleagues. Then they look within the family's grief for a newsworthy angle to fit their organisation's news agenda (Duncan and Newton, 2017). This is a stark view of what journalists do when they report traumatised people's stories, but it is not the whole picture. With the right to report at these tragic times come responsibilities to those in the story and those affected by it. Therefore, although the task may be exploitative and intrusive the journalist has a duty to perform it sensitively, responsibly and respectfully. The rules on privacy, intrusion and harassment help them to do this by making them aware of their responsibilities.

Are these the only rules news organisations need to think about when reporting trauma?

No, they need to consider accuracy, truth, and taste and offence. One of the worst errors a journalist can make is to get the deceased's personal details wrong. Spelling a loved one's name wrongly may be a mistake to the reporter and editor but to the family it is highly insulting. Seeking personal details from neighbours who may provide the news organisation with inaccurate or misleading information can be equally injurious to the family (Duncan and Newton, 2017). Additionally, although taste is not regulated by the Editors' Code, news organisations should be aware of its effect on their audience as well as on traumatised people. This applies more to visual content than text but not exclusively. News desks should weigh up decisions to publish graphic content by considering whether it is in the public interest to do so. Is it important that the public know the reality because a greater good may emerge from informing them? Or, has the news organisation decided to publish the content because they think it might interest the public, i.e. for gratuitous or sensational reasons to increase clicks, shares, circulation or viewing figures? It is important that news teams strike a balance in these situations, especially when making split-second decisions due to 24/7 news cycles and the pressure to be first.

What can happen to news organisations and journalists who break the rules?

They can be reprimanded by the professional body that regulates them. This can range from having to publish a correction or apology to being fined substantial sums of money, although that is rare. Ofcom has the power to shorten or take away a broadcast organisation's licence if they are persistent offenders. IPSO can order prominent printed apologies and corrections to uphold complaints. They also run a low-cost arbitration process to avoid court action in media law disputes. IMPRESS takes a similar approach, although they have developed their own code of ethics, which could result in different interpretations of certain situations.

Regardless of the sanction, receiving a complaint about their work can have an adverse effect on individual journalists. Consequently, most strive to behave well and avoid breaking the rules.

How are complaints dealt with?

This depends on who the regulator is. Mostly, they try to resolve the issue with the complainant through mediation, and if that fails an adjudication panel may review the complaint. They make a decision on whether to uphold or reject it by weighing up evidence from both sides in relation to specific clauses from their codes that the news organisation is accused of breaching. Detailed explanations of the various complaints procedures can be found on the regulatory bodies' websites.

Can you summarise the guidance available on covering death, funerals and inquests?

Most sudden deaths occur in public places and therefore are not wholly private matters. Consequently, they affect the community in which a person lived. Journalists, therefore, have a dual responsibility: to minimise harm to grieving relatives and friends, and to do their duty by reporting on the death for the public record and to inform the community at large.

Regulators agree that journalists should not break news of a death to traumatised relatives. Therefore to minimise harm and to verify the accuracy of information, it is recommended that news outlets confirm through the police that the family know about the death before contacting relatives, or publishing the name of a person who has died. Journalists should also take care when publishing content, particularly photographs or video footage, in the immediate aftermath in case they inadvertently identify the deceased before the family has been informed, for example showing the number plate of a car involved in a road accident. Ofcom also advise that broadcasters should respect any reasonable arrangements made by the emergency services to supervise media access to victims or their relatives immediately after a tragedy.

Deciding to cover a funeral is a tricky one for news teams because some bereaved relatives welcome their presence and others consider it intrusive and distressing. How journalists behave in such situations is paramount and they should consider the effect it could have on the deceased's family. They must assess relatives' wishes and should seek to determine these through an inter-mediary such as a funeral director or by assessing the circumstances of the death. They should also act sensitively when parts of the funeral occur in public view, such as mourners' arrival at the service. Care should be taken with photographs and filming of people in extreme distress. Ofcom states that news teams should respect requests for them to withdraw at funerals.

In contrast, inquests are public events that journalists are entitled to attend with a view to publishing or broadcasting a story. The deceased's grieving rel-atives and friends may not be aware that news outlets can report the evidence presented at the inquest without seeking their consent. Also, families might not want some of the evidence to appear in the news but the reporter might need to include it to give an accurate account. This can cause distress to rela-tives who may see the media as intruding in their private business and behav-ing ghoulishly. Therefore, journalists should be mindful of this distress when approaching families for a comment and should proceed with sympathy and sensitivity. They should not persist in pursuing, questioning, photographing or filming grieving relatives when asked to stop.

What about suicide?

Suicide is a very complex area for journalists to report and thus requires extra care. Many people see it as a taboo subject and those bereaved by suicide are highly vulnerable. Extensive guidance is available from the numerous media reporting guidelines that can be found by searching the internet. The most pertinent UK guidelines are those produced separately by the National Union of Journalists, Samaritans and the World Health Organization. These cover various topics including copycat behaviour, appropriate and inappropriate language, sensationalising or romanticising suicide, celebrity cases, murder-suicide, and the inclusion of helplines.

Media regulators' rules mostly concentrate on method and location. They state that journalists should not excessively describe, display or photograph the method or location, as this could lead to imitative acts by others. They should be particularly vigilant when they refer to an unusual method that could ap-peal to vulnerable people. However, if the method is key to the findings at an inquest then reporters can include detail as long as it is not excessive. Report-ing locations may lead to them becoming popular places for suicide attempts so journalists should take care to avoid portraying these locations as 'suicide spots.' Journalists are directed that if they must refer to the place then they should do this in general terms instead of giving the exact location. Lastly, a word about language. Most guidelines recommend that journalists avoid using the phrase 'committed suicide.' This implies suicide is a criminal act, which has not been the case in the UK since 1961, and attaches blame, which can be damaging for and to those bereaved by suicide.

What do reporters and broadcasters need to be aware of when working with children? Why are they a significant category requiring protection?

Children should be treated as a special case because they are considered to be minors and therefore not responsible for any decisions they might make. That means they are unable to consent to being interviewed or unable to consider the consequences of speaking to the media. Therefore, journalists should reflect on the potential harm that their reports could have on children in their stories or as part of their audience. The welfare of the child should be given a high priority, not only when reporting the story but in the effect that publication or broadcast might have on them. There is some confusion over what is a child, however. Clauses to protect children in the Editors' Code apply to anyone under 16 whereas Ofcom defines children as people under the age of 15. The law, nonetheless, determines that a child is anyone under the age of 18. So what happens to those young people aged 15–18? Ethically, it would be advisable to treat them with the same care as those under 15, especially when reporting stories of vulnerability such as bullying, sexting, suicide or tragedy.

Journalists should avoid approaching children or photographing them within school grounds without permission from the school authorities. This applies even if a custodial parent/guardian has given their consent. Further complications can arise when one parent decides to speak to the media or allow their child to speak to them and the other parent disagrees. Here, the advice is that the custodial parent has the greater right to consent so the journalist should establish who that is before they proceed. Children should not be questioned about issues involving their own or another child's welfare unless a custodial parent/guardian or similarly responsible adult consents. Also, news organisations are advised to only pay children or their custodial parents/guardians for their story when it is clearly in the child's interest, and editors are warned not to use a custodial parent/guardian's fame or position as the only reason for publishing details of a child's private life. Therefore, gaining consent from a custodial parent/guardian is imperative if reporters or news crews plan to work with children. There may be exceptions to these rules if news outlets can show that publishing such content is clearly in the public interest.

Identification could be an issue too, particularly with groups of children, some of whom might have little or no connection to the story. In this case, especially when news organisations use pictures or video, they should consider whether it is necessary and fair to identify the children in the group. Audiences are accustomed to anonymised footage now so this would seem like an ethical approach.

Care should be taken when news organisations use content published on social media by children. Once again, the key concern is the welfare of the child. Innocuous material that does not impinge on the child's welfare or their time at school is ethically more acceptable than controversial content, such as footage of a playground fight, which could adversely affect a child due to a news outlet re-publishing. Here it is important that media professionals consider the consequences of re-publishing. This applies even if the material is publicly available because by re-publishing they are exposing it to a wider audience than when the child put it on social media.

What rules do we need to be aware of when covering stories about sexual violence and abuse?

Once again, news organisations should be aware of minimising harm, treating those in their stories with dignity and being fair. However, they also have a duty to report accurately and truthfully as victims who contact them may be doing so as a means of seeking justice. Striving to get the balance right is a key factor here. They should also be aware that there are legal protections in place for victims of sexual assault, including children, and news teams should evaluate these as well as the ethical concerns.

Often those who are victims of sexual violence and abuse wish to remain anonymous. They may have struggled to make the decision to go public with their story and might fear the consequences of handing control over to news organisations who will have different priorities from them. Therefore, it is important that journalists respect the dignity and anonymity of victims.

Regulators also warn of the dangers of the 'jigsaw effect' where a news outlet publishes or broadcasts limited information that can be pieced together with that from other news organisations, resulting in the victim being identified. This is particularly important when reporting children. Some information may seem insignificant to the news team but to people who know something about those described in a story it can be enough to lead to speculation about their identity. For example, giving the dates of an offence could, along with other information, compromise anonymity. IPSO advise reporters and news desks to ensure they are aware of the information that is in the public domain from other news outlets and in their own previous reports. They suggest news teams liaise with other publications to agree an approach to prevent jigsaw identification.

However, IPSO recognise that news outlets can do little regarding posts by the public on social media that speculate on a victim's identity. They advise news outlets to consider whether they could safely publish stories involving sexual assault victims on their social media sites, particularly where open to public comments (IPSO, 2018, Sexual Offences). The media are urged to take extra care in sexual offences cases involving children in any capacity, e.g. as victims, witnesses, defendants or perpetrators. Ofcom's advice refers to children under 18 whereas IPSO's guidance applies to children under 16. Both, however, stress the child must not be identified, and the term 'incest' should be avoided, especially when it could lead to identifying the child.

Can you summarise the guidance available around user-generated content and accessing sensitive material through social media?

When news desks receive traumatic user-generated content (UGC) or access it from social media, they must address ethical issues regarding its authenticity, sensitivity, transparency, safety, and rights and permissions. Verifying content in order to avoid inaccuracies and misleading the audience with unconfirmed information is the main challenge, particularly when covering tragic breaking news. One method is to upload it immediately, telling the audience it is not fully verified, whilst news teams attempt to assess its credibility with help from their users. However, this relies on news desks updating the UGC's status, which could be overlooked in pressurised newsrooms. Consequently, there is a risk of spreading inaccurate content and misinforming the audience. The safest method is to contact the actual creator to assess whether it is genuine before uploading it onto a news site. News outlets have a responsibility to their audience to admit when they have been unable to verify UGC completely. However, the drive to be first with breaking news can cause tensions, with journalists being tempted to take a chance without full verification. For the ethical journalist who wishes to adhere to truth telling, accuracy should be prioritised over speed. Equally, as journalists are accountable for their actions, they should be honest about where the UGC has come from and how they verified it, for example, by giving the creator's name and not merely the social media source. News outlets should not use statements that they are unable to verify content *independently* as ethical get-out clauses. Inaccuracies, misleading the audience and a lack of transparency can cause the public to lose trust in news outlets.

Journalists should also be sensitive to those who provide UGC, to their safety and to their emotional state. When contacting the contributor, especially those in dangerous places or traumatic situations, the journalist should warn them about taking risks when gathering content. In some cases, news outlets should assess whether they should even contact someone when searching for UGC as doing so could put that person at risk. Some contributors could be in a highly emotional state, especially if they have witnessed a tragic incident. Additionally, reaching out to those involved in a traumatic experience for UGC can potentially cause harm. It might involve the journalist breaking distressing news to the person, or they might have suffered the loss of a loved one. Therefore, news desks and reporters should ask themselves whether this is the right time to be contacting vulnerable people for UGC. Lastly, news outlets should be cautious about using content from ordinary citizens' social media accounts. Taking photographs or other digital content from a site set to private without consent is unacceptable, according to the Editors' Code. However, journalists should be cautious even when taking material from a public site where consent is not required. By doing so they can cause the family significant harm, as they might be unaware that the news outlet can do this without their knowledge. It is important here to think about the consequences of the action.

Can you give an example of a 'grey' area where the rules are unclear?

Grey areas arise because journalists are unsure which is the 'right' action to take and for whom. There are many stakeholders in a story but one has to take priority over others and who that is depends on conflicting factors. Each situation needs to be treated on its own merits. Thus, journalists can appear to make surprising and even apparently unprofessional choices when faced with difficult dilemmas. An example is how often reporters can contact traumatised people to request an interview. Journalists regularly use Facebook Messenger or Twitter to reach bereaved people after a tragedy like the Manchester Arena bombing. But what happens when they receive no response? Can the reporter contact them again? Codes advise against persistent contact, but what does that actually mean? Unlike the traditional death knock where there is a clear yes or no on the doorstep, communicating through social media can lead to confusing, grey areas. If, after no response from the family, the journalist, with the best of motives, sent another message via Facebook or Twitter or even made a phone call, would that amount to persistence, resulting in harassment? This uncertainty could make some journalists question whether they are breaking the rules, leaving them in a quandary about what to do next. If they stick to the advice in the codes and do not make further contact, most likely a story will still appear, but without the family's involvement, based only on information from emergency services or less dependable sources, some of which might be inaccurate. Thus, the grieving family might feel they are losing control over what they see as their private situation. They could suffer even when the reporter follows the rules. The journalist has behaved appropriately, but they have still caused harm and possibly compromised truth telling because they have failed to get information from the best source – the family. The situation lacks clarity and results in a grey area.

Six takeaways from this chapter

- The story is important but so are the people who appear in it or helped with research, especially when they are vulnerable. Therefore, review your behaviour, what you reported, and make positive changes for the future.
- Strive to be accurate and truthful. Inaccuracies have a serious adverse effect on vulnerable people.
- Where possible, minimise harm to those in your stories by thinking about the consequences of your reporting and publishing.
- Do your duty by following the code of conduct that applies to your branch of the media. Seek additional advice from media reporting guidelines like the ones listed below. If you are unsure about the ethical issues around a story, seek help from IPSO or Ofcom helplines or organisations like Samaritans that work to protect vulnerable people.
- If you are an inexperienced reporter, speak to your editor about stories where you are unsure if you are about to cross, or have crossed, an ethical boundary.
- Be accountable for your actions. Ask yourself if you followed the rules. Did you think about the consequences of your reporting? If you got it wrong in terms of your code of conduct and professional standards, then try to make it right.

References and useful resources

BBC (n.d.). Editorial Guidelines. Retrieved from www.bbc.co.uk/editorialguidelines/.
Dant, G. (1998). Knocking on death's door. *Press Gazette*, 24 April, p. 14.
Duncan, S., and Newton, J. (2017). *Reporting Bad News: Negotiating the Boundaries between Intrusion and Fair Representation in Media Coverage of Death*. New York: Peter Lang.
Independent Monitor for the Press (2017). Standards Code. Retrieved from www.impress.press/standards/standards-code.html.

Independent Press Standards Organisation (2017). Editors' Code of Practice. Retrieved from www.ipso.co.uk/editors-code-of-practice/.

Independent Press Standards Organisation (2017). Social Media Guidance. Retrieved from www.ipso.co.uk/member-publishers/guidance-for-journalists-and-editors/social-media-guidance/.

Independent Press Standards Organisation (2018). Editors' Codebook. Retrieved from www.editorscode.org.uk/the_code_book.php

Independent Press Standards Organisation (2018). Guidance on Reporting of Sexual Offences. Retrieved from www.ipso.co.uk/member-publishers/guidance-for-journalists-and-editors/guidance-on-reporting-of-sexual-offences/.

National Association for People Abused in Childhood (2016). Media Guidelines for Reporting Child Abuse. Retrieved from https://napac.org.uk/wp-content/uploads/2016/06/NAPAC-media-guidelines-FINAL-Jan-2016.pdf.

National Union of Journalists (2014). Responsible Reporting on Mental Health, Mental Illness and Death by Suicide. Retrieved from www.nuj.org.uk/news/mental-health-and-suicide-reporting-guidelines/.

Office of Communications (2017). Broadcasting Code. Retrieved from www.ofcom.org.uk/tv-radio-and-on-demand/broadcast-codes/broadcast-code.

Samaritans (n.d.). Media Guidelines for the Reporting of Suicide. Retrieved from www.samaritans.org/media-centre/media-guidelines-reporting-suicide.

World Health Organization (2017). Preventing Suicide: A Resource for Media Professionals. Retrieved from www.who.int/mental_health/suicide-prevention/resource_booklet_2017/en/.

Zero Tolerance (n.d.). Advice for Journalists. Retrieved from www.zerotolerance.org.uk/work-journalists/.

12
The tips

How to cover sensitive stories: key points

Use these as a checklist when covering a sensitive story:

- *Prepare.* Know the basics of the story, check facts meticulously when you are there. Inaccuracy will cause distress.
- *Acknowledge.* When covering a bereavement, a sincere 'sorry' for what has happened is a decent thing to say.
- *Attitude.* Approach with humanity. Be attentive, sensitive and respectful. Expect varied responses and reactions and always treat people with dignity.
- *Empathy.* Think how you would feel in their position. Never fake, avoid over-empathising and maintain professional boundaries.
- *Fatigue.* They may be exhausted and in turmoil. Make allowances: avoid over-filming, speak clearly, allow breaks, check they are comfortable with what you are asking of them.
- *Language.* Avoid saying 'I know how you feel.' You don't. Don't diagnose, blame, criticise, or make assumptions.
- *Control.* Traumatic events can disempower. Always stop and think: how can I give them some control over how I am working with them? Explain, involve but don't overwhelm.
- *Listen.* Use active listening skills. Listen rather than talk. Do not rush people or appear distracted by your phone or deadline.
- *Manage expectations.* Be open, honest and transparent. Be clear on consent.
- *Emotional reactions.* Do not provoke tears, but don't be afraid of them. Sit quietly. If they break down, ask what you can do to help.
- *Interview.* Prepare them for what you would like to ask, listen to their opinions. Avoid being overly interrogative. If they relive an event, allow your questions to draw them gently back into the 'here and now.'

- *Re-visiting.* Don't assume they 'get over it.' Apply the same level of consideration when you re-visit people's sensitive stories.
- *The story.* Be mindful of how you word your report. Avoid the language of blame or sensation. Contact them after the story has been published or broadcast to thank them.
- *Look after yourself, and each other.* It matters.

Index